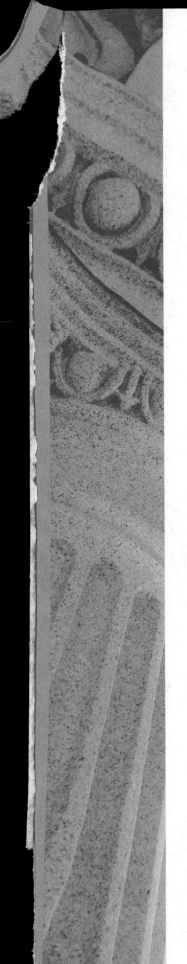

M

Music

D1214665

Library of Congress Classification
2010

LIBRARY OF
CONGRESS

Prepared by the Policy and Standards Division

LIBRARY OF CONGRESS
Cataloging Distribution Service
Washington, D.C.

This edition cumulates all additions and changes to Class M through Weekly List 2010/21, dated May 26, 2010. Additions and changes made subsequent to that date are published in weekly lists posted on the World Wide Web at

<http://www.loc.gov/aba/cataloging/classification/weeklylists/>

and are also available in *Classification Web*, the online Web-based edition of the Library of Congress Classification.

Library of Congress Cataloging-in-Publication Data

Library of Congress.
  Library of Congress classification. M. Music / prepared by the Policy and Standards Division, Library Services. — 2010 ed.
      p. cm.
  "This edition cumulates all additions and changes to Class M through Weekly list 2010/21, dated May 26, 2010. Additions and changes made subsequent to that date are published in weekly lists posted on the World Wide Web ... and are also available in Classification Web, the online Web-based edition of the Library of Congress classification"—T.p. verso.
  Includes index.
  ISBN 978-0-8444-9511-8
  1. Classification, Library of Congress. 2. Classification—Books—Music.
3. Classification—Music. I. Library of Congress. Policy and Standards Division. II. Title. III. Title: Languages of Eastern Asia, Africa, Oceania. IV. Title: Hyperborean, Indian, and artificial languages.

 Z696.U5M 2010
 025.4'678—dc22

                                                        2010024894

For sale by the Library of Congress Cataloging Distribution Service, 101 Independence Avenue, S.E., Washington, DC 20540-4910. Product catalog available on the Web at **www.loc.gov/cds**.

PREFACE

Class M was created by Oscar G.T. Sonneck, first chief of the Music Division of the Library of Congress, and was one of the first schedules to be adopted in the new classification scheme the Library began developing late in the year 1900. The Music Division began to use Class M in 1902, and the first edition was published in 1904. A revised edition, also called the second edition, was published in 1917; it was reprinted twice with supplementary pages for additions and changes, first in 1957 and then in 1968. In 1978 the third edition was published as an integrated schedule that incorporated additions and changes made through June 1977. New editions were published in 1998 and 2007; each of these editions cumulated changes that were made since the previous edition was published. This 2010 edition cumulates changes made since the publication of the 2007 edition.

Classification numbers or spans of numbers that appear in parentheses are formerly valid numbers that are now obsolete. Numbers or spans that appear in angle brackets are optional numbers that have never been used at the Library of Congress but are provided for other libraries that wish to use them. In most cases, a parenthesized or angle-bracketed number is accompanied by a "see" reference directing the user to the actual number that the Library of Congress currently uses, or a note explaining Library of Congress practice.

Access to the online version of the full Library of Congress Classification is available on the World Wide Web by subscription to *Classification Web*. Details about ordering and pricing may be obtained from the Cataloging Distribution Service at

<http://www.loc.gov/cds/>

New or revised numbers and captions are added to the L.C. Classification schedules as a result of development proposals made by the cataloging staff of the Library of Congress and cooperating institutions. Upon approval of these proposals by the weekly editorial meeting of the Policy and Standards Division, new classification records are created or existing records are revised in the master classification database. Weekly lists of newly approved or revised classification numbers and captions are posted on the World Wide Web at

<http://www.loc.gov/aba/cataloging/classification/weeklylists/>

Geraldine Ostrove, senior cataloging policy specialist in the Policy and Standards Division, is responsible for coordinating the overall intellectual and editorial content of class M and its various subclasses. Kent Griffiths, assistant editor of classification schedules, is responsible for creating new classification records, maintaining the master database, and creating index terms for the captions.

Barbara B. Tillett, Chief
Policy and Standards Division

June 2010

OUTLINE

Music
    Literature on music - Continued

	Music
	Music printed or copied in manuscript in the United States or the colonies before 1860
	Through 1820
1.A1	General
1.A11	Collections of sheet music bound into volumes by their original owners
	1820-1860
	Sheet music for copyright deposit
	Contained in about 300 volumes arranged by district court and year
1.A12I	Instrumental
1.A12V	Vocal
1.A12Z	Instrumental and vocal
1.A13	General
1.A15	Collections of sheet music bound into volumes by their original owners
(1.A18)	Manuscripts not assigned to other classes
	Class manuscripts and manuscript facsimiles intended as performance editions with printed music
	For music printed or copied in manuscript in the United States or the colonies before 1860 see M1.A1+
	For music printed or copied in manuscript before 1700 see M1490
	For copyists' manuscripts and their facsimiles of Roman Catholic liturgical music see M2147
	For copyists' manuscripts and their facsimiles of Orthodox liturgical music see M2156
	For manuscripts of Protestant church liturgical music see M2161+
	For manuscripts of individual compositions and sketches, and collections of manuscripts by one or more composers see ML96
	Collections
	Including collections with commentary or other literary matter
1.A5-Z	Miscellaneous
	Class here collections by two or more composers too varied to assign to a more specific class
	Musical sources
	For obsolete numbers formerly used for musical sources, see Table MZ1
	Class here scholarly collections of historical sources
	Including facsimile editions, transcriptions into modern notation, etc.
	Class collections for a single instrument with the instrument, e.g. Organ music, M6
2	General

Collections
    Musical sources -- Continued

2.1   Copyists' manuscripts

                     Class manuscripts intended as performance editions with published works

                     For copyists' manuscripts written in the United States before 1820 see M1.A1

                     For copyists' manuscripts written outside of the United States before 1700 see M1490

                     For copyists' manuscripts and their facsimiles of Roman Catholic liturgical music see M2147

                     For copyists' manuscripts and their facsimiles of Orthodox liturgical music see M2156

2.3.A-Z   By region or country, A-Z

    Collected works of individual composers

3   Complete editions

3.1   Selections

                     Class here collections too varied to assign to a more specific class

3.3   First editions

                     Class here first editions by composers listed below. Class first editions by other composers by medium of performance or other appropriate class

                     J.S. Bach, W.F. Bach, Beethoven, Berlioz, Brahms, Chopin, Debussy, Dvořák, Fauré, Stephen Foster, Handel, J. Haydn, Kuhnau, Lanner, Liszt, C.F. Loewe, MacDowell, Mendelssohn, W.A. Mozart, Nevin, Puccini, Purcell, Schubert, Schumann, Scriabin, O.G.T. Sonneck, E. Strauss, Johann Strauss (1804-1849), Johann Strauss (1825-1899), Josef Strauss, Wagner, Weber

    Instrumental music

              Class manuscripts and manuscript facsimiles intended as performance editions with printed music

(4)   Selections too miscellaneous for special classes

              For general collections of instrumental and vocal music by two or more composers see M1.A5+

              For collections of scholarly historical sources by two or more composers see M2

              For general collections of instrumental music by two or more composers see M5

              For general collections of secular and sacred vocal music by two or more composers see M1495

Instrumental music -- Continued

5   Collections

Class here collections of works by two or more composers for various combinations of instruments

Including collections containing chamber music and larger instrumental works

For collections for two or more different combinations of solo instruments see M177+

One solo instrument

Keyboard instruments

Organ

For electronic organ, except works for specific seasons and occasions see M14.8+

For reed organ see M15+

6   Miscellaneous collections

Class here collections by two or more composers containing original works and arrangements

Original compositions

7   General collections

Class here collections that cannot be assigned to a more specific class

8-11.2   By form or type

Class here collections and separate works

8   Sonatas

8.5   Symphonies

9   Suites. Variation forms

Including passacaglias, chaconnes, etc.

10   Fugues

Including those with preludes

11   Pieces

Class here only separate works not assigned to classes for specific forms or occasions

11.2   Pedal pieces

Arrangements

12   Collections

13   Separate works

Service music

Class here service music for all religions

For recital works with religious aspects, see M6-M13

For collections containing both secular and service music, see M6 , M7 , M12

14   Organ accompaniments

Class here accompaniments to psalms, hymns, chants, etc.

Instrumental music
One solo instrument
Keyboard instruments
Organ
Service music -- Continued
14.3   Pieces
Class here works composed for general liturgical use,
e.g., chorale and hymn preludes, organ masses,
elevations, offertories, postludes, etc.
For works intended for specific seasons and
occasions see M14.4.A+
Specific seasons and occasions
Including electronic organ
14.4.A-Z   Collections. By season, occasion, etc., A-Z
For two seasons or occasions, cutter for the first
14.4.A1   Three or more seasons, etc.
14.4.A4   Advent
14.4.C5   Christmas
14.4.E2   Easter
14.4.E6   Epiphany
14.4.F8   Funeral music
14.4.H2   Harvest. Thanksgiving
14.4.H5   Holy communion
14.4.H6   Holy Week
14.4.L5   Lent. Passiontide
14.4.P4   Palm Sunday
Passiontide see M14.4.L5
Pentecost Festival see M14.4.W4
Thanksgiving see M14.4.H2
14.4.W3   Wedding music
14.4.W4   Whitsuntide. Pentecost Festival
14.5.A-Z   Separate works. By season, occasion, etc., A-Z
For two seasons or occasions, cutter for the first
14.5.A1   Three or more seasons, etc.
14.5.A4   Advent
14.5.C5   Christmas
14.5.E2   Easter
14.5.F8   Funeral music
14.5.H2   Harvest. Thanksgiving
14.5.H5   Holy communion
14.5.H6   Holy Week
14.5.L5   Lent. Passiontide
14.5.P4   Palm Sunday
Passiontide see M14.5.L5
Pentecost Festival see M14.5.W4
Thanksgiving see M14.5.H2
14.5.W3   Wedding music

Instrumental music

One solo instrument

Keyboard instruments

Organ

Specific seasons and occasions

Separate works. By season, occasion, etc., A-Z --
Continued

14.5.W4   Whitsuntide. Pentecost Festival

For organ music for radio see M1527.5+

For organ music for silent films and music not intended
for specific motion pictures see M176

(14.6)   For organ music for specific motion picture sound
tracks
see M1527+

For organ music for television see M1527.7+

Electronic organ

For specific religious seasons and occasions see
M14.4+

14.8   Collections

14.85   Separate works

15-19   Reed organ (Table M2)

Piano, harpsichord, clavichord, etc.

For piano, three or more hands see M198+

20   Miscellaneous collections

Class here collections by two or more composers
containing original works and arrangements

Civil War (United States)

Class here collections and separate works published in
the United States during the Civil War era and
related to it by title or otherwise

Cf. M1637+ Vocal music and instrumental
arrangements of vocal music

20.C58   General

20.C59   Union

20.C61   Confederate

20.E7   World War I

Class here collections and separate works

Cf. M1646 Vocal music and instrumental
arrangements of vocal music

Original compositions

General collections

Class here collections that can not be assigned to a
more specific class

21   Two or more composers

22   One composer

Cf. M23+ collections in a specific form

	Instrumental music
	One solo instrument
	Keyboard instruments
	Piano, harpsichord, clavichord, etc.
	Original compositions -- Continued
	By form or type
	Class here collections and separate works
23	Sonatas
24	Suites
25	Pieces
	Class here only separate works that cannot be assigned to a more specific class
25.2	Double keyboard, Janko keyboard, etc.
25.3	Two pianos, one performer
	Piano, 1 hand
26	Left hand
26.2	Right hand
27	Variation forms
	Including passacaglias, chaconnes, etc.
28	Marches
	Dances
30	General
31	Two-rhythm (polka, etc.)
32	Three-rhythm (waltz, etc.)
	Arrangements
	Including transcriptions
	For arrangements of works for piano, 1 hand see M26+
32.8	General collections
	Class here collections that cannot be assigned to a more specific class
	By form or type
	Class here collections and separate works
	Operas, oratorios, cantatas, etc.
	Class here piano scores
	For piano music for silent films and music not intended for specific motion picture sound tracks see M176
	For piano vocal scores of operas see M1503+
	For piano scores and piano vocal scores of ballets see M1523
	For piano music for specific motion picture sound tracks see M1527+
	For piano music for radio see M1527.5
	For piano music for television see M1527.7+
33	Complete works
33.5	Excerpts

Instrumental music
  One solo instrument
    Keyboard instruments
      Piano, harpsichord, clavichord, etc.
        Arrangements
          By form or type -- Continued

34	Transcriptions, paraphrases, generally for concert purposes, of operas, oratorios, cantatas, etc.
	Class here complete works and excerpts
	For detached overtures see M35.5
	For potpourris, medleys, fantasies on operas, etc. see M39
	Orchestral music. Band music
	Class here symphonies, suites, overtures, marches, dances, etc., and detached overtures, entr'actes, etc.
	For arrangements of potpourris, etc. see M39
35	Complete works
35.5	Excerpts
(36.5)	Continuo realizations
	see M177
	Concertos, etc.
	Class here concertos, etc. for any instrument(s) and any accompaniment, arranged entirely for one piano
	For concertos in which the accompaniment is arranged for keyboard intrument, the solo part(s) remaining unchanged, see the classes for solo(s) with piano in M1005+ M1105+ M1205+
37	Complete works
37.5	Excerpts
38	Chamber music, part songs, and music for one instrument
38.2	Works for double keyboard, Janko keyboard, Solovox, etc.
38.3	Simplified editions of piano music for two hands
38.5	Songs, etc.
	For transcriptions, paraphrases, etc. of operas, oratorios, cantatas, etc. see M34
39	Potpourris. Medleys
	Class here original works and arrangements
	For works with titles such as "Theme and variations", Variations on ..., etc. see M27
39.5	Two pianos, one performer
39.6	Piano, 1 hand
	Stringed instruments
40-44	Violin (Table M2)

	Instrumental music
	One solo instrument
	Stringed instruments
	Violin -- Continued
44.3	Simplified editions
45-49	Viola (Table M2)
50-54	Violoncello (Table M2)
54.3	Simplified editions
	Double bass
55	Miscellaneous collections
	Original compositions
56	Collections
57	Separate works
58	Arrangements
	Class here collections and separate works
59.A-Z	Other. By instrument, A-Z
	Prior to 1978 not subdivided by individual stringed
	instrument
	Ban hu see M59.P3
59.B4	Baryton
59.C36	Campanula
59.C5	Ching hu. Jing hu
59.E7	Er hu
59.G83	Gŭdulka
59.H3	Haegŭm
59.H37	Hardanger fiddle
	Jing hu see M59.C5
59.L9	Lyra viol
59.N3	Nan hu
59.P3	Pan hu. Ban hu
59.S6	Sǭ dūang
59.S67	Sō sām sāi
59.V53	Viol
	Class here works for unspecified viol
59.V54	Viola da gamba
59.V56	Viola d'amore
59.5	Unspecified stringed instrument
	Wind instruments
60-64	Flute (Table M2)
	Including alto flute, bass flute, contrabass flute
	For piccolo see M110.P5
65-69	Oboe (Table M2)
70-74	Clarinet (Table M2)
	Including alto clarinet, basset clarinet, bass clarinet,
	contrabass clarinet
75-79	Bassoon. Contrabassoon (Table M2)
80-84	Horn (Table M2)

Instrumental music
One solo instrument
Wind instruments -- Continued

85-89	Trumpet. Cornet (Table M2)
90-94	Trombone (Table M2)
	Including alto trombone, bass trombone
95-99	Tuba (Table M2)
100-104	Saxhorn (Table M2)
105-109	Saxophone (Table M2)
110.A-Z	Other. By instrument, A-Z
	Prior to 1956 not subdivided by individual wind instrument
	For unspecified wind instrument see M111
110.A47	Alphorn
(110.A88)	Auto horn
	Bagpipe see M145
110.B33	Baritone. Euphonium
110.B35	Basset horn
110.B57	Birbynė
110.C5	Coach horn
	Cornet see M85+
110.C78	Crumhorn
110.C83	Csakan
	Di zi see M110.T6
110.E5	English horn
	Euphonium see M110.B33
110.F43	Fife
110.F5	Flageolet
110.F52	Flaviol
110.F53	Flügelhorn
110.G83	Guan
110.H4	Heckelphone
(110.H7)	Hsiao
	see M110.X53
110.I94	Iwabue
110.K4	Kaval
(110.K8)	Kuan
	see M110.G83
110.L9	Lur
110.M44	Melodica
(110.M7)	Mouth organ
	see M175.H3
110.M87	Musette (Oboe)
110.N38	Native American flute
110.N65	Nōkan
110.O3	Ocarina
110.P36	Panpipes
110.P46	Penny whistle

	Instrumental music
	One solo instrument
	Wind instruments
	Other. By instrument, A-Z -- Continued
110.P5	Piccolo
(110.P54)	P'illyul
	see M110.P58
110.P56	Pipe
	Class here the English instrument and similar duct flutes
	not classified separately
110.P58	P'iri. P'illyul
110.Q46	Quena
110.R4	Recorder
110.R98	Ryūteki
110.S39	Serpent
110.S45	Shakuhachi
110.S47	Shehnai
110.S5	Shofar
110.S6	Suo na
110.T3	Taegŭm
110.T36	Tanso
110.T6	Titsŭ tzu. Di zi
110.X53	Xiao
111	Unspecified wind instrument
	Plucked instruments
115-119	Harp (Table M2)
120-124	Banjo (Table M2)
125-129	Guitar (Table M2)
130-134	Mandolin (Table M2)
135-139	Zither (Table M2)
	Lute
140	Collections
141	Separate works
142.A-Z	Other. By instrument, A-Z
	Prior to 1978 not subdivided by individual plucked
	instrument
142.A7	Appalachian dulcimer
142.A8	Archlute
142.A87	Autoharp
142.B2	Balalaika
142.B3	Bandurria
142.B33	Bass guitar
142.B5	Biwa
142.C38	Cavaquinho
142.C44	Celtic harp
142.C49	Cheng. Zheng
142.C5	Ch'in. Qin

Instrumental music
One solo instrument
Plucked instruments
Other. By instrument, A-Z -- Continued

142.C58	Cittern
142.D55	Dobro
142.D6	Dömbra
(142.D8)	Dulcimer
	see M175.D84
	Dulcimer, Appalachian see M142.A7
142.E4	Electric guitar
	For bass guitar see M142.B33
142.E5	English guitar
142.G8	Gusli
142.H2	Harp-lute
142.H3	Hawaiian guitar
142.H9	Hyŏn' gŭm
142.I3	Ichigenkin
142.K36	Kanklės
142.K37	Kantele
142.K39	Kayagŭm
142.K55	Kobza
142.K58	Kŏmun'go
142.K59	Kopuz
142.K595	Kora
142.K6	Koto
(142.L9)	Lyra viol
	see M59.L9
142.M25	Mandola
142.M3	Mbira
142.O9	Oud
142.P6	Pi pa
	Qin see M142.C5
142.S45	Shamisen
142.S5	Sitar
(142.S7)	Santūr
	see M175.S26
142.T25	Tambura (Fretted lute)
142.T3	Tar (Lute)
142.T5	Theorbo
142.U5	Ukulele
142.V53	Vihuela
142.V55	Vina
(142.Y35)	Yang ch'in
	see M175.Y3
142.Y83	Yue qin
	Zheng see M142.C49

	Instrumental music
	One solo instrument -- Continued
	Percussion instruments. Other instruments
	For electronic organ see M14.8+
	For ondes Martenot see M175.O5
	For theremin see M175.T5
	For other electronic instruments see M1473
145	Bagpipe
146	Percussion. Drum
	Including drum set, snare drum, tympani, etc., and works for one performer playing two or more different percussion instruments
147	Bells, glockenspiel, etc.
(149)	Children's instruments. Button-key accordion
	For toy orchestra, see M1420
	For button-key accordion, see M154
(153)	Whistling pieces
	see M175.3
154	Concertina. Button-key accordion
165	Glass harmonica
172	Carillons. Chimes
174.A-Z	Mechanical instruments. By instrument, A-Z
	Prior to 1978 not subdivided by individual mechanical instrument
(174.A3)	Aeolian
174.B37	Barrel organ
(174.M4)	Metrostile
	see M20+
174.M85	Music box
(174.P4)	Pianola
	see M20+
(174.P5)	Pianola educational series
	see MT257
(174.R4)	Rythmic pianola
	see M20+
175.A-Z	Other. By instrument, A-Z
	Prior to 1956 not subdivided by individual instrument
	For varying or unspecified solo instrument see M175.5
175.A4	Accordion
175.A5	Apollo harp
(175.A8)	Autoharp
	see M142.A87
175.B17	Bambuso sonoro
175.B2	Bandoneon. Bayan
(175.B3)	Barrel organ
	see M174.B37

Instrumental music
  One solo instrument
    Percussion instruments. Other instruments
      Other. By instrument, A-Z -- Continued

	Bayan see M175.B2
	Button-key accordion see M154
175.C3	Calliope
175.C35	Castanets
175.C44	Celesta
175.C5	Cimbalom
175.C54	Clavioline
(175.C6)	Musique concrète
	see M1473
	Concertina see M154
175.C76	Crotales
175.D84	Dulcimer
175.H3	Harmonica
175.H45	Heliphon
(175.H8)	Hu qin
	see M59.E7
175.H9	Hurdy-gurdy
175.J4	Jew's harp
175.K45	Khim
(175.L87)	Lur
	see M110.L9
175.M3	Mandolin harp
	Marimba see M175.X6
175.M38	Melodeon
(175.M4)	Metrostile
	see M20+
175.M9	Musical saw
175.O5	Ondes Martenot
175.O6	Orphéal
175.S26	Santūr
175.S5	Sheng
175.S55	Shō
175.S74	Steel drum
(175.T35)	Tape
	see M1473
175.T5	Theremin
175.T56	Tinglik
175.T69	Toy piano
	Vibraharp see M175.X6
	Vibraphone see M175.X6
175.X6	Xylophone. Marimba. Vibraharp. Vibraphone
175.Y3	Yang qin
175.Y36	Yanggŭm

Instrumental music

One solo instrument -- Continued

175.3   Whistling pieces

Class here works for one or more whistlers with or without accompaniment

175.5   Varying solo instrument. Unspecified solo instrument

Class here collections of works for three or more different solo instruments or for unspecified solo instrument, and separate works for unspecified solo instrument

For music for unspecified stringed instrument see M59.5

For music for unspecified wind instrument see M111

176   Motion picture music

Class here instrumental music for silent films and music not meant for specific motion picture sound tracks

For vocal excerpts from music for specific motion pictures see M1505+

For music for specific motion pictures, including musicals either originally composed or adapted from stage versions see M1527+

176.5   Radio and television music

Class here instrumental music not intended for specific programs

For music composed for specific radio programs see M1527.5+

For music composed for specific television programs see M1527.7+

Two or more solo instruments

Class here scores and parts for chamber music and other ensembles principally for one player to a part

Classify individual works in which the number of players varies from movement to movement according to the total number of players

Cf. M990 Chamber music for instruments of the 18th century and earlier that are generally not used in the modern symphony orchestra

Collections for various numbers of solo instruments

For two or more organs see M180+

177   Miscellaneous collections
178   Original compositions
179   Arrangements

Duets

Organ

Class here works for one or more organs, two or more players

Including electronic organ

180   Collections

Instrumental music
  Two or more solo instruments
    Duets
      Piano, harpsichord, etc., and one other instrument
        Stringed instrument
          Double bass -- Continued
238   Separate works
239.A-Z   Other. By other instrument, A-Z
239.C36   Campanula
239.P37   Pardessus de viole
(239.Q6)   Quinton
                  see M239.P37
239.T74   Treble viol
239.V54   Viola da gamba
239.V56   Viola d'amore
239.V58   Viola pomposa
239.V62   Violone
        Wind instrument
          Including continuo played by two performers (e.g.
            harpsichord and violoncello) in addition to the
            featured instrument
240-244   Flute (Table M2)
                Including alto flute, bass flute, contrabass flute
                For piccolo, see M270.P45 , M271.P45
              Oboe
                For English horn, see M270.E5 , M271.E5
245   Collections
              Separate works
246   Original compositions
(246.2)   English horn
247   Arrangements
248-252   Clarinet (Table M2)
                Including alto clarinet, basset clarinet, bass clarinet,
                  contrabass clarinet
              Bassoon. Contrabassoon
                Class here original works and arrangements
253   Collections
254   Separate works
255-259   Horn (Table M2)
              Trumpet. Cornet
260   Collections
261   Separate works
              Trombone
                Including alto trombone, bass trombone
262   Collections
263   Separate works
              Tuba

Instrumental music
Two or more solo instruments
Duets
Piano, harpsichord, etc., and one other instrument
Wind instrument
Tuba -- Continued

264	Collections
265	Separate works
	Saxhorn
266	Collections
267	Separate works
	Saxophone
268	Collections
269	Separate works
	Other. By other instrument, A-Z
270.A-Z	Collections

Prior to 1978 not subdivided by individual wind
instrument

(270.A2)	General
270.A4	Alto horn
270.B3	Bagpipe
270.B37	Baritone. Euphonium
270.B4	Basset horn
270.B8	Bugle
	Cornet see M260+
270.C6	Cornett
270.C8	Csakan
270.E5	English horn
(270.E9)	Euphonium

see M270.B37

270.F7	Flügelhorn
270.G7	Gralla
270.M4	Mellophone
(270.M7)	Mouth organ

see M284.H3

270.O24	Oboe da caccia
270.O26	Oboe d'amore
270.O3	Ocarina
270.P3	Panpipes
270.P45	Piccolo
270.P5	Pipe
270.R4	Recorder
270.S45	Shakuhachi
270.S47	Shinobue
270.S5	Shofar
(270.S95)	Syrinx

see M270.P3

M

Instrumental music
  Two or more solo instruments
    Duets
      Piano, harpsichord, etc., and one other instrument
        Wind instrument
          Other. By other instrument, A-Z
            Collections -- Continued

270.T3	Tárogató
270.T45	Tenor horn
271.A-Z	Separate works
	Prior to 1978 not subdivided by individual wind instrument
271.A4	Alto horn
271.B3	Bagpipe
271.B37	Baritone. Euphonium
271.B4	Basset horn
271.B8	Bugle
271.C6	Cornett
271.C8	Csakan
271.E5	English horn
	Euphonium see M271.B37
271.F7	Flügelhorn
271.G7	Gralla
271.M4	Mellophone
(271.M7)	Mouth organ
	see M285.H3
271.O24	Oboe da caccia
271.O26	Oboe d'amore
271.O3	Ocarina
271.P3	Panpipes
271.P45	Piccolo
271.P5	Pipe
271.R4	Recorder
271.S45	Shakuhachi
271.S47	Shinobue
271.S5	Shofar
(271.S95)	Syrinx
	see M271.P3
271.T3	Tárogató
271.T45	Tenor horn

      Plucked instrument
        Including continuo played by two performers (e.g. theorbo
          and bassoon) in addition to the featured instrument
        Harp

272	Collections
273	Separate works

        Banjo

Instrumental music
Two or more solo instruments
Duets
Piano, harpsichord, etc., and one other instrument
Plucked instrument
Banjo -- Continued

274	Collections
275	Separate works
	Guitar
276	Collections
277	Separate works
	Mandolin
278	Collections
279	Separate works
	Zither
280	Collections
281	Separate works
	Other. By other instrument, A-Z
282.A-Z	Collections

Prior to 1978 not subdivided by individual plucked instrument

282.B3	Balalaika
(282.C5)	Cimbalom
	see M284.C5
(282.D4)	Dulcimer
	see M284.D85
282.D64	Dömbra
282.H4	Harp-lute guitar
282.L88	Lute
282.R33	Rabāb
282.T3	Tar (Lute)
283.A-Z	Separate works

Prior to 1978 not subdivided by individual plucked instrument

283.B3	Balalaika
(283.C5)	Cimbalom
	see M285.C5
(283.D4)	Dulcimer
	see M285.D85
283.D64	Dömbra
	Dulcimer see M285.D85
283.H4	Harp-lute guitar
283.L88	Lute
283.R33	Rabāb
283.T3	Tar (Lute)
	Other. By other instrument, A-Z

M

	Instrumental music
	Two or more solo instruments
	Duets
	Piano, harpsichord, etc., and one other instrument
	Other. By other instrument, A-Z -- Continued
284.A-Z	Collections
	Prior to 1956 not subdivided by individual "other" instrument
	For unspecified melody instrument see M285.5
284.A3	Accordion
(284.B3)	Balalaika
	see M282.B3
284.B33	Bandoneon
284.B4	Bells
284.C4	Celesta
(284.C43)	Chord organ
	see M284.E4
284.C45	Cimbalom
284.C5	Clavioline
284.C6	Computer. Synthesizer
284.C94	Cymbals
284.D8	Drum
	Including snare drum
284.D83	Drum set
284.D85	Dulcimer
284.E4	Electronic instrument
	Class here works for pre-recorded sound and works not assigned to other classes for specific electronic instruments or devices
284.G6	Glass harmonica
284.G65	Glockenspiel
284.H3	Harmonica. Mouth organ
284.H35	Hawaiian guitar
(284.K4)	Kettledrums
	see M284.T5
	Marimba see M284.X9
(284.M6)	Mouth organ
	see M284.H3
284.O5	Ondes Martenot
284.P4	Percussion
	Class here works for one performer playing two or more different percussion instruments
	Piano accordion see M284.A3
	Snare drum see M284.D8
	Synthesizer see M284.C6
	Tape see M284.E4
284.T5	Timpani

Instrumental music
Two or more solo instruments
Duets
Piano, harpsichord, etc., and one other instrument
Other. By other instrument, A-Z
Collections -- Continued

(284.V5)	Vibraphone
	see M284.X9
284.X9	Xylophone. Marimba. Vibraphone
285.A-Z	Separate works
	Prior to 1956 not subdivided by individual "other" instrument
	For unspecified melody instrument see M285.6
285.A3	Accordion
(285.B3)	Balalaika
	see M282.B3
285.B33	Bandoneon
285.B4	Bells
285.C4	Celesta
(285.C43)	Chord organ
	see M285.E4
285.C45	Cimbalom
285.C5	Clavioline
285.C6	Computer. Synthesizer
285.C94	Cymbals
285.D8	Drum
	Including snare drum
285.D83	Drum set
285.D85	Dulcimer
285.E4	Electronic instrument
	Class here works for pre-recorded sound and works not assigned to other classes for specific electronic instruments or devices
285.G6	Glass harmonica
285.G65	Glockenspiel
285.H3	Harmonica. Mouth organ
285.H35	Hawaiian guitar
(285.K4)	Kettledrums
	see M285.T5
	Marimba see M285.X9
(285.M6)	Mouth organ
	see M285.H3
285.O5	Ondes Martenot
285.P4	Percussion
	Class here works for one performer playing two or more different percussion instruments
	Piano accordion see M285.A3

	Instrumental music
	Two or more solo instruments
	Duets
	Piano, harpsichord, etc., and one other instrument
	Other. By other instrument, A-Z
	Separate works -- Continued
	Snare drum see M285.D8
	Synthesizer see M285.C6
	Tape see M285.E4
285.T5	Timpani
(285.V5)	Vibraphone
	see M285.X9
285.X9	Xylophone. Marimba. Vibraphone
	Unspecified melody instrument
285.5	Collections
285.6	Separate works
	Two stringed instruments
286	Collections
287	Separate works
	Two wind instruments
288	Collections
289	Separate works
	One stringed and one wind instrument
290	Collections
291	Separate works
	Two plucked instruments
292	Collections
293	Separate works
	One stringed and one plucked instrument
294	Collections
295	Separate works
	One wind and one plucked instrument
296	Collections
297	Separate works
298	Other combinations of specified instruments
	Class here works for two performers that cannot be assigned to other classes
	For accordion duets see M1362
298.5	Unspecified instruments. Combinations of specified and unspecified instruments
	Trios
300-304	Organ and two other instruments (Table M2)
	For organ(s) three players see M180+
305-309	Reed organ and two other instruments (Table M2)

Instrumental music
Two or more solo instruments
Trios -- Continued
Piano, harpsichord, etc., and two other instruments
Including continuo played by two performers (e.g.
harpsichord and violoncello, theorbo and bassoon) in
addition to the featured instruments
For two or more pianos, three or more performers
see M216
Stringed instruments

310	Miscellaneous collections
	Class here collections containing both original works and arrangements
	Original compositions
311	General collections
	Special collections. Separate works
312	Piano, violin or viola, and violoncello
312.4	Other combinations
	Class here separate works only
	Arrangements
313	Collections
314	Separate works
315-319	Wind instruments (Table M2)
320-324	Stringed and wind instruments (Table M2)
325-329	Plucked instruments (Table M2)
330-334	Stringed and plucked instruments (Table M2)
335-339	Wind and plucked instruments (Table M2)
340-344	Other combinations (Table M2)
349-353	Stringed instruments (Table M2)
	Wind instruments
355	Miscellaneous collections
	Class here collections containing both original works and arrangements
	Original compositions
356	Collections
	Separate works
357	General
357.2	Woodwinds only
357.4	Brasses only
	Arrangements
358	Collections
359	Separate works
360-364	Stringed and wind instruments (Table M2)
365-369	Plucked instruments (Table M2)
370-374	Stringed and plucked instruments (Table M2)
375-379	Wind and plucked instruments (Table M2)
380-384	Stringed, wind, and plucked instruments (Table M2)

M

Instrumental music
   Two or more solo instruments
      Trios -- Continued

385   Other combinations of specified instruments
             Class here works for three performers that cannot be
                assigned to other classes

386   Unspecified instruments. Combinations of specified and
             unspecified instruments

        Quartets

400-404   Organ and three other instruments (Table M2)
405-409   Reed organ and three other instruments (Table M2)
          Piano, harpsichord, etc., and three other instruments
             Including continuo played by two performers (e.g.,
                harpsichord and violoncello, theorbo and bassoon) in
                addition to the featured instruments
           Stringed instruments

410   Miscellaneous collections
              Class here collections containing both original works
                and arrangements
            Original compositions

411   General collections
             Special collections. Separate works

412   Violin, viola, and violoncello
412.2   Three violins
412.4   Other combinations
                Class here separate works only
            Arrangements

413   Collections
414   Separate works
415-419   Wind instruments (Table M2)
420-424   Stringed and wind instruments (Table M2)
425-429   Plucked instruments (Table M2)
430-434   Stringed and plucked instruments (Table M2)
435-439   Wind and plucked instruments (Table M2)
440-444   Stringed, wind, and plucked instruments (Table M2)
445-449   Other combinations (Table M2)
          Stringed instruments

450   Miscellaneous collections
               Class here collections containing both original works and
                arrangements
            Original compositions

451   General collections
             Special collections. Separate works

452   Two violins, viola, violoncello
452.2   Four violins
452.4   Other combinations
                Class here separate works only

Instrumental music
　　Two or more solo instruments
　　　　Quartets
　　　　　　Stringed instruments -- Continued
　　　　　　　　Arrangements

| 453 | Collections |
| 454 | Separate works |

　　　　　　Wind instruments

| 455 | Miscellaneous collections |

　　　　　　　　　　Class here collections containing both original works and
　　　　　　　　　　　arrangements
　　　　　　　　Original compositions

| 456 | Collections |

　　　　　　　　Separate works

457	General
457.2	Woodwinds only
457.4	Brasses only

　　　　　　　　Arrangements

458	Collections
459	Separate works
460-464	Stringed and wind instruments (Table M2)
465-469	Plucked instruments (Table M2)
470-474	Stringed and plucked instruments (Table M2)
475-479	Wind and plucked instruments (Table M2)
480-484	Stringed, wind, and plucked instruments (Table M2)
485	Other combinations of specified instruments

　　　　　　　　Class here works for four performers that cannot be
　　　　　　　　　assigned to other classes

| 486 | Unspecified instruments. Combinations of specified and unspecified instruments |

　　　　Quintets

| 500-504 | Organ and four other instruments (Table M2) |
| 505-509 | Reed organ and four other instruments (Table M2) |

　　　　　　Piano, harpsichord, etc., and four other instruments
　　　　　　　　Including continuo played by two performers (e.g.,
　　　　　　　　　harpsichord and violoncello, theorbo and bassoon) in
　　　　　　　　　addition to the featured instruments
　　　　　　Stringed instruments

| 510 | Miscellaneous collections |

　　　　　　　　Class here collections containing both original works
　　　　　　　　　and arrangements
　　　　　　　Original compositions

| 511 | General collections |

　　　　　　　Special collections. Separate works

| 512 | Two violins, viola, violoncello |
| 512.2 | Four violins |

	Instrumental music
	Two or more solo instruments
	Quintets
	Piano, harpsichord, etc., and four other instruments
	Stringed instruments
	Original compositions
	Special collections. Separate works -- Continued
512.4	Other combinations
	Class here separate works only
	Arrangements
513	Collections
514	Separate works
515-519	Wind instruments (Table M2)
520-524	Stringed and wind instruments (Table M2)
525-529	Plucked instruments (Table M2)
530-534	Stringed and plucked instruments (Table M2)
535-539	Wind and plucked instruments (Table M2)
540-544	Stringed, wind, and plucked instruments (Table M2)
545-549	Other combinations (Table M2)
550-554	Stringed instruments (Table M2)
	Wind instruments
555	Miscellaneous collections
	Class here collections containing both original works and arrangements
	Original compositions
556	Collections
	Separate works
557	General
557.2	Woodwinds only
557.4	Brasses only
	Arrangements
558	Collections
559	Separate works
560-564	Stringed and wind instruments (Table M2)
565-569	Plucked instruments (Table M2)
570-574	Stringed and plucked instruments (Table M2)
575-579	Wind and plucked instruments (Table M2)
580-584	Stringed, wind, and plucked instruments (Table M2)
585	Other combinations of specified instruments
	Class here works for five performers that cannot be assigned to other classes
586	Unspecified instruments. Combinations of specified and unspecified instruments
	Sextets
600-604	Organ and five other instruments (Table M2)
605-609	Reed organ and five other instruments (Table M2)

Instrumental music
  Two or more solo instruments
    Sextets -- Continued
      Piano, harpsichord, etc., and five other instruments
        Including continuo played by two performers (e.g.,
          harpsichord and violoncello, theorbo and bassoon) in
          addition to the featured instruments

610-614	Stringed instruments (Table M2)
615-619	Wind instruments (Table M2)
620-624	Stringed and wind instruments (Table M2)
625-629	Plucked instruments (Table M2)
630-634	Stringed and plucked instruments (Table M2)
635-639	Wind and plucked instruments (Table M2)
640-644	Stringed, wind, and plucked instruments (Table M2)
645-649	Other combinations (Table M2)
650-654	Stringed instruments (Table M2)

      Wind instruments

655	Miscellaneous collections

        Class here collections containing both original works and
          arrangements
        Original compositions

656	Collections

          Separate works

657	General
657.2	Woodwinds only
657.4	Brasses only

        Arrangements

658	Collections
659	Separate works
660-664	Stringed and wind instruments (Table M2)
665-669	Plucked instruments (Table M2)
670-674	Stringed and plucked instruments (Table M2)
675-679	Wind and plucked instruments (Table M2)
680-684	Stringed, wind, and plucked instruments (Table M2)
685	Other combinations of specified instruments

        Class here works for six performers that cannot be
          assigned to other classes

686	Unspecified instruments. Combinations of specified and unspecified instruments

    Septets

700-704	Organ and six other instruments (Table M2)
705-709	Reed organ and six other instruments (Table M2)

      Piano, harpsichord, etc., and six other instruments
        Including continuo played by two performers (e.g.,
          harpsichord and violoncello, theorbo and bassoon) in
          addition to the featured instruments

710-714	Stringed instruments (Table M2)

	Instrumental music
	Two or more solo instruments
	Septets
	Piano, harpsichord, etc., and six other instruments -- Continued
715-719	Wind instruments (Table M2)
720-724	Stringed and wind instruments (Table M2)
725-729	Plucked instruments (Table M2)
730-734	Stringed and plucked instruments (Table M2)
735-739	Wind and plucked instruments (Table M2)
740-744	Stringed, wind, and plucked instruments (Table M2)
745-749	Other combinations (Table M2)
750-754	Stringed instruments (Table M2)
	Wind instruments
755	Miscellaneous collections
	Class here collections containing both original works and arrangements
	Original compositions
756	Collections
	Separate works
757	General
757.2	Woodwinds only
757.4	Brasses only
	Arrangements
758	Collections
759	Separate works
760-764	Stringed and wind instruments (Table M2)
765-769	Plucked instruments (Table M2)
770-774	Stringed and plucked instruments (Table M2)
775-779	Wind and plucked instruments (Table M2)
780-784	Stringed, wind, and plucked instruments (Table M2)
785	Other combinations of specified instruments
	Class here works for seven performers that cannot be assigned to other classes
786	Unspecified instruments. Combinations of specified and unspecified instruments
	Octets
800-804	Organ and seven other instruments (Table M2)
805-809	Reed organ and seven other instruments (Table M2)
	Piano, harpsichord, etc., and seven other instruments
	Including continuo played by two performers (e.g., harpsichord and violoncello, theorbo and bassoon) in addition to the featured instruments
810-814	Stringed instruments (Table M2)
815-819	Wind instruments (Table M2)
820-824	Stringed and wind instruments (Table M2)
825-829	Plucked instruments (Table M2)

	Instrumental music
	Two or more solo instruments
	Octets
	Piano, harpsichord, etc., and seven other instruments -- Continued
830-834	Stringed and plucked instruments (Table M2)
835-839	Wind and plucked instruments (Table M2)
840-844	Stringed, wind, and plucked instruments (Table M2)
845-849	Other combinations (Table M2)
850-854	Stringed instruments (Table M2)
	Wind instruments
855	Miscellaneous collections
	Class here collections containing both original works and arrangements
	Original compositions
856	Collections
	Separate works
857	General
857.2	Woodwinds only
857.4	Brasses only
	Arrangements
858	Collections
859	Separate works
860-864	Stringed and wind instruments (Table M2)
865-869	Plucked instruments (Table M2)
870-874	Stringed and plucked instruments (Table M2)
875-879	Wind and plucked instruments (Table M2)
880-884	Stringed, wind, and plucked instruments (Table M2)
885	Other combinations of specified instruments
	Class here works for eight performers that cannot be assigned to other classes
886	Unspecified instruments. Combinations of specified and unspecified instruments
	Nonets and larger chamber music combinations
900-904	Organ and eight or more other instruments (Table M2)
905-909	Reed organ and eight or more other instruments
	Piano, harpsichord, etc., and eight or more other instruments
	Including continuo played by two performers (e.g., harpsichord and violoncello, theorbo and bassoon) in addition to the featured instruments
910-914	Stringed instruments (Table M2)
915-919	Wind instruments (Table M2)
920-924	Stringed and wind instruments (Table M2)
925-929	Plucked instruments (Table M2)
930-934	Stringed and plucked instruments (Table M2)
935-939	Wind and plucked instruments (Table M2)

Instrumental music
Two or more solo instruments
Nonets and larger chamber music combinations
Piano, harpsichord, etc., and eight or more other
instruments -- Continued

940-944	Stringed, wind, and plucked instruments (Table M2)
945-949	Other combinations (Table M2)
950-954	Stringed instruments (Table M2)
	Wind instruments
955	Miscellaneous collections

Class here collections containing both original works and
arrangements

Original compositions

956	Collections
	Separate works
957	General
957.2	Woodwinds only
957.4	Brasses only
	Arrangements
958	Collections
959	Separate works
960-964	Stringed and wind instruments (Table M2)
965-969	Plucked instruments (Table M2)
970-974	Stringed and plucked instruments (Table M2)
975-979	Wind and plucked instruments (Table M2)
980-984	Stringed, wind, and plucked instruments (Table M2)
985	Other combinations of specified instruments

Class here works for nine or more solo performers that
cannot be assigned to other classes

986	Unspecified instruments. Combinations of specified and unspecified instruments
990	Early instruments

Class here chamber music for two or more instruments of the
18th century and earlier

For solo recorders in various combinations, see M355+ ,
M455+ , etc.

For early instruments in combination with modern
instruments, see M177+

For one early instrument and harpsichord continuo, see
M239, M270+ M282+ M284+

For one early instrument and organ continuo see
M182+

(991)	Orchestral music including obsolete instruments not classified with music for modern orchestra

see M1000+

(992)	Two or more solo obsolete instruments

see M177+ , M990

Instrumental music
Two or more solo instruments
Early instruments -- Continued
(993)   Orchestral music not classified with music for modern
orchestra
see M1000+
Orchestra
Including works for chamber orchestra
1000   Collections
Class here collections too varied to assign to more specific
classes
Class collections in a specific form with the form, e.g.,
collections of symphonies in M1001
Original compositions
Class collections of a particular form or type with individual
works
1001   Symphonies
1002   Symphonic poems
1003   Suites. Variation forms
Including separately published suites from operas, ballets,
etc.
Including passacaglias, chaconnes, etc.
1004   Overtures
Including separately published opera preludes, entr'actes,
and overtures
Solo instrument(s) with orchestra
Class here concertos and similar works, both original and
arranged
1004.5   Collections for different solo instruments
Class here scores, parts, and solo(s) with keyboard
instrument
Collections of cadenzas
1004.6   Different solo instruments
1004.7.A-Z   The same solo instrument. By instrument, A-Z
One solo instrument. Two or more of the same solo
instrument
Keyboard instruments
Organ
1005   Scores. Parts
1005.5.A-Z   Cadenzas
By composer of concerto, A-Z
1006   Solo(s) with keyboard instrument
Piano, harpsichord, clavichord, etc.
1010   Scores. Parts
1010.5.A-Z   Cadenzas. By composer of concerto, A-Z
1011   Solo(s) with keyboard instrument
Stringed instruments

	Instrumental music
	Orchestra
	Original compositions
	Solo instrument(s) with orchestra
	One solo instrument. Two or more of the same solo instrument
	Stringed instruments -- Continued
	Violin
1012	Scores. Parts
1012.5.A-Z	Cadenzas. By composer of concerto, A-Z
1013	Solo(s) with keyboard instrument
	Viola
1014	Scores. Parts
1014.5.A-Z	Cadenzas. By composer of concerto, A-Z
1015	Solo(s) with keyboard instrument
	Violoncello
1016	Scores. Parts
1016.5.A-Z	Cadenzas. By composer of concerto, A-Z
1017	Solo(s) with keyboard instrument
1018	Double bass
	Class here scores, parts, cadenzas, and solo(s) with keyboard instrument
1019.A-Z	Other. By solo instrument, A-Z
	Class here scores, parts, cadenzas, and solo(s) with keyboard instrument
	Prior to 1978 not subdivided by individual solo stringed instrument
	Ban hu see M1019.P3
1019.C5	Ching hu. Jing hu
1019.C55	Chung hu. Zong hu
1019.E8	Er hu
	Gao hu see M1019.K32
	Jing hu see M1019.C5
1019.K32	Kao hu. Gao hu
1019.P3	Pan hu. Ban hu
1019.V54	Viola da gamba
1019.V56	Viola d'amore
	Zong hu see M1019.C55
	Wind instruments
	Flute
	Including alto flute, bass flute, contrabass flute
	For piccolo, see M1034.P5 , M1034.5.P5 , M1035.P5
1020	Scores. Parts
1020.5.A-Z	Cadenzas. By composer of concerto, A-Z
1021	Solo(s) with keyboard instrument

Instrumental music
  Orchestra
    Original compositions
      Solo instrument(s) with orchestra
        One solo instrument. Two or more of the same solo
          instrument
          Wind instruments -- Continued
            Oboe
              For English horn, see M1034.E5 , M1034.5.E5 ,
                M1035.E5

1022	Scores. Parts
1022.5.A-Z	Cadenzas. By composer of concerto, A-Z
1023	Solo(s) with keyboard instrument

            Clarinet
              Including alto clarinet, basset clarinet, bass clarinet,
                contrabass clarinet

1024	Scores. Parts
1024.5.A-Z	Cadenzas. By composer of concerto, A-Z
1025	Solo(s) with keyboard instrument

            Bassoon. Contrabassoon

1026	Scores. Parts
1026.5.A-Z	Cadenzas. By composer of concerto, A-Z
1027	Solo(s) with keyboard instrument

            Horn

1028	Scores. Parts
1028.5.A-Z	Cadenzas. By composer of concerto, A-Z
1029	Solo(s) with keyboard instrument

            Trumpet. Cornet

1030	Scores. Parts
1030.5.A-Z	Cadenzas. By composer of concerto, A-Z
1031	Solo(s) with keyboard instrument

            Trombone
              Including alto trombone, bass trombone

1032	Scores. Parts
1032.5.A-Z	Cadenzas. By composer of concerto, A-Z
1033	Solo(s) with keyboard instrument

            Other. By solo instrument, A-Z

1034.A-Z	Scores. Parts

              Prior to 1978 not subdivided by individual solo wind
                instrument

1034.B37	Baritone. Euphonium
1034.B38	Basset horn
1034.C5	Chalumeau
	Cornet see M1030
	Di zi see M1034.T6
1034.E5	English horn
	Euphonium see M1034.B37

Instrumental music
Orchestra
Original compositions
Solo instrument(s) with orchestra
One solo instrument. Two or more of the same solo instrument
Wind instruments
Other. By solo instrument, A-Z
Scores. Parts -- Continued

1034.F6	Flügelhorn
1034.H4	Heckelphone
1034.K8	Kuan
1034.O26	Oboe d'amore
1034.P35	Panpipes
1034.P5	Piccolo
1034.R4	Recorder
1034.R66	Roopill
1034.S4	Saxophone
	Class here saxophones in all registers
1034.S5	Shakuhachi
1034.T3	Tárogató
1034.T6	Ti tzu. Di zi
1034.T8	Tuba
1034.5.A-Z	Cadenzas. By composer of concerto, A-Z
	Prior to 1978 not subdivided by individual solo wind instrument
1034.5.B37	Baritone. Euphonium
1034.5.B38	Basset horn
1034.5.C5	Chalumeau
	Cornet see M1030.5.A+
	Di zi see M1034.5.T6
1034.5.E5	English horn
	Euphonium see M1034.5.B37
1034.5.F6	Flügelhorn
1034.5.H4	Heckelphone
1034.5.K8	Kuan
1034.5.O26	Oboe d'amore
1034.5.P35	Panpipes
1034.5.P5	Piccolo
1034.5.R4	Recorder
1034.5.R66	Roopill
1034.5.S4	Saxophone
	Class here saxophones in all registers
1034.5.S5	Shakuhachi
1034.5.T3	Tárogató
1034.5.T6	Ti tzu. Di zi
1034.5.T8	Tuba

	Instrumental music
	Orchestra
	Original compositions
	Solo instrument(s) with orchestra
	One solo instrument. Two or more of the same solo instrument
	Wind instruments
	Other. By solo instrument, A-Z -- Continued
1035.A-Z	Solo(s) with keyboard instrument
	Prior to 1978 not subdivided by individual solo wind instrument
1035.B37	Baritone. Euphonium
1035.B38	Basset horn
1035.C5	Chalumeau
	Cornet see M1031
	Di zi see M1035.T6
1035.E5	English horn
	Euphonium see M1035.B37
1035.F6	Flügelhorn
1035.H4	Heckelphone
1035.K8	Kuan
1035.O26	Oboe d'amore
1035.P35	Panpipes
1035.P5	Piccolo
1035.R4	Recorder
1035.R66	Roopill
1035.S4	Saxophone
	Class here saxophones in all registers
1035.S5	Shakuhachi
1035.T3	Tárogató
1035.T6	Ti tzu. Di zi
1035.T8	Tuba
	Plucked instruments
	Harp
1036	Scores. Parts
1036.5.A-Z	Cadenzas. By composer of concerto, A-Z
1037	Solo(s) with keyboard instrument
1037.4.A-Z	Other. By solo instrument, A-Z
	Class here scores, parts, cadenzas, and solo(s) with keyboard instrument
	Prior to 1978 solo plucked instruments other than harp were classified in M1038+
1037.4.B3	Balalaika
1037.4.B36	Banjo
1037.4.C3	Canun
1037.4.C58	Cithara
1037.4.D64	Dömbra

Instrumental music
  Orchestra
    Original compositions
      Solo instrument(s) with orchestra
        One solo instrument. Two or more of the same solo instrument
          Plucked instruments
            Other. By solo instrument, A-Z -- Continued

1037.4.E44	Elecric guitar
1037.4.G8	Guitar
1037.4.K68	Koto
1037.4.M3	Mandolin
1037.4.P5	Pi pa
1037.4.S58	Sitar
1037.4.T3	Tar (Lute)
1037.4.U4	Ukulele
1037.4.Z6	Zither

          Percussion instruments
            Including works for one or more soloists playing two or more percussion instruments
            Prior to 1978 used for plucked solo instruments other than harp
            For one soloist playing one percussion instrument see M1039.4.A+

1038	Scores. Parts

            Prior to 1978 used for plucked solo instruments other than harp

1038.5.A-1038.Z	Cadenzas. By composer of concerto, A-Z

            Prior to 1978 used for plucked solo instruments other than harp

1039	Solo(s) with keyboard instrument

            Prior to 1978 used for plucked solo instruments other than harp

1039.4.A-Z	Other. By solo instrument, A-Z

            Class here scores, parts, cadenzas, and solo(s) with keyboard instrument

1039.4.A3	Accordion
1039.4.B3	Bandoneon
1039.4.B4	Bayan
1039.4.C55	Cimbalom
1039.4.D85	Dulcimer

	Instrumental music
	Orchestra
	Original compositions
	Solo instrument(s) with orchestra
	One solo instrument. Two or more of the same solo instrument
	Other. By solo instrument, A-Z -- Continued
1039.4.E35	Electronics
	Class here works for one or more performers playing two or more different electronic instruments or devices, and works for one instrument not assigned to a more specific class, e.g., M1039.4.O5 , Ondes Martenot; M1039.4.S95 , Synthesizer
1039.4.E37	Electronic organ
(1039.4.E38)	Electronics
	see M1039.4.E35
1039.4.E4	Electronium
1039.4.G58	Glass harmonica
1039.4.G87	Gusli
1039.4.H3	Harmonica
(1039.4.H83)	Hu ch'in
	see M1019.E8
1039.4.H87	Hurdy-gurdy
	Marimba
	see M1039.4.X9
(1039.4.M6)	Mouth organ
	see M1039.4.H3
1039.4.O5	Ondes Martenot
1039.4.P5	Pianola
	Pre-recorded tape see M1039.4.T3
1039.4.S26	Santūr
1039.4.S5	Sheng
1039.4.S95	Synthesizer
1039.4.T3	Tape
	Including pre-recorded tape
1039.4.T7	Trautonium
	Vibraphone
	see M1039.4.X9
1039.4.X9	Xylophone. Vibraphone. Marimba
1039.4.Y35	Yang qin
1039.5	Unspecified instrument
	Class here scores, parts, cadenzas, and solos with keyboard instrument
	Two or more different solo instruments
1040	Scores. Parts
1040.5.A-Z	Cadenzas. By composer of concerto, A-Z

Instrumental music
Orchestra
Original compositions
Solo instrument(s) with orchestra
Two or more different solo instruments -- Continued
1041   Solos with keyboard instrument
1042   Concertos for orchestra
Pieces
1045   General
Class here works that cannot be assigned to a more
specific class
1046   Marches
Dances
1047   General
1048   Two-rhythm (polka, etc.)
1049   Three-rhythm (waltz, etc.)
Arrangements
Class here works that cannot be assigned to a more specific
class
For arrangements for solo instrument(s) with orchestra
see M1004.5+
1060   General
1070   Excerpts
Including entirely instrumental arrangements of works
originally with vocal parts
1075   Potpourris, fantaisies, etc.
String orchestra
1100   Miscellaneous collections. General collections
Original compositions
Including special collections
1101   Symphonies
1102   Symphonic poems
1103   Suites. Variation forms
Including passacaglias, chaconnes, etc.
1104   Overtures
Including separately published opera preludes, entr'actes,
and overtures
Solo instrument(s) with string orchestra
Class here concertos and similar works, both original and
arranged
Collections for different solo instruments
Prior to 1978 used for all works for solo instruments
accompanied by string orchestra
1105   Scores. Parts
Prior to 1978 used for all works for solo instrument(s)
accompanied by string orchestra

                     Instrumental music
                       String orchestra
                         Original compositions
                           Solo instrument(s) with string orchestra
                            Collections for different solo instruments -- Continued

1106	Solo(s) with keyboard instrument
	Prior to 1978 used for all works for solo instrument(s) originally accompanied by string orchestra
	One solo instrument. Two or more of the same solo instrument
	Prior to 1978 solo instrument(s) with string orchestra accompaniment was classified in M1105+
	Keyboard instruments
	Organ
1108	Scores. Parts
1108.5.A-Z	Cadenzas
	By composer of concerto, A-Z
1109	Solo(s) with keyboard instrument
	Piano, harpsichord, clavichord, etc.
1110	Scores. Parts
1110.5.A-Z	Cadenzas. By composer of concerto, A-Z
1111	Solo(s) with keyboard instrument
	Stringed instruments
	Violin
1112	Scores. Parts
1112.5.A-Z	Cadenzas. By composer of concerto, A-Z
1113	Solo(s) with keyboard instrument
	Viola
1114	Scores. Parts
1114.5.A-Z	Cadenzas. By composer of concerto, A-Z
1115	Solo(s) with keyboard instrument
	Violoncello
1116	Scores. Parts
1116.5.A-Z	Cadenzas. By composer of concerto, A-Z
1117	Solo(s) with keyboard instrument
1118	Double bass
	Class here scores, parts, cadenzas, and solo(s) with keyboard instrument
1119.A-Z	Other. By solo instrument, A-Z
	Class here scores, parts, cadenzas, and solo(s) with keyboard instrument
1119.H37	Hardanger fiddle
1119.N36	Nan hu
1119.V54	Viola da gamba
1119.V56	Viola d'amore
1119.V6	Violoncello piccolo
	Wind instruments

M

Instrumental music
  String orchestra
    Original compositions
      Solo instrument(s) with string orchestra
        One solo instrument. Two or more of the same solo
          instrument
         Wind instruments -- Continued
          Flute
            Including alto flute, bass flute, contrabass flute
              For piccolo, see M1134.P5 , M1134.5.P5 , M1135.P5

1120	Scores. Parts
1120.5.A-Z	Cadenzas. By composer of concerto, A-Z
1121	Solo(s) with keyboard instrument

          Oboe
            For English horn, see M1134.E5 , M1134.5.E5 ,
              M1135.E5

1122	Scores. Parts
1122.5.A-Z	Cadenzas. By composer of concerto, A-Z
1123	Solo(s) with keyboard instruments

          Clarinet
            Including alto clarinet, bass clarinet, basset clarinet,
              contrabass clarinet

1124	Scores. Parts
1124.5.A-Z	Cadenzas. By composer of concerto, A-Z
1125	Solo(s) with keyboard instrument

          Bassoon. Contrabassoon

1126	Scores. Parts
1126.5.A-Z	Cadenzas. By composer of concerto, A-Z
1127	Solo(s) with keyboard instrument

          Horn

1128	Scores. Parts
1128.5.A-Z	Cadenzas. By composer of concerto, A-Z
1129	Solo(s) with keyboard instrument

          Trumpet. Cornet

1130	Scores. Parts
1130.5	Cadenzas
1131	Solo(s) with keyboard instrument

          Trombone
            Including alto trombone, bass trombone

1132	Scores. Parts
1132.5.A-Z	Cadenzas. By composer of concerto, A-Z
1133	Solo(s) with keyboard instrument

          Other. By solo instrument, A-Z

1134.A-Z	Scores. Parts
1134.B37	Baritone. Euphonium
1134.C5	Chalumeau
	Cornet see M1130

Instrumental music
String orchestra
Original compositions
Solo instrument(s) with string orchestra
One solo instrument. Two or more of the same solo instrument
Wind instruments
Other. By solo instrument, A-Z
Scores. Parts -- Continued

1134.E5	English horn
	Euphonium see M1134.B37
1134.F7	Flügelhorn
1134.O26	Oboe d'amore
1134.P5	Piccolo
1134.R4	Recorder
1134.S4	Saxophone
1134.S5	Shakuhachi
1134.T8	Tuba
	Cadenzas. By composer of concerto, A-Z
1134.5.B37	Baritone. Euphonium
1134.5.C5	Chalumeau
	Cornet see M1130.5
1134.5.E5	English horn
	Euphonium see M1134.5.B37
1134.5.F7	Flügelhorn
1134.5.O26	Oboe d'amore
1134.5.P5	Piccolo
1134.5.R4	Recorder
1134.5.S4	Saxophone
1134.5.S5	Shakuhachi
1134.5.T8	Tuba
	Solo(s) with keyboard instrument
1135.B37	Baritone. Euphonium
1135.C5	Chalumeau
	Cornet see M1131
1135.E5	English horn
	Euphonium see M1135.B37
1135.F7	Flügelhorn
1135.O26	Oboe d'amore
1135.P5	Piccolo
1135.R4	Recorder
1135.S4	Saxophone
1135.S5	Shakuhachi
1135.T8	Tuba
	Plucked instruments
	Harp
1136	Scores. Parts

Instrumental music
String orchestra
Original compositions
Solo instrument(s) with string orchestra
One solo instrument. Two or more of the same solo instrument
Plucked instruments
Harp -- Continued

1136.5.A-Z	Cadenzas. By composer of concerto, A-Z
1137	Solo(s) with keyboard instrument
1137.4.A-Z	Other. By solo instrument, A-Z
	Class here scores, parts, cadenzas, and solo(s) with keyboard instrument
1137.4.A6	Appalachian dulcimer
1137.4.G8	Guitar
1137.4.K36	Kantele
1137.4.L88	Lute
1137.4.M3	Mandolin
1137.4.O9	Oud
1137.4.P7	Psaltery

Percussion instruments
For obsolete numbers formerly used under this span see Table MZ2
Class here works for one or more soloists playing one or more percussion instruments

1138	Scores. Parts
1138.5.A-Z	Cadenzas. By composer of concerto, A-Z
1139	Solo(s) with keyboard instrument
1139.4.A-Z	Other. By solo instrument, A-Z
	Class here scores, parts, cadenzas, and solo(s) with keyboard instrument
1139.4.A3	Accordion
1139.4.B3	Bandoneon
1139.4.C5	Cimbalom
1139.4.C6	Concertina
1139.4.D85	Dulcimer
1139.4.E35	Electronics
	Class here works for one performer using two or more different electronic instruments or devices, or for electronic media that cannot be assigned a more specfic class, e. g., M1139.4.O5
1139.4.H3	Harmonica
(1139.4.M6)	Mouth organ
	see M1139.4.H3
1139.4.O5	Ondes Martenot
1139.4.W5	Wind controller

Instrumental music
String orchestra
Original compositions
Solo instrument(s) with string orchestra
One solo instrument. Two or more of the same solo
instrument -- Continued

1139.5	Unspecified solo instrument
	Class here scores, parts, cadenzas, and solos with keyboard instrument
	Two or more different solo instruments
1140	Scores. Parts
1140.5.A-Z	Cadenzas. By composer of concerto, A-Z
1141	Solos with keyboard instrument
1142	Concertos for string orchestra
	Pieces
	Class here works that cannot be assigned to a more specific class
1145	General
1146	Marches
	Dances
1147	General
1148	Two-rhythm (polka, etc.)
1149	Three-rhythm (waltz, etc.)
1160	Arrangements
	For arrangements for solo instrument(s) with string orchestra see M1105+
	Band
1200	Miscellaneous collections. General collections
	Original compositions
	Including special collections
1201	Symphonies
1202	Symphonic poems
1203	Suites. Variation forms
	Including passacaglias, chaconnes, etc.
1204	Overtures
	Including separately published opera preludes, entr'actes, and overtures
	Solo instrument(s) with band
1205	Scores. Parts
1206	Solo(s) with keyboard instrument
1242	Concertos for band
	Pieces
1245	General
1247	Marches
	Dances
1247.9	General
1248	Two-rhythm (polka, etc.)

Instrumental music
Band
Original compositions
Pieces
Dances -- Continued
1249   Three-rhythm (waltzes, etc.)
Arrangements
1254   Symphonies, symphonic poems, suites, etc.
1255   Overtures
Including separately published opera preludes, entr'actes,
and overtures
1257   Solo instrument(s) with band
Class here scores, parts, cadenzas, and solo(s) with
keyboard instrument
Pieces
1258   General
1260   Marches
Dances
1262   General
1264   Two-rhythm (polka, etc.)
1266   Three-rhythm (waltz, etc.)
1268   Potpourris, fantaisies, etc.
1269   Marching routines
1270   Fife or bugle and drum music, field music, etc.
Other ensembles
For ensembles of electronic instruments, aleatory music,
or mixed media see M1470+
Reduced orchestra
Class here works originally composed with accompaniment
for reduced orchestra
Including works for music hall, salon, etc., orchestra, in which
the piano is generally the leading instrument
Including dance orchestra music received prior to July 1,
1944
For dance orchestra music received after July 1, 1944
see M1356+
For lead sheets see M1356.2
1350   General
(1352)   Church orchestra
see M1350
1353   Solos with keyboard instrument
(1355)   Song orchestration (vaudeville, etc.)
see M1356-M1356.2
Dance orchestra or instrumental ensemble
Including popular music of all countries
For music copyrighted or received prior to July 1, 1944
see M1350+

	Instrumental music
	Other ensembles
	Dance orchestra or instrumental ensemble -- Continued
1356	General
1356.2	Lead sheets
(1357)	Moving picture orchestra

For music for silent films and music not intended for specific motion picture sound tracks see M176

For music composed for specific motion picture sound tracks, including musicals either originally composed for motion pictures or adapted from stage versions see M1527+

1360	Plucked instrument orchestras

Including works for soloist(s) with accompaniment of orchestra of plucked instruments

1362	Accordion ensemble. Accordion band

Including music for two or more accordions

1363	Steel band
1365	Minstrel music

Class here instrumental and vocal music

1366	Jazz ensembles

Class here instrumental duets, trios, etc.

For jazz for solo instruments see M6+

For jazz vocals see M1622 , M1630.18-M1630.2 , M1680.18-M1680.2 , etc.

	Instrumental music for children
	One instrument
1375	Organ. Reed organ

For electronic organ see M14.8+

	Piano, harpsichord, etc.
1378	Collections
1380	Separate works
1385.A-Z	Other, A-Z
1385.A4	Accordion
1385.A8	Autoharp
1385.B34	Bandoneon
1385.B35	Banjo
1385.C6	Clarinet
1385.D6	Double bass
1385.D7	Drum
1385.E4	Electronic organ
1385.F6	Flute
1385.G7	Guitar
1385.H3	Harp
1385.H6	Horn
	Marimba see M1385.X9
1385.M3	Melody instrument. Unspecified solo instrument

Instrumental music

Instrumental music for children

One instrument

Other, A-Z -- Continued

1385.P5	Percussion
	Class here works for one percussionist playing two or more different percussion instruments
1385.R3	Recorder
1385.T76	Trombone
1385.T78	Trumpet
1385.T8	Tuba
1385.U5	Ukulele
	Unspecified solo instrument see M1385.M3
	Vibraharp see M1385.X9
	Vibraphone see M1385.X9
1385.V35	Viola
1385.V4	Violin
1385.V45	Violoncello
1385.X9	Xylophone. Marimba. Vibraharp. Vibraphone

Duets

Piano, harpsichord, etc.

Class here works for one or more keyboard instruments, two or more performers

1389	Collections
1390	Separate works

Violin and keyboard instrument. Viola and keyboard instrument

1393	Collections
1395	Separate works
1400	Violoncello and keyboard instrument. Double bass and keyboard instrument
1405	Wind instrument and keyboard instrument
1410	Other
1413-1417	Trios, quartets, etc. (Table M2)
1420	Orchestra. Band
	Including toy orchestra
(1430)	Gamelan
	see M985

Instrumental music -- Continued

(1450)   Dance music
                    For music for social dancing see M1356+
                    For folk, national and ethnic dances see M1627+
                    For other dances for specific instrumental or vocal mediums of
                        performance see the appropriate class, e.g., Piano, M30+
                    For music to accompany instruction in ballet, gymnastics,
                        rhythmic movement, etc., see MT950
                    For dance steps and dance instruction see GV1580+
                    Cf. M1520+ Music composed for theatrical dances such as
                        ballets and for pantomines, masques, pageants, etc.

1455   Dancer(s) with orchestra or other accompaniment
                    Class here concertos and similar concert works, e.g., for tap
                        dancer
                    For ballets and other choreographed dances,
                        pantomimes, masques, pageants, etc. see M1520+

(1457)   Dance poems with chamber music accompaniment
                    see M1455
                    For ballets and other choreographed dances,
                        pantomimes, masques, pageants, etc. see M1520+

(1459)   Dance poems with piano
                    see M1455

                Aleatory music. Electronic music. Mixed media

1470   Aleatory music
                    Class here works that are mainly or entirely indeterminate
                        where neither the medium of performance nor the
                        number of performers is specified

1473   Electronic music
                    Class here works solely for one or more electronic
                        instruments or devices
                    For works for instrument(s) and/or voice(s) with electronics,
                        see the class for the other instrument(s) or voice(s), e.g.,
                        electronic instrument and piano, M284.E4 , M285.E4;
                        quartets including a performer on electronics, M485 ;
                        songs with electronics, M1613.3
                    For works for electric violin, see M40-M44.3 ; for electric
                        guitar, see M125-M129 , etc.
                    For electronic organ see M14.8+

(1475.A-Z)   Music for ether-wave instruments. By instrument, A-Z
                    see M1473

(1475.M2)   Ondes Martenot
                    see M175.O5

(1475.T4)   Theremin
                    see M175.T5

Instrumental music
Electronic music. Aleatory music. Mixed media
1480   Mixed media
Class here works combining various musical, dramatic, and
visual elements not assigned to classes for types of
dramatic music
Including works with projected color, light, or images; spoken,
danced, mimed parts, etc.
1490   Music printed or copied in manuscript before 1700
Class here instrumental and vocal music
For music printed or copied before 1700 in the American
colonies, later the United States see M1.A1+
Vocal music
Including manuscripts and manuscript facsimiles intended as
performance editions
1495   Collections
Class here collections containing both secular and sacred
music by two or more composers
Secular vocal music
1497   Collections
Class here collections by two or more composers too varied
to be assigned to a more specific class
Dramatic music
For sacred dramatic music see M2000+
Operas
Including operettas, Singspiele, musicals, etc.
For Chinese operas see M1805.3+
For North Korean revolutionary operas see M1819.3
Complete works
1500   Scores. Parts
1501   Concert arrangements
Vocal scores. Chorus scores
1502   Without accompaniment
Accompaniment of keyboard instrument
1503   General
1503.5   Concert arrangements
1504   College operas
Excerpts
Including vocal or predominantly vocal excerpts from
works composed for specific motion picture sound
tracks
For excerpts of instrumental or predominantly
instrumental motion picture music see M1527.2
1505   Original accompaniment
Arranged accompaniment
1506   Orchestra or other ensemble
Keyboard instrument

Vocal music
Secular vocal music
Dramatic music
Operas
Excerpts
Arranged accompaniment
Keyboard instrument -- Continued
1507   Collections
1508   Separate works. By title of opera, musical, etc.
Vocal and chorus scores without accompaniment
1508.1   Collections
1508.2   Separate works
1509   Operatic scenes
Class here independent works not detached from larger works
For opera excerpts see M1505+
Incidental music
Complete works
1510   Scores. Parts
1512   Vocal and chorus scores without accompaniment
1513   Vocal scores with keyboard instrument
Excerpts
1515   Original accompaniment
Arranged accompaniment
1516   Orchestra or other ensemble
Keyboard instrument
1517   Collections
1518   Separate works. By title of play, etc.
Ballets, etc.
Class here music composed for theatrical dances of all types and for pantomimes, masques, pageants, etc.
Complete works
1520   Scores. Parts
1522   Vocal and chorus scores without accompaniment
1523   Keyboard scores. Vocal scores with keyboard instrument
(1523.5)   Pantomime hymns, etc.
see M2000-M2007
Excerpts
1524   Original accompaniment
Arranged accompaniment
1525   Orchestra or other ensemble
1526   Keyboard instrument

Vocal music
Secular vocal music
Dramatic music -- Continued
Motion picture music
Class here music composed for specific motion picture
sound tracks
Including musicals for specific motion picture sound tracks,
either originally composed or adapted from stage
versions
For instrumental music for silent films and music not
composed for specific motion picture sound
tracks see M176

| 1527 | Complete works |
| 1527.2 | Excerpts |

Class here instrumental, or predominantly instrumental,
excerpts
For vocal excerpts see M1505+
Radio music
Class here music composed for specific programs
For music not intended for specific programs see
M176.5

| 1527.5 | Complete works |

Including vocal themes for programs

| 1527.6 | Excerpts |

Television music
Class here music composed for specific programs
For music not intended for specific programs see
M176.5

| 1527.7 | Complete works |
| 1527.8 | Excerpts |

Two or more solo voices
Accompaniment of orchestra, other ensemble, or
electronics

1528	Scores. Parts
1528.5	Vocal scores without accompaniment
1529	Vocal scores with keyboard instrument

Accompaniment of one instrument or unaccompanied
Class here works whose performance by solo voices is
specifically indicated
For part songs, glees, madrigals, etc., that may be
performed by either solo voices or chorus see
M1547+
Two solo voices

| 1529.2 | Collections |
| 1529.3 | Separate works |

Three or more solo voices

| 1529.4 | Collections |

	Vocal music
	Secular vocal music
	Two or more solo voices
	Accompaniment of one instrument or unaccompanied
	Three or more solo voices -- Continued
1529.5	Separate works
	Choruses
	Including choral works with vocal soloists and secular oratorios
	Accompaniment of orchestra or other ensemble
	Including choral works with vocal soloists
	Mixed voices
	Complete works
	Scores. Parts
	Orchestral accompaniment
1530	General
1530.3	With recitation
1531	Other accompaniment
	Class here works with accompaniment of string orchestra, band, other ensemble of two or more instruments, or electronics
1532	Vocal and chorus scores without accompaniment
	Vocal scores with keyboard instrument
1533	General
1533.3	With recitation
	Excerpts
1534	Original accompaniment
	Arranged accompaniment
1535	Orchestra or other ensemble
	Vocal scores with keyboard instrument
1536	Collections
1537	Separate works
1537.5	Vocal and chorus scores without accompaniment
	Men's voices
	Complete works
	Scores. Parts
	Orchestral accompaniment
1538	General
1538.3	With recitation
	Other accompaniment
	Class here works with accompaniment of string orchestra, band, other ensemble of two or more instruments, or electronics
1539	General
1539.3	With recitation
	Vocal scores with keyboard instrument
1540	General

Vocal music
  Secular vocal music
    Choruses
      Accompaniment of orchestra or other ensemble
        Men's voices
          Complete works
            Vocal scores with keyboard instrument -- Continued

1540.3	With recitation
1540.5	Vocal and chorus scores without accompaniment
	Excerpts
1541	Orchestral accompaniment
1542	Vocal scores with keyboard instrument
1542.5	Vocal and chorus scores without accompaniment

        Treble voices
          Class here works for women's voices, works for women's and children's voices together, and works for treble voices whose choral medium is not otherwise specified.
         Complete works
          Scores. Parts
            Orchestral accompaniment

1543	General
1543.3	With recitation
1543.5	Other accompaniment

              Class here works with accompaniment of string orchestra, band, other ensemble of two or more instruments, or electronics
            Vocal scores with keyboard instrument

1544	General
1544.3	With recitation
1544.5	Vocal and chorus scores without accompaniment
	Excerpts
1545	Accompaniment other than solo keyboard
1546	Vocal scores with keyboard instrument
1546.3	Vocal and chorus scores without accompaniment
1546.5	Children's voices

          Class here works primarily for concert performance
          For choruses, songs, etc., for children with original accompaniment other than orchestra or other ensemble see M1997+
      Accompaniment of one instrument or unaccompanied
        Class here choruses, with or without solo voices, and part songs that may be performed by either chorus or solo voices
        For works whose performance by solo voices is specifically indicated see M1529.2+

1547	Collections of accompanied and unaccompanied works

Vocal music
Secular vocal music
Choruses
Accompaniment of one instrument or unaccompanied --
Continued
Accompaniment of keyboard instrument
Collections
Including collections that contain some works with
accompaniment of other solo instrument

1548	Two or more types of chorus
1549	Mixed voices
	For obsolete numbers formerly used for number of vocal parts, see Table MZ3
1550	Men's voices
	For obsolete numbers formerly used for number of vocal parts, see Table MZ3
1551	Treble voices
	For obsolete numbers formerly used for number of vocal parts, see Table MZ3

Separate works

1552	Mixed voices
	For obsolete numbers formerly used for number of vocal parts, see Table MZ4
1560	Men's voices
	For obsolete numbers formerly used for number of vocal parts, see Table MZ4
1570	Treble voices
	For obsolete numbers formerly used for number of vocal parts, see Table MZ4

Accompaniment of one instrument other than keyboard
instrument

1574	Two or more types of chorus
	Class here collections only
1575	Mixed voices
1576	Men's voices
1577	Treble voices

Unaccompanied
Collections

1578	Two or more types of chorus
1579	Mixed voices
	For obsolete numbers formerly used for number of vocal parts, see Table MZ3
1580	Men's voices
	For obsolete numbers formerly used for number of vocal parts, see Table MZ3

Vocal music
Secular vocal music
Choruses
Accompaniment of one instrument or unaccompanied
Unaccompanied
Collections -- Continued

1581	Treble voices
	For obsolete numbers formerly used for number of vocal parts, see Table MZ3
	Separate works
1582	Mixed voices
	For obsolete numbers formerly used for number of vocal parts, see Table MZ5
1590	Men's voices
	For obsolete numbers formerly used for number of vocal parts, see Table MZ5
1600	Treble voices
	For obsolete numbers formerly used for number of vocal parts, see Table MZ5
1608	Choruses, etc., in tonic sol-fa notation
1609	Unison choruses
(1610)	Cantatas, choral symphonies, etc., for unaccompanied chorus with or without solo voices
	For unaccompanied secular works see M1578+
	For unaccompanied sacred works see M2081+

One solo voice
Class here songs, solo cantatas, etc.
Including works with obligato chorus
Accompaniment of orchestra or other instrumental ensemble
Original compositions
Collections
Including collections of original works and arrangements

1611	Scores. Parts
1612	Vocal scores with keyboard instrument

Separate works
Class here individual works and sets of works
Scores. Parts

1613	Orchestral accompaniment

Vocal music
Secular vocal music
One solo voice
Accompaniment of orchestra or other instrumental
ensemble
Original compositions
Separate works
Scores. Parts -- Continued
1613.3   Other accompaniment
Class here works with accompaniment of string
orchestra, band, other ensemble of two or
more instruments, or electronics
For accompaniment of keyboard instrument
and one other instrument see M1621.3
For accompaniment of continuo with one
plucked and one bass instrument see
M1623+
1614   Vocal scores with keyboard instrument
Arrangements
Collections
1615   Scores. Parts
1616   Vocal scores with keyboard instrument
For accompaniment of keyboard instrument and
one other instrument see M1621.3
Separate works
For accompaniment of keyboard instrument and
one other instrument see M1621.3
1617   Scores. Parts
1618   Vocal scores with keyboard instrument
Accompaniment of keyboard instrument, keyboard and
one other instrument, or unaccompanied
Including continuo with additional bass instrument
Collections
Two or more composers
1619   General
1619.5.A-Z   Individual poets, A-Z
1620   One composer
Separate works
Class here individual works and sets of works
For song cycles see M1621.4
1621   Keyboard instrument accompaniment
1621.2   Unaccompanied
1621.3   Accompaniment of keyboard instrument and one
other instrument
Class here original works and arrangements
1621.4   Song cycles

Vocal music
　　Secular vocal music
　　　　One solo voice
　　　　　　Accompaniment of keyboard instrument, keyboard and
　　　　　　　　one other instrument, or unaccompanied
　　　　　　　　Separate works -- Continued

(1621.5-.9)	By vocal register 　　see M1619+
1622	Vaudeville, music-hall, etc. songs

　　　　　　　　　　Class here songs published between 1850 and 1923
　　　　　　　　　　For vaudeville, music-hall, etc. songs published after
　　　　　　　　　　　　1923, see popular music under the country of
　　　　　　　　　　　　origin in M1628+
　　　　　　　　　　For vaudeville, music-hall, etc. songs published before
　　　　　　　　　　　　1850 see the class for medium of performance in
　　　　　　　　　　　　M1528+ and M1611+
　　　　　　Accompaniment of one instrument other than keyboard
　　　　　　　　instrument
　　　　　　　　Including continuo with lute, etc. and additional bass
　　　　　　　　　　instrument
　　　　　　　　Collections
　　　　　　　　　　Plucked instrument

1623	General
1623.4	Harp
1623.5	Lute
(1623.7)	Two or more other instruments 　　see M1613.3
1623.8	Other instrument
(1623.9)	Two or more other instruments 　　see M1613.3

　　　　　　　　Separate works
　　　　　　　　　　Plucked instrument

1624	General
1624.4	Harp
1624.5	Lute
1624.7	Wind instrument
1624.8	Other instrument
(1624.9)	Two or more other instruments 　　see M1613.3

　　　　One solo voice... Recitations with music
　　　　　　Class here secular and sacred works without chorus with
　　　　　　　　separate parts for any solo vocalization not sung

Vocal music
Secular vocal music
Recitations with music -- Continued
1625   Accompaniment of orchestra or other ensemble
For secular recitations with mixed chorus and
orchestra or other ensemble see M1530.3
For secular recitations with men's chorus and
orchestra or other ensemble see M1538.3
For secular recitations with treble chorus and
orchestra or other ensemble see M1543.3
For sacred recitations with mixed chorus and
orchestra or other ensemble see M2020.3
1626   Accompaniment of one instrument
Including keyboard instrument, whether original or
arranged, and piano scores without text
For keyboard-vocal scores of secular recitations with
mixed chorus see M1533.3
For keyboard-vocal scores of secular recitations with
men's chorus see M1540.3
For keyboard-vocal scores of secular recitations with
treble chorus see M1544.3
For vocal and chorus scores of sacred recitations
with mixed chorus see M2023.3
Folk, national, and ethnic music
Class here folk, national, ethnic, patriotic, political songs,
popular music, etc., not classified in M1900-M1985
Including solo songs, part songs, collections of texts with the
tunes indicated, unaccompanied songs, and instrumental
arrangements
For composers' settings of folk music and songs, see the
class for the medium of performance, e.g., choruses,
M1530+ ; one solo voice, M1611+
International
For music concerning the entire hemisphere of North
and South America see M1680+
1627   Collections
1627.15   Separate works
Foreign broadsides
(1627.2)   Collections
(1627.3)   Separate works
1627.5.A-Z   Famous persons. By person, A-Z
Class here works about or inspired by the person
For persons in the United States, see M1659+
North America
United States

	Vocal music
	Secular vocal music
	Folk, national, and ethnic music
	North America
	United States -- Continued
1628	Songsters
	Class here collections of songs generally without the music, but with indications of the tunes
	Broadsides
	Class here works with or without music
1628.2	Collections
1628.3	Separate works
1629	General collections
	For separate songs (general) see M1630
	For collections of cowboy songs cataloged after 1997 see M1977.C6
1629.3.A-Z	National holidays, A-Z
	Class here collections and separate works
1629.3.A1	Two or more holidays
	Armistice Day see M1629.3.V4
1629.3.C5	Christmas
1629.3.C6	Columbus Day
1629.3.E3	Easter
1629.3.E5	Election Day
1629.3.F4	Flag Day
1629.3.F5	Fourth of July. Independence Day
1629.3.G8	Groundhog Day
(1629.3.I5)	Independence Day
	see M1629.3.F5
1629.3.L3	Labor Day
1629.3.L5	Lincoln's Birthday
1629.3.M3	Memorial Day
1629.3.N4	New Year's Day
1629.3.S3	Saint Patrick's Day
1629.3.T4	Thanksgiving Day
1629.3.V4	Veterans Day. Armistice Day
1629.3.W3	Washington's Birthday
1629.5	Patriotic, national, etc. songs, combined in medleys
	Collections by region or state
	Class here collections from the region or state
	For songs about states and cities see M1657+
1629.6.A-Z	By region, A-Z
1629.7.A-.W	By state, A-W (Table M1)
	Cf. M1657 Collection of songs about states and cities
	Cf. M1658.A+ Separate songs, by state

	Vocal music
	Secular vocal music
	Folk, national, and ethnic music
	North America
	United States -- Continued
1630	Separate works (General)
	Class here works not classified by topic or title
	For general collections see M1629
	Popular music
1630.18	Collections
1630.2	Separate works
	Class here individual songs and sets of songs
	Songs of particular historical interest
1630.3.A-Z	By title, A-Z
1630.3.A5	America (My country 'tis of thee)
1630.3.A6	America the beautiful
1630.3.B3	Battle hymn of the Republic
1630.3.C6	Columbia the gem of the ocean
1630.3.D4	Dixie
1630.3.H3	Hail Columbia
1630.3.H6	Home, sweet home
	My country 'tis of thee see M1630.3.A5
	Star-spangled banner
	Class arrangements not specified below with the class for the medium of performance, e.g., M1258, band settings
1630.3.S68	The Anacreontic song
	By date of edition
1630.3.S69	Broadsides
	By date of edition
1630.3.S7	Song and part song editions
	By Muller number to 1864 (Joseph Muller, The Star spangled banner, 1935); then by date and initial if necessary
1630.3.S72	Keyboard arrangements
	Class here editions with or without words for one or more keyboard instruments, two or more hands
1630.3.S74	Keyboard variations, fantasies, etc.
1630.3.S76	Anacreontic parodies
	Class here texts other than F.S. Key's
1630.3.S78	Other tunes
	Class here tunes other than the Anacreontic Ode Including J. Hewitt, The Star spangled banner, 1819
1630.3.Y2	Yankee Doodle
	Events, celebrations, etc. (Chronological)

	Vocal music
	Secular vocal music
	Folk, national, and ethnic music
	North America
	United States
	Songs of particular historical interest
	Events, celebrations, etc. (Chronological) -- Continued
1631	American Revolution, 1775-1783
1632	1783-1812
	War of 1812
1633	Collections
1634	Separate works
	Mexican War, 1846-1848
1635	Collections
1636	Separate works
	Civil War, 1861-1865
	General
1637	Collections
(1637.2)	National Peace Jubilee and Music Festival see M1642.2
1638	Separate works
(1638.2)	World's Peace Jubilee and International Musical Festival see M1642.3
	Union
1639	Collections
1640	Separate works
	Confederate
1641	Collections
1642	Separate works
	Peace Jubilees, Boston
1642.2	National Peace Jubilee and Music Festival, 1869
1642.3	World's Peace Jubilee and International Musical Festival, 1872
	Spanish-American War, 1898
1643	Collections
1644	Separate works
1645	Relations with Mexico, 1914-1917
1646	World War, 1914-1918
	World War, 1939-1945
1647	Before December 1941
1648	December 1941-1945
1649	Korean War, 1950-1953
1650	Vietnam War, 1961-1975
1652	American Revolution Bicentennial, 1776-1976

	Vocal music
	Secular vocal music
	Folk, national, and ethnic music
	North America
	United States
	Songs of particular historical interest
	Events, celebrations, etc. (Chronological) -- Continued
1653	September 11 Terrorist Attacks, 2001
	States and cities
	Class here songs about states and cities
	For collections of songs by region see M1629.6.A+
	For collections of songs by state see M1629.7.A+
1657	Collections
	Class here collections representing three or more states, cities, etc.
	Individual states and cities
	Class here collections and separate works
1658.A-.W	By state, A-W (Table M1)
1658.5.A-Z	By city, A-Z
	Famous persons. By person, A-Z
	Class here works about or inspired by the person
1659.A-Z	Presidents, statesmen, generals, etc.
1659.5.A-Z	Others
	Political movements, parties, campaign songs, etc.
1659.7	Collections
1659.8	Nonpartisan
	Republican
1660	Collections
1661	Separate works
	Democratic
1662	Collections
1663	Separate works
	Other. By topic, A-Z
	Including labor organizations, etc.
1664.A-Z	Collections
1664.A35	Abolitionist movement
1664.A5	American cooperative movement
1664.A55	American Independent Party
	American Party see M1664.K5
	Anti-prohibition movement see M1664.P82
1664.C6	Communist Party of the United States of America
1664.F15	Farmer-Labor Party
1664.F2	Farmers' Alliance (U.S.). National Farmers' Alliance and Industrial Union

M

Vocal music
Secular vocal music
Folk, national, and ethnic music
North America
United States
Political movements, parties, campaign songs, etc.
Other. By topic, A-Z
Collections -- Continued

1664.F4	Federal Party (U.S.)
1664.F8	Free-Soil Party (U.S.)
1664.G8	Greenback Labor Party
1664.K5	Know-nothing Party. American Party
1664.K7	Ku-Klux Klan
1664.L3	Labor organizations

Class here songs of the American Federation of
Labor (A.F.L.); Committee for Industrial
Organization (C.I.O.); Industrial Workers of
the World (I.W.W.); Knights of Labor; etc.
Cf. M1977.L3 Labor songs

1664.N3	National Recovery Administration
1664.P6	Populist Party (U.S.)
1664.P7	Progressive Party (1912)
	Prohibition and anti-prohibition movements
1664.P8	Prohibition movement
1664.P82	Anti-prohibition movement
1664.S4	Single tax movement
1664.S67	Socialist parties
1664.T8	Townsend National Recovery Plan, Inc.
1664.W4	Whig Party (U.S.)
1664.W8	Woman's suffrage movement
1665.A-Z	Separate works
1665.A35	Abolitionist movement
1665.A5	American cooperative movement
1665.A55	American Independent Party
	American Party see M1665.K5
	Anti-prohibition movement see M1665.P82
1665.C6	Communist Party of the United States of America
1665.F15	Farmer-Labor Party
1665.F2	Farmers' Alliance (U.S.). National Farmers' Alliance and Industrial Union
1665.F4	Federal Party (U.S.)
1665.F8	Free-Soil Party (U.S.)
1665.G8	Greenback Labor Party
1665.K5	Know-nothing Party. American Party
1665.K7	Ku-Klux Klan

Vocal music
Secular vocal music
Folk, national, and ethnic music
North America
United States
Political movements, parties, campaign songs, etc.
Other. By topic, A-Z
Separate works -- Continued

1665.L3	Labor organizations
	Class here songs of the American Federation of Labor (A.F.L.); Committee for Industrial Organization (C.I.O.); Industrial Workers of the World (I.W.W.); Knights of Labor; etc.
	Cf. M1978.L3 Labor songs
1665.N3	National Recovery Administration
1665.P6	Populist Party (U.S.)
1665.P7	Progressive Party (1912)
	Prohibition and anti-prohibition movements
1665.P8	Prohibition movement
1665.P82	Anti-prohibition movement
1665.S4	Single tax movement
1665.S67	Socialist parties
1665.T8	Townsend National Recovery Plan, Inc.
1665.W4	Whig Party (U.S.)
1665.W8	Woman's suffrage movement
	Patriotic and other national songs arranged for keyboard instrument
	Class other instrumental arrangements not classified in M5+ with the song
	For the Star-spangled banner see M1630.3.S72
1666	Collections
1667	Separate works
	Ethnic music
1668	General
	Acadian see M1668.8
	African American see M1670+
	American Indian see M1669
1668.1	British American
	Cajun see M1668.8
1668.2	Irish American
1668.3	German American
1668.4	Hispanic American
1668.6	Scandinavian American
1668.7	Slavic American
1668.8	French American
	Including Cajun and Acadian
1668.9.A-Z	Other, A-Z

M

	Vocal music
	Secular vocal music
	Folk, national, and ethnic music
	North America
	United States
	Ethnic music
	Other, A-Z -- Continued
(1668.9.A27)	Acadian
	see M1668.8
	African American see M1670+
	American Indian see M1669
1668.9.A67	Arab American
(1668.9.C26)	Cajun
	see M1668.8
1668.9.E8	Eskimo
	Cf. M1629.7.A+ Eskimo in Alaska
1668.9.G73	Greek American
1668.9.H8	Hungarian American
1668.9.I8	Italian American
1668.9.J5	Jewish American
1668.9.L4	Latvian American
1668.9.L6	Lithuanian American
1668.9.R64	Romanian American
1668.9.V5	Vietnamese American
1669	American Indian
	African American
	Class here accompanied and unaccompanied works
	Including spirituals
1670	Collections
1671	Separate works
	Territories, A-Z
	For obsolete numbers formerly used under this span
	see Table MZ6
1672.A-Z	Collections
1672.C2	Canal Zone
	Cf. Panama, M1684.P2 , M1685.P218
1672.G8	Guam
	Puerto Rico see M1681.P6+
	Samoa, American see M1844.S2+
1672.V5	Virgin Islands of the United States
1673.A-Z	Separate works
1673.C2	Canal Zone
	Cf. Panama, M1685.P2 , M1685.P22
1673.G8	Guam
	Puerto Rico see M1681.P6+
	Samoa, American see M1844.S2+
1673.V5	Virgin Islands of the United States

	Vocal music
	Secular vocal music
	Folk, national, and ethnic music
	North America
	United States -- Continued
1675.A-Z	American songs on foreign wars, etc., in which the United States has not participated. By event, A-Z
1675.C8	Cuban revolution, 1895-1898
1675.R85	Russo-Japanese War, 1904-1905
1676.A-Z	Patriotic societies and organizations, A-Z
1676.A1	General
	40 and 8 see M1676.Q3
	American Legion and Auxiliary
1676.A5	American Legion
1676.A52	Auxiliary
1676.B5	Blue Star Mothers
1676.D3	Daughters of the American Revolution
1676.D4	Daughters of Union Veterans of the Civil War
1676.D45	Daughters of Utah Pioneers
1676.D5	Death Valley '49ers
1676.D6	Disabled American Veterans
1676.F5	Filipino Federation of America
1676.G6	Gold Star Mothers, American, Inc.
1676.G7	Grand Army of the Republic
1676.J4	Jewish War Veterans of the United States of America
1676.L97	Lyceum League
1676.M48	Military Order of the Loyal Legion of the United States
1676.M5	Military Order of the Purple Heart
1676.N3	National Guard Association of the United States
	Order of Sons of Italy in America see M1676.S56
1676.P3	Pershing Rifles
1676.Q3	Quarante hommes et huit chevaux, Société des (40 and 8)
1676.S54	Society of Mayflower Descendants
1676.S55	Society of the Cincinnati
1676.S56	Order of Sons of Italy in America
1676.S6	Sons of the American Revolution
1676.S7	Sons of Union Veterans of the Civil War
1676.T8	Transylvanians, Society of
1676.U6	Union League of America
1676.U7	United Daughters of the Confederacy
1676.U77	United Service Organizations (U.S.) (USO)
	Veterans of Foreign Wars of the United States and Ladies' Auxiliary
1676.V4	Veterans of Foreign Wars of the United States

Vocal music
Secular vocal music
Folk, national, and ethnic music
North America
United States
Patriotic societies and organizations, A-Z
Veterans of Foreign Wars of the United States

1676.V42	Ladies' Auxiliary
1677	Old folks concerts of Father Kemp
1677.2.A-Z	Exhibitions. By place, A-Z, and date
	Including worlds' fairs and exhibitions elsewhere in North America
1677.2.C3 1893	Chicago. World's Columbian Exposition
1677.2.C3 1933	Chicago. Century of Progress International Exposition
1677.2.C3 1948	Chicago. Railroad Fair
1677.2.C6 1936	Cleveland. Great Lakes Exposition
1677.2.M65 1967	Montreal. Expo 67
1677.2.N4 1939	New York. World's Fair
1677.2.P4 1876	Philadelphia. Centennial Exhibition
1677.2.S25 1904	St. Louis. Louisiana Purchase Exposition
1677.2.S28 1968	San Antonio. Hemisfair
1677.2.S3 1915	San Diego. Panama-California Exposition
1677.2.S4 1939	San Francisco. Golden Gate International Exposition
1677.2.S43 1962	Seattle. Century 21 Exposition
1677.2.S65 1974	Spokane. Expo 74
1677.3.A-Z	Dedication of patriotic monuments, etc. By place, A-Z
1677.3.M67	Mount Rushmore National Memorial
1677.3.N4	New York, N.Y.
1677.3.P4	Philadelphia
(1677.4)	United States American Revolution Bicentennial, 1776-1976
	see M1652
(1677.8)	Other topics
	Canada
	General
1678	Collections
1679	Separate works
	Popular music
1679.18	Collections
1679.2	Separate works
	North and South America
	Class here music concerning the entire hemisphere
	For individual regions or countries, see the region or country
1680	General

	Vocal music
	Secular vocal music
	Folk, national, and ethnic music
	North and South America -- Continued
	Popular music
	Including music published in the United States in Spanish
	for distribution in other countries
1680.18	Collections
1680.2	Separate works
	West Indies. Caribbean Area
1681.A1-.A12	General
	Class here collections and separate works
1681.A5-Z	By island, country, etc., A-Z
	Bahamas
1681.B3	General
	Popular music
1681.B318	Collections
1681.B32	Separate works
	Barbados
1681.B34	General
	Popular music
1681.B3418	Collections
1681.B342	Separate works
	British Virgin Islands see M1681.V5+
	Cuba
1681.C9	General
	Popular music
1681.C918	Collections
1681.C92	Separate works
(1681.C93-.C932)	Curaçao
	see M1681.N48+
	Dominican Republic
1681.D8	General
	Popular music
1681.D818	Collections
1681.D82	Separate works
	Guadeloupe
1681.G8	General
	Popular music
1681.G818	Collections
1681.G82	Separate works
	Haiti
1681.H2	General
	Popular music
1681.H218	Collections
1681.H22	Separate works
	Jamaica

	Vocal music
	Secular vocal music
	Folk, national, and ethnic music
	West Indies. Caribbean Area
	By island, country, etc., A-Z
	Jamaica -- Continued
1681.J3	General
	Popular music
1681.J318	Collections
1681.J32	Separate works
	Martinique
1681.M32	General
	Popular music
1681.M3218	Collections
1681.M322	Separate works
	Netherlands Antilles
1681.N48	General
	Popular music
1681.N4818	Collections
1681.N482	Separate works
	Puerto Rico
1681.P6	General
	Popular music
1681.P618	Collections
1681.P62	Separate works
	Saint Lucia
1681.S17	General
	Popular music
1681.S1718	Collections
1681.S172	Separate works
	Saint Kitts and Nevis
1681.S8	General
	Popular music
1681.S818	Collections
1681.S82	Separate works
	Trinidad and Tobago
1681.T7	General
	Popular music
1681.T718	Collections
1681.T72	Separate works
	British Virgin Islands
1681.V5	General
	Popular music
1681.V518	Collections
1681.V52	Separate works
	Bermuda Islands
1681.5	General

	Vocal music
	Secular vocal music
	Folk, national, and ethnic music
	Bermuda Islands -- Continued
	Popular music
1681.518	Collections
1681.52	Separate works
	Mexico
	General
1682	Collections
1683	Separate works
	Popular music
1683.18	Collections
1683.2	Separate works
	Central America
1684.A1-.A2	General
	Class here collections and separate works
1684.A3-Z	By region or country, A-Z
	Subclasses for individual countries continue at M1685
	Costa Rica
	General
1684.C6	Collections
	Guatemala
	General
1684.G9	Collections
	Honduras
	General
1684.H5	Collections
	Nicaragua
	General
1684.N4	Collections
	Panama
	General
1684.P2	Collections
	El Salvador
	General
1684.S2	Collections
1685.A-Z	By region or country, A-Z
	Subclasses for individual countries begin at M1684.A5
	Costa Rica
	General
1685.C6	Separate works
	Popular music
1685.C618	Collections
1685.C62	Separate works
	Guatemala
	General

M

	Vocal music
	Secular vocal music
	Folk, national, and ethnic music
	Central America
	By region or country, A-Z
	Guatemala
	General -- Continued
1685.G9	Separate works
	Popular music
1685.G918	Collections
1685.G92	Separate works
	Honduras
	General
1685.H5	Separate works
	Popular music
1685.H518	Collections
1685.H52	Separate works
	Nicaragua
	General
1685.N4	Separate works
	Popular music
1685.N418	Collections
1685.N42	Separate works
	Panama
	General
1685.P2	Separate works
	Popular music
1685.P218	Collections
1685.P22	Separate works
	El Salvador
	General
1685.S2	Separate works
	Popular music
1685.S218	Collections
1685.S22	Separate works
	South America
1686	General
	By region or country, A-Z
	Subclasses for individual countries continue at M1688
	Argentina
	General
1687.A7	Collections
	Bolivia
	General
1687.B6	Collections
	Brazil see M1689+
	British Guyana see M1687.G9

Vocal music
Secular vocal music
Folk, national, and ethnic music
South America
By region or country, A-Z -- Continued
Chile see M1691+
Colombia
General
1687.C6   Collections
Ecuador
General
1687.E2   Collections
Guyana
General
1687.G9   Collections
Paraguay
General
1687.P2   Collections
Peru see M1693+
Suriname
General
1687.S9   Collections
Uruguay
General
1687.U6   Collections
Venezuela
General
1687.V3   Collections
1688.A-Z   By region or country, A-Z
Subclasses for individual regions and countries begin at M1687
Argentina
General
1688.A7   Separate works
Popular music
1688.A718   Collections
1688.A72   Separate works
Bolivia
General
1688.B6   Separate works
Popular music
1688.B618   Collections
1688.B62   Separate works
British Guyana see M1688.G89+
Brazil see M1689+
Chile see M1691+
Colombia

Vocal music
Secular vocal music
Folk, national, and ethnic music
South America
By region or country, A-Z
Colombia -- Continued
General
1688.C6   Separate works
Popular music
1688.C618   Collections
1688.C62   Separate works
Ecuador
General
1688.E2   Separate works
Popular music
1688.E218   Collections
1688.E22   Separate works
Guyana
General
1688.G9   Separate works
Popular music
1688.G918   Collections
1688.G92   Separate works
Paraguay
General
Separate works
Popular music
1688.P218   Collections
1688.P22   Separate works
Peru see M1693+
Suriname
General
1688.S9   Separate works
Popular music
1688.S918   Collections
1688.S92   Separate works
Uruguay
General
1688.U6   Separate works
Popular music
1688.U618   Collections
1688.U62   Separate works
Venezuela
General
1688.V3   Separate works
Popular music
1688.V318   Collections

	Vocal music
	Secular vocal music
	Folk, national, and ethnic music
	South America
	By region or country, A-Z
	Venezuela
	Popular music -- Continued
1688.V32	Separate works
	Brazil
	General
1689	Collections
1690	Separate works
	Popular music
1690.18	Collections
1690.2	Separate works
	Chile
	General
1691	Collections
1692	Separate works
	Popular music
1692.18	Collections
1692.2	Separate works
	Peru
	General
1693	Collections
1694	Separate works
	Popular music
1694.18	Collections
1694.2	Separate works
(1697)	Pan America. Latin America
	see M1680+
	Europe
	For obsolete numbers formerly used under this span see Table MZ7
1698	General
	Austria
	General
1702	Collections
1703	Separate works
	Popular music
1703.18	Collections
1703.2	Separate works
	Czech Republic
	For Slovakia see M1708+
	General
1704	Collections
1705	Separate works

Vocal music
  Secular vocal music
    Folk, national, and ethnic music
      Europe
        Czech Republic -- Continued
          Popular music

1705.18	Collections
1705.2	Separate works

        Czechoslovakia see M1704+
        Hungary
          General

1706	Collections
1707	Separate works

          Popular music

1707.18	Collections
1707.2	Separate works

        Slovakia
          For Czechoslovakia see M1704+
          General

1708	Collections
1709	Separate works

          Popular music

1709.18	Collections
1709.2	Separate works

        Balkan Peninsula
          Bulgaria
            General

1712	Collections
1713	Separate works

            Popular music

1713.18	Collections
1713.2	Separate works

          Greece
            General

1714	Collections
1715	Separate works

            Popular music

1715.18	Collections
1715.2	Separate works

          Montenegro
            General

1716	Collections
1717	Separate works

            Popular music

1717.18	Collections
1717.2	Separate works

          Romania

Vocal music
Secular vocal music
Folk, national, and ethnic music
Europe
Balkan Peninsula
Romania -- Continued
General

1718	Collections
1719	Separate works

Popular music

1719.18	Collections
1719.2	Separate works

Yugoslavia. Serbia and Montenegro
For Montenegro see M1716+
General

1720	Collections
1721	Separate works

Popular music

1721.18	Collections
1721.2	Separate works

Slovenia
General

1721.3	Collections
1721.4	Separate works

Popular music

1721.5	Collections
1721.6	Separate works

Croatia
General

1722.3	Collections
1722.4	Separate works

Popular music

1722.5	Collections
1722.6	Separate works

Bosnia and Hercegovina
General

1723.3	Collections
1723.4	Separate works

Popular music

1723.5	Collections
1723.6	Separate works

Albania
General

1724	Collections
1725	Separate works

Popular music

1725.18	Collections

M

Vocal music
　Secular vocal music
　　Folk, national, and ethnic music
　　　Europe
　　　　Balkan Peninsula
　　　　　Albania
　　　　　　Popular music -- Continued
1725.2　　　　　　　Separate works
　　　　　Macedonia (Republic)
　　　　　　General
1725.3　　　　　　　Collections
1725.4　　　　　　　Separate works
　　　　　　Popular music
1725.5　　　　　　　Collections
1725.6　　　　　　　Separate works
　　　　　Belgium
　　　　　　General
1726　　　　　　　Collections
1727　　　　　　　Separate works
　　　　　　Popular music
1727.18　　　　　　　Collections
1727.2　　　　　　　Separate works
　　　　　　Local, A-Z
1728.A-Z　　　　　　　Collections
1729.A-Z　　　　　　　Separate works
　　　　　Finland
　　　　　　General
1729.3　　　　　　　Collections
1729.4　　　　　　　Separate works
　　　　　　Popular music
1729.5　　　　　　　Collections
1729.6　　　　　　　Separate works
　　　　　France
　　　　　　General
1730　　　　　　　Collections
1731　　　　　　　Separate works
　　　　　　Popular music
1731.18　　　　　　　Collections
1731.2　　　　　　　Separate works
　　　　　　Local, A-Z
1732.A-Z　　　　　　　Collections
1733.A-Z　　　　　　　Separate works
　　　　　Germany
　　　　　　General
1734　　　　　　　Collections
1735　　　　　　　Separate works
　　　　　　Popular music

	Vocal music
	Secular vocal music
	Folk, national, and ethnic music
	Europe
	Germany
	Popular music -- Continued
1735.18	Collections
1735.2	Separate works
	Local, A-Z
1736.A-Z	Collections
1737.A-Z	Separate works
	Great Britain. Ireland
	General
1738	Collections
1739	Separate works
	Popular music
1739.18	Collections
1739.2	Separate works
1739.3	Broadsides
	England
	General
1740	Collections
1741	Separate works
	Popular music
1741.18	Collections
1741.2	Separate works
	Wales
	General
1742	Collections
1743	Separate works
	Popular music
1743.18	Collections
1743.2	Separate works
	Ireland
	General
1744	Collections
1745	Separate works
	Popular music
1745.18	Collections
1745.2	Separate works
	Northern Ireland
	General
1745.3	Collections
1745.4	Separate works
	Popular music
1745.5	Collections
1745.6	Separate works

M

                    Vocal music
                        Secular vocal music
                            Folk, national, and ethnic music
                                Europe
                                    Great Britain. Ireland -- Continued
                                        Scotland
                                            General
1746   Collections
1747   Separate works
                                            Popular music
1747.18   Collections
1747.2   Separate works
                                        Crown dependencies
1747.3   Isle of Man
1747.4   Channel Islands
                                    Italy
                                        General
1748   Collections
1749   Separate works
                                        Popular music
1749.18   Collections
1749.2   Separate works
                                        Local, A-Z
1750.A-Z   Collections
1751.A-Z   Separate works
                                    Netherlands
                                        General
1752   Collections
1753   Separate works
                                        Popular music
1753.18   Collections
1753.2   Separate works
                                        Local, A-Z
1754.A-Z   Collections
1755.A-Z   Separate works
                                    Poland
                                        General
1755.3   Collections
1755.4   Separate works
                                        Popular music
1755.5   Collections
1755.6   Separate works
                                    Russia. Soviet Union. Russia (Federation)
                                        For former Soviet republics in Asia see M1824+
                                        General
1756   Collections
1757   Separate works

	Vocal music
	Secular vocal music
	Folk, national, and ethnic music
	Europe
	Russia. Soviet Union. Russia (Federation) -- Continued
	Popular music
1757.18	Collections
1757.2	Separate works
	Latvia
	General
1758	Collections
1759	Separate works
	Popular music
1759.18	Collections
1759.2	Separate works
	Ukraine
	General
1764	Collections
1765	Separate works
	Popular music
1765.18	Collections
1765.2	Separate works
1766.A-Z	Other former Soviet republics (Europe), A-Z
	Subclasses for individual regions or countries continue at M1767
	For obsolete numbers formerly used under this span see Table MZ7
	Belarus
	General
1766.B4	Collections
	Estonia
	General
1766.E6	Collections
	Lithuania
	General
1766.L4	Collections
	Moldova
	General
1766.M5	Collections
1767.A-Z	Other former Soviet republics (Europe), A-Z
	Subclasses for individual countries begin at M1766
	For obsolete numbers formerly used under this span see Table MZ7
	Belarus
	General
1767.B4	Separate works
	Popular music

	Vocal music
	Secular vocal music
	Folk, national, and ethnic music
	Europe
	Other former Soviet republics (Europe), A-Z
	Belarus
	Popular music -- Continued
1767.B418	Collections
1767.B42	Separate works
	Estonia
	General
1767.E6	Separate works
	Popular music
1767.E618	Collections
1767.E62	Separate works
	Lithuania
	General
1767.L4	Separate works
	Popular music
1767.L418	Collections
1767.L42	Separate works
	Moldova
	General
1767.M5	Separate works
	Popular music
1767.M518	Collections
1767.M52	Separate works
	Scandinavia
	General
1768	Collections
1769	Separate works
	Popular music
1769.18	Collections
1769.2	Separate works
	Denmark
	General
1770	Collections
1771	Separate works
	Popular music
1771.18	Collections
1771.2	Separate works
	Iceland
	General
1771.3	Collections
1771.4	Separate works
	Popular music
1771.5	Collections

Vocal music
  Secular vocal music
    Folk, national, and ethnic music
      Europe
        Scandinavia
          Iceland
            Popular music -- Continued

1771.6	Separate works
	Norway
	General
1772	Collections
1773	Separate works
	Popular music
1773.18	Collections
1773.2	Separate works
	Sweden
	General
1774	Collections
1775	Separate works
	Popular music
1775.18	Collections
1775.2	Separate works
	Greenland
	General
1776	Collections
1777	Separate works
	Prior to 1970 used for collections of national music from Spain and Portugal
	Popular music
1777.18	Collections
1777.2	Separate works
	Spain
	General
1779	Collections
1780	Separate works
	Popular music
1780.18	Collections
1780.2	Separate works
	Portugal
	For works cataloged before 1970 see M1777-M1778
	General
1781	Collections
1782	Separate works
	Popular music
1782.18	Collections
1782.2	Separate works
	Switzerland

	Vocal music
	Secular vocal music
	Folk, national, and ethnic music
	Europe
	Switzerland -- Continued
	General
1784	Collections
1785	Separate works
	Popular music
1785.18	Collections
1785.2	Separate works
	Local, A-Z
1786.A-Z	Collections
1787.A-Z	Separate works
1788.A-1789.Z	Other European countries, A-Z
	Subclasses for individual countries continue at M1789
	Liechtenstein
	General
1788.L76	Collections
	Luxembourg
	General
1788.L8	Collections
	Malta
	General
1788.M43	Collections
	Monaco
	General
1788.M63	Collections
1789.A-Z	Other European countries, A-Z
	Subclasses for individual countries begin at M1788
	Liechtenstein
	General
1789.L56	Separate works
	Popular music
1789.L5618	Collections
1789.L562	Separate works
	Luxembourg
	General
1789.L8	Separate works
	Popular music
1789.L818	Collections
1789.L82	Separate works
	Malta
	General
1789.M3	Separate works
	Popular music
1789.M318	Collections

	Vocal music
	Secular vocal music
	Folk, national, and ethnic music
	Europe
	Other European countries, A-Z
	Malta
	Popular music -- Continued
1789.M32	Separate works
	Monaco
	General
1789.M6	Separate works
	Popular music
1789.M618	Collections
1789.M62	Separate works
	Asia
1795	General
	For general collections of music from the Arab countries see M1828
	Saudi Arabia
	General
1797	Collections
1798	Separate works
	Popular music
1798.18	Collections
1798.2	Separate works
	Armenia
	General
1800	Collections
1801	Separate works
	Popular music
1801.18	Collections
1801.2	Separate works
	China
	For general collections of the music of Tibet see M1824.T5
	For general separate works and popular music of Tibet see M1825.T5+
	General
1804	Collections
1805	Separate works
	Popular music
1805.18	Collections
1805.2	Separate works
	Chinese operas
	Including Beijing opera
1805.3	General
1805.4.A-Z	Local types and styles. By region, A-Z

	Vocal music
	Secular vocal music
	Folk, national, and ethnic music
	Asia -- Continued
	Taiwan
	General
1806	Collections
1807	Separate works
	Popular music
1807.18	Collections
1807.2	Separate works
	India
	General
1808	Collections
1809	Separate works
	Popular music
1809.18	Collections
1809.2	Separate works
	Israel. Palestine
	Cf. M1850+ Music of the Jews
	General
1810	Collections
1811	Separate works
	Popular music
1811.18	Collections
1811.2	Separate works
	Japan
	General
1812	Collections
1813	Separate works
	Popular music
1813.18	Collections
1813.2	Separate works
	Korea. South Korea
	General
1816	Collections
1817	Separate works
	Popular music
1817.18	Collections
1817.2	Separate works
	Korea (North)
	General
1818	Collections
1819	Separate works
	Popular music
1819.18	Collections
1819.2	Separate works

	Vocal music
	Secular vocal music
	Folk, national, and ethnic music
	Asia
	Korea (North) -- Continued
1819.3	Revolutionary operas
	Iran
	General
1820	Collections
1821	Separate works
	Popular music
1821.18	Collections
1821.2	Separate works
	Philippines
	General
1822	Collections
1823	Separate works
	Popular music
1823.18	Collections
1823.2	Separate works
1824-1825	Other regions or countries, A-Z
1824.A-Z	Individual regions or countries, A-Z
	Subclasses for individual regions and countries continue at M1825
	For obsolete numbers formerly used under this span see Table MZ8
	Afghanistan
	General
1824.A3	Collections
	Azerbaijan
	General
1824.A9	Collections
	Bangladesh
	General
1824.B32	Collections
	Brunei
	General
1824.B7	Collections
	Burma
	General
1824.B8	Collections
	Cambodia
	General
1824.C3	Collections
	Cyprus
	General
1824.C9	Collections

	Vocal music
	Secular vocal music
	Folk, national, and ethnic music
	Asia
	Other regions or countries, A-Z
	Individual regions or countries, A-Z -- Continued
	Georgia
	General
1824.G28	Collections
	Indonesia
	General
1824.I5	Collections
	Iraq
	General
1824.I75	Collections
	Kazakhstan
	General
1824.K39	Collections
	Kurdistan
	General
1824.K87	Collections
	Kyrgyzstan
	General
1824.K96	Collections
	Laos
	General
1824.L3	Collections
	Lebanon
	General
1824.L4	Collections
	Malaysia
	General
1824.M34	Collections
	Mongolia
	General
1824.M5	Collections
	Nepal
	General
1824.N5	Collections
	Papua New Guinea
	General
1824.P36	Collections
	Singapore
	General
1824.S7	Collections
	Sri Lanka. Ceylon
	General

Vocal music
Secular vocal music
Folk, national, and ethnic music
Asia
Other regions or countries, A-Z
Individual regions or countries, A-Z
Sri Lanka. Ceylon
General -- Continued

1824.S8	Collections
	Syria
	General
1824.S9	Collections
	Thailand. Siam
	General
1824.T48	Collections
	Tibet
	General
1824.T5	Collections
	Turkey
	General
1824.T8	Collections
	Turkmenistan
	General
1824.T9	Collections
	Vietnam
	General
1824.V5	Collections
	Yemen
	General
1824.Y45	Collections

Individual regions or countries, A-Z
Subclasses for individual regions and countries begin
at M1824
For obsolete numbers formerly used under this span
see Table MZ8
Afghanistan
General

1825.A3	Separate works
	Popular music
1825.A318	Collections
1825.A32	Separate works
	Azerbaijan
	General
1825.A98	Separate works
	Popular music
1825.A9818	Collections
1825.A982	Separate works

	Vocal music
	Secular vocal music
	Folk, national, and ethnic music
	Asia
	Other regions or countries, A-Z
	Individual regions or countries, A-Z -- Continued
	Bangladesh
	General
1825.B32	Separate works
	Popular music
1825.B3218	Collections
1825.B322	Separate works
	Brunei
	General
1825.B7	Separate works
	Popular music
1825.B718	Collections
1825.B72	Separate works
	Burma
	General
1825.B8	Separate works
	Popular music
1825.B818	Collections
1825.B82	Separate works
	Cambodia
	General
1825.C3	Separate works
	Popular music
1825.C318	Collections
1825.C32	Separate works
	Cyprus
	General
1825.C9	Separate works
	Popular music
1825.C918	Collections
1825.C92	Separate works
	Georgia
	General
1825.G28	Separate works
	Popular music
1825.G2818	Collections
1825.G282	Separate works
	Indonesia
	General
1825.I5	Separate works
	Popular music
1825.I518	Collections

	Vocal music
	Secular vocal music
	Folk, national, and ethnic music
	Asia
	Other regions or countries, A-Z
	Individual regions or countries, A-Z
	Indonesia
	Popular music -- Continued
1825.I52	Separate works
	Iraq
	General
1825.I75	Separate works
	Popular music
1825.I7518	Collections
1825.I752	Separate works
	Kazakhstan
	General
1825.K39	Separate works
	Popular music
1825.K3918	Collections
1825.K392	Separate works
	Kurdistan
	General
1825.K87	Separate works
	Popular music
1825.K8718	Collections
1825.K872	Separate works
	Kyrgyzstan
	General
1825.K96	Separate works
	Popular music
1825.K9618	Collections
1825.K962	Separate works
	Laos
	General
1825.L3	Separate works
	Popular music
1825.L318	Collections
1825.L32	Separate works
	Lebanon
	General
1825.L4	Separate works
	Popular music
1825.L418	Collections
1825.L42	Separate works
	Malaysia
	General

M

Vocal music
Secular vocal music
Folk, national, and ethnic music
Asia
Other regions or countries, A-Z
Individual regions or countries, A-Z
Malaysia
General -- Continued
1825.M34   Separate works
Popular music
1825.M3418   Collections
1825.M342   Separate works
Mongolia
General
1825.M5   Separate works
Popular music
1825.M518   Collections
1825.M52   Separate works
Nepal
General
1825.N52   Separate works
Popular music
1825.N5218   Collections
1825.N522   Separate works
Papua New Guinea
General
1825.P36   Separate works
Popular music
1825.P3618   Collections
1825.P362   Separate works
Singapore
1825.S7   Separate works
Popular music
1825.S718   Collections
1825.S72   Separate works
Sri Lanka. Ceylon
General
1825.S8   Separate works
Popular music
1825.S818   Collections
1825.S82   Separate works
Syria
General
1825.S9   Separate works
Popular music
1825.S918   Collections
1825.S92   Separate works

```
                              Vocal music
                                Secular vocal music
                                  Folk, national, and ethnic music
                                    Asia
                                      Other regions or countries, A-Z
                                        Individual regions or countries, A-Z -- Continued
                                          Thailand. Siam
                                            General
1825.T48                                      Separate works
                                            Popular music
1825.T4818                                    Collections
1825.T482                                     Separate works
                                          Tibet
                                            General
1825.T5                                       Separate works
                                            Popular music
1825.T518                                     Collections
1825.T52                                      Separate works
                                          Turkey
                                            General
1825.T8                                       Separate works
                                            Popular music
1825.T818                                     Collections
1825.T82                                      Separate works
                                          Turkmenistan
                                            General
1825.T9                                        Separate works
                                            Popular music
1825.T918                                     Collections
1825.T92                                      Separate works
                                          Vietnam
                                            General
1825.V5                                       Separate works
                                            Popular music
1825.V518                                     Collections
1825.V52                                      Separate works
                                          Yemen
                                            General
1825.Y45                                      Separate works
                                            Popular music
1825.Y4518                                    Collections
1825.Y452                                     Separate works
```

	Vocal music
	Secular vocal music
	Folk, national, and ethnic music -- Continued
1828	Arab countries
	Class here general collections of music from the Arab world
	For music of Saudi Arabia see M1797+
	For music of individual Arab countries of Asia see M1824+
	For music of individual Arab countries of Africa see M1838.A+
	Africa
	For obsolete numbers formerly used under this span see Table MZ8
1830	General
1831.A-Z	By ethnic group, A-Z

Class here music of individual Black African ethnic groups; for music of two or more groups published together, see General or the country; for music of White African groups, see the country, e.g., Afrikaners, see South Africa

For obsolete numbers formerly used under this span see Table MZ20

1831.A4	Akan
1831.B27	Bafia
1831.B345	Bamun
1831.B35	Bantu-speaking peoples
1831.B37	Baule
1831.B43	Batwa
1831.B49	Bemba
1831.B59	Bisa
1831.C5	Chokwe
1831.C52	Chopi
1831.D55	Dinka
1831.D56	Diola
1831.D6	Dogon
1831.E4	Ekonda
1831.E9	Ewe
1831.F3	Fan (Cameroon). Fang (Cameroon). Fe'fe'
1831.F33	Fang (West Africa)
	Fe'fe' see M1831.F3
1831.F8	Fula
1831.G2	Gã
1831.G47	Gere. Ngere
1831.G87	Guro
1831.H39	Hausa
1831.I3	Idoma
	Kabiye see M1831.K3

	Vocal music
	Secular vocal music
	Folk, national, and ethnic music
	Africa
	By ethnic group, A-Z -- Continued
1831.K3	Kabre. Kabiye
1831.K82	Kuba
1831.L82	Luba
1831.M3	Mandingo
1831.M4	Mbuti
1831.M45	Mende
1831.N33	Ndau
1831.N44	Ngbaka
	Ngere see M1831.G47
1831.N95	Nzakara
1831.R98	Ruund
1831.S26	San
1831.S5	Shona
1831.S68	Sotho
1831.S93	Swahili-speaking peoples
1831.T53	Tida. Tibbu
1831.T64	Toma
1831.T66	Topoke
1831.T76	Tsonga
1831.T82	Tuaregs
1831.T87	Tutsi
1831.X5	Xhosa
1831.Y67	Yoruba
1831.Z8	Zulu
(1832)	Individual regions, tribes, and languages
	For languages, see the region, country, or ethnic group
	For ethnic groups see M1831.A+
	For regions see M1834+
	By region or country
	Prior to 1978 indigenous music by region was classified in M1831
	South Africa
	For Transvaal and other countries and districts formerly part of South Africa see M1838.A+
1834	General
	Popular music
1834.18	Collections
1834.2	Separate works
1838.A-Z	Other, A-Z
	For obsolete numbers formerly used under this span see Table MZ8

Vocal music
Secular vocal music
Folk, national, and ethnic music
Africa
By region or country
Other, A-Z -- Continued
Algeria
Prior to 1957 used for African regions and countries
other than South Africa

1838.A4	General
	Popular music
1838.A418	Collections
1838.A42	Separate works
	Angola
1838.A5	General
	Popular music
1838.A518	Collections
1838.A52	Separate works
	Belgian Congo see M1838.C67+
	Burkina Faso. Upper Volta
1838.B85	General
	Popular music
1838.B8518	Collections
1838.B852	Separate works
	Burundi
1838.B87	General
	Popular music
1838.B8718	Collections
1838.B872	Separate works
	Cape Verde
1838.C25	General
	Popular music
1838.C2518	Collections
1838.C252	Separate works
	Central African Republic. Central African Empire
1838.C45	General
	Popular music
1838.C4518	Collections
1838.C452	Separate works
	Chad
1838.C5	General
	Popular music
1838.C518	Collections
1838.C52	Separate works
	Congo (Democratic Republic). Belgian Congo. Zaire
1838.C67	General

	Vocal music
	Secular vocal music
	Folk, national, and ethnic music
	Africa
	By region or country
	Other, A-Z
	Congo (Democratic Republic). Belgian Congo. Zaire -- Continued
	Popular music
1838.C6718	Collections
1838.C672	Separate works
	Côte d'Ivoire see M1838.I9+
	Egypt
1838.E3	General
	Popular music
1838.E318	Collections
1838.E32	Separate works
	Ethiopia
1838.E8	General
	Popular music
1838.E818	Collections
1838.E82	Separate works
	Gabon
1838.G3	General
	Popular music
1838.G318	Collections
1838.G32	Separate works
	Ghana
1838.G5	General
	Popular music
1838.G518	Collections
1838.G52	Separate works
	Guinea
1838.G85	General
	Popular music
1838.G8518	Collections
1838.G852	Separate works
	Ivory Coast. Côte d'Ivoire
1838.I9	General
	Popular music
1838.I918	Collections
1838.I92	Separate works
	Kenya
1838.K45	General
	Popular music
1838.K4518	Collections
1838.K452	Separate works

	Vocal music
	Secular vocal music
	Folk, national, and ethnic music
	Africa
	By region or country
	Other, A-Z -- Continued
	Liberia
1838.L5	General
	Popular music
1838.L518	Collections
1838.L52	Separate works
	Libya
1838.L75	General
	Popular music
1838.L7518	Collections
1838.L752	Separate works
	Madagascar. Malagasy Republic
1838.M3	General
	Popular music
1838.M318	Collections
1838.M32	Separate works
	Malagasy Republic see M1838.M3+
	Malawi. Nyasaland
1838.M34	General
	Popular music
1838.M3418	Collections
1838.M342	Separate works
	Mali
1838.M36	General
	Popular music
1838.M3618	Collections
1838.M362	Separate works
	Mauritania
1838.M38	General
	Popular music
1838.M3818	Collections
1838.M382	Separate works
	Morocco
1838.M6	General
	Popular music
1838.M618	Collections
1838.M62	Separate works
	Niger
1838.N47	General
	Popular music
1838.N4718	Collections
1838.N472	Separate works

	Vocal music
	Secular vocal music
	Folk, national, and ethnic music
	Africa
	By region or country
	Other, A-Z -- Continued
	Nigeria
1838.N5	General
	Popular music
1838.N518	Collections
1838.N52	Separate works
	Nyasaland see M1838.M34+
	Rhodesia see M1838.Z34+
	Rwanda
1838.R9	General
	Popular music
1838.R918	Collections
1838.R92	Separate works
	Senegal
1838.S45	General
	Popular music
1838.S4518	Collections
1838.S452	Separate works
	Sierra Leone
1838.S53	General
	Popular music
1838.S5318	Collections
1838.S532	Separate works
	Somalia
1838.S65	General
	Popular music
1838.S6518	Collections
1838.S652	Separate works
	Sudan
1838.S83	General
	Popular music
1838.S8318	Collections
1838.S832	Separate works
	Tanzania
1838.T35	General
	Popular music
1838.T3518	Collections
1838.T352	Separate works
	Togo
1838.T6	General
	Popular music
1838.T618	Collections

Vocal music
Secular vocal music
Folk, national, and ethnic music
Africa
By region or country
Other, A-Z
Togo
Popular music -- Continued

1838.T62	Separate works
	Tunisia
1838.T8	General
	Popular music
1838.T818	Collections
1838.T82	Separate works
	Uganda
1838.U34	General
	Popular music
1838.U3418	Collections
1838.U342	Separate works
	Zambia. Rhodesia
1838.Z34	General
	Popular music
1838.Z3418	Collections
1838.Z342	Separate works
	Australia
	General
1840	Collections
1841	Separate works
	Popular music
1841.18	Collections
1841.2	Separate works
	New Zealand
	General
1842	Collections
1843	Separate works
	Popular music
1843.18	Collections
1843.2	Separate works
	Pacific Islands
1844.A1	General
1844.A2-Z	By island or group, A-Z
	For obsolete numbers used under this span see Table MZ8
	Cook Islands
1844.C54	General
	Popular music
1844.C5418	Collections

	Vocal music
	Secular vocal music
	Folk, national, and ethnic music
	Pacific Islands
	By island or group, A-Z
	Cook Islands
	Popular music -- Continued
1844.C542	Separate works
	Fiji Islands
1844.F45	General
	Popular music
1844.F4518	Collections
1844.F452	Separate works
	Gilbert and Ellice Islands
1844.G54	General
	Popular music
1844.G5418	Collections
1844.G542	Separate works
	New Hebrides. Vanuatu
1844.N5	General
	Popular music
1844.N518	Collections
1844.N52	Separate works
	Samoa
1844.S2	General
	Popular music
1844.S218	Collections
1844.S22	Separate works
	Sandwich Island (Vanuatu) see M1844.N5+
	Sandwich Islands
	see M1629.7.H4, M1658.H4
	Solomon Islands
1844.S6	General
	Popular music
1844.S618	Collections
1844.S62	Separate works
	Tahiti
1844.T3	General
	Popular music
1844.T318	Collections
1844.T32	Separate works
	Tonga
1844.T6	General
	Popular music
1844.T618	Collections
1844.T62	Separate works
	Vanuatu see M1844.N5+

	Vocal music
	Secular vocal music
	Folk, national, and ethnic music
	Pacific Islands -- Continued
(1845)	Primitive music not elsewhere classified
	see the region or country
	Indian Ocean Islands
1846.A1	General
1846.A5-Z	By island, A-Z
	Mauritius
1846.M4	General
	Popular music
1846.M418	Collections
1846.M42	Separate works
	Réunion
1846.R4	General
	Popular music
1846.R418	Collections
1846.R42	Separate works
	Seychelles
1846.S45	General
	Popular music
1846.S4518	Collections
1846.S452	Separate works
	Jews
	For Jews in Israel or Palestine see M1810+
1850	General
1851	Zionist, Hasidic, and other movements
	By language
1852	Yiddish
1853	Other dialects
	Songs of specific groups or on specific topics
	Class here solo songs and part songs
	For national, ethnic, and political songs, and songs
	about famous persons see M1627+
	Fraternal society songs
	Class here sacred and secular songs
	Freemasons
	Collections
(1900.M3)	General
	By order, rite, etc.
	Class here only those orders, rites, etc. listed below.
	Arrange other collections by composer, title, or
	compiler
1900.M31	Blue Lodge
1900.M32	Chapter
1900.M35	Commandery

	Vocal music
	Secular vocal music
	Songs of specific groups or on specific topics
	Fraternal society songs
	Freemasons
	Collections
	By order, rite, etc. -- Continued
	Eastern Star see M1905.E3
1900.M37	Scottish Rite (Masonic order)
1900.M38	Mystic Order of Veiled Prophets of the Enchanted Realm
1900.M4	Mystic Shrine. Ancient Arabic Order of the Nobles of the Mystic Shrine for North America
1900.M41	DeMolay for Boys
1900.M42	Ancient Egyptian Order of Scioto
	Rainbow, Order of, for Girls see M1905.R3
	Separate works
(1901.M3)	General
	By order, rite, etc.
	Class here only those orders, rites, etc. listed below. Arrange other separate works by composer or title
1901.M31	Blue Lodge
1901.M32	Chapter
1901.M35	Commandery
	Eastern Star, Order of see M1906.E3
1901.M37	Scottish Rite (Masonic order)
1901.M38	Mystic Order of Veiled Prophets of the Enchanted Realm
1901.M4	Mystic Shrine. Ancient Arabic Order of the Nobles of the Mystic Shrine for North America
1901.M41	DeMolay for Boys
1901.M42	Ancient Egyptian Order of Scioto
	Rainbow for Girls see M1906.R3
(1901.R7)	Royal Order of Jesters
	Other
	Collections. By society, A-Z
	For obsolete numbers formerly used under this span see Table MZ9
1905.A1	General
1905.A46	Alhambra, Order of
1905.A55	Amaranth, Order of
1905.B5	B'nai B'rith
1905.D5	Deutscher Orden der Harugari (German Order of Harugari)
1905.E2	Eagles, Fraternal Order of

	Vocal music
	Secular vocal music
	Songs of specific groups or on specific topics
	Fraternal society songs
	Other
	Collections. By society, A-Z -- Continued
1905.E3	Eastern Star, Order of
1905.E5	Elks (Fraternal order)
	German Order of Harugari see M1905.D5
	Grange see M1905.P3
1905.J6	Job's Daughters, International Order of
1905.K5	Knights of Columbus
1905.K54	Knights of Malta
1905.K55	Knights of Pythias
1905.K6	Knights of the Golden Eagle
	Modern Woodmen of America see M1905.W7
1905.M7	Moose, Loyal Order of
	National Grange see M1905.P3
1905.O3	Odd Fellows, Independent Order of
1905.P2	P.E.O. Sisterhood
1905.P3	Patrons of Husbandry. National Grange
1905.R3	Rainbow, Order of, for Girls
1905.R33	Rebekah Assemblies, International Association of, IOOF
1905.W6	Woman's Benefit Association of the Maccabees
1905.W7	Supreme Forest Woodmen Circle (U.S.), Modern Woodmen of America, and other foresters' fraternal organizations
	Separate works. By society, A-Z
	For obsolete numbers formerly used under this span see Table MZ9
1906.A46	Alhambra, Order of
1906.A55	Amaranth, Order of
1906.B5	B'nai B'rith International
1906.D5	Deutscher Orden der Harugari (German Order of Harugari)
1906.E2	Eagles, Fraternal Order of
1906.E3	Eastern Star, Order of
1906.E5	Elks (Fraternal order)
	German Order of Harugari see M1906.D5
	Grange see M1906.P3
1906.J6	Job's Daughters, International Order of
1906.K5	Knights of Columbus
1906.K54	Knights of Malta
1906.K55	Knights of Pythias
1906.K6	Knights of the Golden Eagle
	Modern Woodman of America see M1906.W7

Vocal music
Secular vocal music
Songs of specific groups or on specific topics
Fraternal society songs
Other
Separate works. By society, A-Z -- Continued

1906.M7	Moose, Loyal Order of
	National Grange see M1906.P3
1906.O3	Odd Fellows, Independent Order of
1906.P2	P.E.O. Sisterhood
1906.P3	Patrons of Husbandry. National Grange
1906.R3	Rainbow, Order of, for Girls
1906.R33	Rebekah Assemblies, International Association of, IOOF
1906.W6	Woman's Benefit Association of the Maccabees
1906.W7	Supreme Forest Woodmen Circle (U.S.), Modern Woodmen of America, and other foresters' fraternal organizations

Other societies, organizations, and clubs, A-Z
For patriotic societies and organizations in the United States see M1676.A+

1920.A-Z	Collections
	For obsolete numbers formerly used under this span see Table MZ9
	Names listed below are given as examples
1920.A35	Alcoholics Anonymous
1920.A433	American Association of Retired Persons. AARP
1920.A44	American Cancer Society
1920.F4	4-H clubs
1920.G5	Gideon's International. Christian Commercial Travelers' Association of America
1920.I55	International Business Machines Corporation
1920.K5	Kiwanis clubs. Kiwanis International
1920.L6	Lions clubs. Lions International
1920.N13	National Federation of Music Clubs
1920.P2	National PTA (U.S.)
1920.R6	Rotary clubs. Rotary International
1920.S54	Society for the Preservation and Encouragement of Barber Shop Quartet Singing in America
1920.U48	United Nations Children's Fund. UNICEF
1921.A-Z	Separate works
	For obsolete numbers formerly used under this span see Table MZ9
	Names listed below are given as examples
1921.A35	Alcoholics Anonymous
1921.A433	American Association of Retired Persons. AARP
1921.A44	American Cancer Society

	Vocal music
	Secular vocal music
	Songs of specific groups or on specific topics
	Other societies, organizations, and clubs, A-Z
	Separate works -- Continued
1921.F4	4-H clubs
1921.G5	Gideon's International. Christian Commercial Travelers' Association of America
1921.I55	International Business Machines Corporation
1921.K5	Kiwanis clubs. Kiwanis International
1921.L6	Lions clubs. Lions International
1921.N13	National Federation of Music Clubs
1921.P2	National PTA (U.S.)
1921.R6	Rotary clubs. Rotary International
1921.S54	Society for the Preservation and Encouragement of Barber Shop Quartet Singing in America
1921.U48	United Nations Children's Fund. UNICEF
	Students' songs
	Class here college and university songs
	For songs of primary and secondary schools see M1992+
	International
1940	Collections
1941	Separate works
	United States
1945	Miscellaneous collections
	Men's colleges and universities
	Collections
1946	Various institutions
1948.A-Z	Individual institutions. By name of institution, A-Z
1950.A-Z	Separate works. By name of institution, A-Z
	Women's colleges and universities
	Collections
1952	Various institutions
1954.A-Z	Individual institutions. By name of institution, A-Z
1956.A-Z	Separate works. By name of institution, A-Z
	Coeducational colleges and universities
	Class here institutions founded as coeducational
	For colleges, etc. originally for men see M1946+
	For colleges, etc. originally for women see M1952+
	Collections
1957	Various institutions
1958.A-Z	Individual institutions. By name of institution, A-Z
1959.A-Z	Separate works. By name of institution, A-Z

	Vocal music
	Secular vocal music
	Songs of specific groups or on specific topics
	Students' songs
	United States -- Continued
1960.A-Z	Fraternities and sororities. By name of fraternity or sorority, A-Z
	Subdivide by chapter and imprint date
	Countries outside the U. S.
1961	Austria. Hungary. Germany. Switzerland
1962	France. Belgium
1964	Great Britain. Ireland
1966	Netherlands
1967	Italy. Spain. Portugal
1970	Canada
1972	Russia. Soviet Union. Russia (Federation)
1973.A-Z	Other. By country, A-Z
1973.A9	Australia
1973.C5	Chile
1973.F5	Finland
1973.G8	Guam
1973.J35	Japan
1973.L3	Latvia
1973.L78	Lithuania
	Montenegro see M1973.Y8
1973.N7	Norway
	Serbia see M1973.Y8
1973.S9	Sweden
1973.T26	Taiwan
1973.V45	Venezuela
1973.Y8	Yugoslavia. Serbia. Montenegro
	By topic, A-Z
1977.A-Z	Collections
1977.A4	Aeronautics. Aviation
1977.A6	Animals
1977.A65	Antiques
	Archery see M1977.S705
1977.A7	Artists
1977.A8	Atoms
	Automobile racing see M1977.S707
	Autumn see M1977.S413
	Aviation see M1977.A4
1977.B3	Balloons
	Baseball see M1977.S713
	Basketball see M1977.S714
1977.B38	Bawdy songs
1977.B4	Beauticians

M

	Vocal music
	Secular vocal music
	Songs of specific groups or on specific topics
	By topic, A-Z
	Collections -- Continued
1977.B5	Birds
1977.B53	Birthdays
	Bowling see M1977.S715
	Boxing see M1977.S716
1977.B6	Boy Scouts of America, Camp Fire Girls, Girl Scouts of the United States of America, Wandervogel, etc.
1977.B7	Brotherhood Week
1977.B8	Bullfights
	Camp Fire Girls see M1977.B6
1977.C3	Camping
1977.C34	Canals
	Cars (Automobiles) see M1977.M6
1977.C4	Cemeteries
1977.C43	Chemistry
1977.C45	Circus
1977.C46	Civil defense
1977.C47	Civil rights
	Comic songs see M1977.H7
1977.C48	Communism
1977.C5	Community
	Conduct of life see M1977.M55
1977.C53	Conservation. Ecology. Pollution
1977.C55	Convicts. Prisoners. Ex-convicts
1977.C6	Cowboy songs
	Prior to 1998 collections of American cowboy songs were classified in M1629
	For other cowboy songs cataloged before 1998, see M1627+ M1630, M1630.18+ M1678+ M1680+
1977.C7	Crime. Criminals
	Cycling see M1977.S7165
1977.D4	Democracy
1977.D7	Drinking songs
	Ecology see M1977.C53
1977.E3	Economic conditions
1977.E33	Education
1977.E68	Emigration. Immigration
1977.E7	Epicures. Gourmets
	Ethics see M1977.M55
	Ex-convicts see M1977.C55
1977.E84	Eyes

	Vocal music
	Secular vocal music
	Songs of specific groups or on specific topics
	By topic, A-Z
	Collections -- Continued
1977.F2	Farmers
	For Patrons of Husbandry and National Grange see M1905.P3
	For 4-H clubs see M1920.F4
1977.F26	Fathers
1977.F38	Fire prevention
1977.F4	Fire fighters
1977.F5	Fishers
1977.F54	Flowers
	Football see M1977.S718
	Football, Rugby see M1977.S7265
1977.F6	Foresters. Forest fires
1977.G3	Gambling
1977.G38	Gays
1977.G46	Geography
	Girl Scouts of the United States of America see M1977.B6
	Golf see M1977.S72
	Gourmets see M1977.E7
1977.G9	Gymnastics
1977.H3	Halloween
1977.H4	Health
1977.H5	Hiking
1977.H58	Hobbies
1977.H6	Hoboes. Tramps
1977.H65	Homemakers. Housewives
	Horse racing see M1977.S723
	Horsemanship see M1977.S722
	Housewives see M1977.H65
1977.H7	Humorous songs
1977.H77	Hunger
1977.H8	Hunting
1977.H85	Husbands
	Immigration see M1977.E68
	Income tax see M1977.T3
1977.I5	Insurance salespeople
1977.J7	Junior republics
1977.J87	Juvenile delinquency
1977.L3	Labor
	Cf. M1664+ songs of labor organizations in the United States
1977.L55	Littering

Vocal music
  Secular vocal music
    Songs of specific groups or on specific topics
      By topic, A-Z
        Collections -- Continued

1977.L8	Lumbermen
1977.M3	Mail carriers
1977.M37	May DaySongs and
1977.M4	Medicine
1977.M44	Men
1977.M5	Miners
1977.M54	Months
1977.M55	Morals. Ethics. Conduct of life
1977.M57	Mothers
1977.M6	Motor transportation. Transportation, Automotive
1977.M63	Mountaineering
1977.M8	Music publishing
1977.M83	Musicians
1977.N38	Nature
1977.N48	Newspaper carriers
1977.N5	Newspapers
1977.N8	Nurses
1977.N83	Nutrition
	Older people see M1977.S45
1977.O5	Olympics
1977.O9	Oysters
1977.P4	Peace
1977.P45	Phonograph
1977.P47	Photography
1977.P5	Physical fitness
1977.P7	Police
	Pollution see M1977.C53
	Postmen see M1977.M3
1977.P74	Printing
	For music publishing see M1977.M8
	Prisoners see M1977.C55
1977.P75	Protest songs
1977.P8	Psychoanalysis
1977.R2	Radio. Television
1977.R3	Railroads
1977.R58	Rivers
	Rodeos see M1977.S726
	Rugby football see M1977.S7265
1977.S15	Safety
1977.S2	Sailors. Sea songs
1977.S25	Saint Valentine's Day
1977.S3	Science

Vocal music
  Secular vocal music
    Songs of specific groups or on specific topics
      By topic, A-Z
        Collections -- Continued
          Sea songs see M1977.S2
          Seasons
            Cf. M1977.W38 Weather

1977.S4	General
1977.S413	Autumn
1977.S417	Spring
1977.S418	Summer
1977.S42	Winter
1977.S43	Secretaries
1977.S45	Senior citizens. Older people
1977.S48	Shepherds
1977.S5	Singing commercials
	Skiing see M1977.S727
	Skydiving see M1977.S73
1977.S55	Smoking
	Soccer see M1977.S75
1977.S6	Soldiers
	For war songs concerning specific U. S. wars see M1631+
1977.S63	Space flight
	Sports
1977.S7	General
1977.S705	Archery
1977.S707	Automobile racing
1977.S713	Baseball
1977.S714	Basketball
1977.S715	Bowling
1977.S716	Boxing
1977.S7165	Cycling
1977.S718	Football
	Football, Rugby see M1977.S7265
1977.S72	Golf
1977.S722	Horsemanship
1977.S723	Horse racing
1977.S726	Rodeos
1977.S7265	Rugby football
1977.S727	Skiing
1977.S73	Skydiving
1977.S75	Soccer
	Spring see M1977.S417
	Summer see M1977.S418
1977.T25	Tailors. Tailoring

Vocal music

  Secular vocal music

    Songs of specific groups or on specific topics

      By topic, A-Z

        Collections -- Continued

1977.T3	Taxation
	Television see M1977.R2
1977.T55	Titanic (Steamship)
1977.T6	Toleration
	Tramps see M1977.H6
1977.T8	Travel
1977.T87	Truck drivers
(1977.T9)	Turners
	see M1977.G9
1977.T97	Typing (Writing)
	Valentine's Day see M1977.S25
1977.V4	Vegetarianism
1977.V5	Voting
	For United States campaign songs see M1659.7+
1977.W3	Waiters
	Wandervogel see M1977.B6
1977.W38	Weather
	Cf. M1977.S4+ Seasons
1977.W4	Weddings
1977.W54	Wine
	Winter see M1977.S42
1977.W57	Witchcraft
1977.W64	Women
	Work see M1977.L3
1977.Z6	Zodiac
1978.A-Z	Separate works
1978.A4	Aeronautics. Aviation
1978.A6	Animals
1978.A65	Antiques
	Archery see M1978.S705
1978.A7	Artists
1978.A8	Atoms
	Automobile racing see M1978.S707
	Autumn see M1978.S413
	Aviation see M1978.A4
1978.B3	Balloons
	Baseball see M1978.S713
	Basketball see M1978.S714
1978.B38	Bawdy songs
1978.B4	Beauticians
1978.B5	Birds
1978.B53	Birthdays

    Vocal music
      Secular vocal music
        Songs of specific groups or on specific topics
          By topic, A-Z
            Separate works -- Continued

	Bowling see M1978.S715
	Boxing see M1978.S716
1978.B6	Boy Scouts of America, Camp Fire Girls, Girl Scouts of the United States of America, Wandervogel, etc.
1978.B7	Brotherhood Week
1978.B8	Bullfights
	Camp Fire Girls see M1978.B6
1978.C3	Camping
1978.C34	Canals
	Cars (Automobiles) see M1978.M6
1978.C4	Cemeteries
1978.C43	Chemistry
1978.C45	Circus
1978.C46	Civil defense
1978.C47	Civil rights
	Comic songs see M1978.H7
1978.C48	Communism
1978.C5	Community
	Conduct of life see M1978.M55
1978.C53	Conservation. Ecology. Pollution
1978.C55	Convicts. Prisoners. Ex-convicts
1978.C6	Cowboy songs
	For separate cowboy songs cataloged before 1998, see M1627.15, M1630, M1630.2, M1679.2, M1680+
1978.C7	Crime. Criminals
	Cycling see M1978.S7165
1978.D4	Democracy
1978.D7	Drinking songs
	Ecology see M1978.C53
1978.E3	Economic conditions
1978.E33	Education
1978.E68	Emigration. Immigration
1978.E7	Epicures. Gourmets
	Ethics see M1978.M55
	Ex-convicts see M1978.C55
1978.E84	Eyes
1978.F2	Farmers
	For Patrons of Husbandry and National Grange see M1905.P3
	For 4-H clubs see M1921.F4

	Vocal music
	Secular vocal music
	Songs of specific groups or on specific topics
	By topic, A-Z
	Separate works -- Continued
1978.F26	Fathers
1978.F38	Fire prevention
1978.F4	Fire fighters
1978.F5	Fishers
1978.F54	Flowers
	Football see M1978.S718
	Football, Rugby see M1978.S7265
1978.F6	Foresters. Forest fires
1978.G3	Gambling
1978.G38	Gays
1978.G46	Geography
	Girl Scouts of the United States of America see M1978.B6
	Golf see M1978.S72
	Gourmets see M1978.E7
1978.G9	Gymnastics
1978.H3	Halloween
1978.H4	Health
1978.H5	Hiking
1978.H58	Hobbies
1978.H6	Hoboes. Tramps
1978.H65	Homemakers. Housewives
	Horse racing see M1978.S723
	Horsemanship see M1978.S722
	Housewives see M1978.H65
1978.H7	Humorous songs
1978.H77	Hunger
1978.H8	Hunting
1978.H85	Husbands
	Immigration see M1978.E68
	Income tax see M1978.T3
1978.I5	Insurance salespeople
1978.J7	Junior republics
1978.J87	Juvenile delinquency
1978.L3	Labor
	Cf. M1664+ songs of labor organizations in the United States
1978.L55	Littering
1978.L8	Lumbermen
1978.M3	Mail carriers
1978.M37	May Day
1978.M4	Medicine

	Vocal music
	Secular vocal music
	Songs of specific groups or on specific topics
	By topic, A-Z
	Separate works -- Continued
1978.M44	Men
1978.M5	Miners
1978.M54	Months
1978.M55	Morals. Ethics. Conduct of life
1978.M57	Mothers
1978.M6	Motor transportation. Transportation, Automotive
1978.M63	Mountaineering
1978.M8	Music publishing
1978.M83	Musicians
1978.N38	Nature
1978.N48	Newspaper carriers
1978.N5	Newspapers
1978.N8	Nurses
1978.N83	Nutrition
	Older people see M1978.S45
1978.O5	Olympics
1978.O9	Oysters
1978.P4	Peace
1978.P45	Phonograph
1978.P47	Photography
1978.P5	Physical fitness
1978.P7	Police
	Pollution see M1978.C53
	Postmen see M1978.M3
1978.P74	Printing
	For music publishing see M1978.M8
	Prisoners see M1978.C55
1978.P75	Protest songs
1978.P8	Psychoanalysis
1978.R2	Radio. Television
1978.R3	Railroads
1978.R58	Rivers
	Rodeos see M1978.S726
	Rugby football see M1978.S7265
1978.S15	Safety
1978.S2	Sailors. Sea songs
1978.S25	Saint Valentine's Day
1978.S3	Science
	Sea songs see M1978.S2
	Seasons
	Cf. M1978.W38 Weather
1978.S4	General

```
                        Vocal music
                          Secular vocal music
                            Songs of specific groups or on specific topics
                              By topic, A-Z
                                Separate works
                                  Seasons -- Continued
1978.S413                             Autumn
1978.S417                             Spring
1978.S418                             Summer
1978.S42                              Winter
1978.S43                          Secretaries
1978.S45                          Senior citizens. Older people
1978.S48                          Shepherds
1978.S5                           Singing commercials
                                  Skiing see M1978.S727
                                  Skydiving see M1978.S73
1978.S55                          Smoking
                                  Soccer see M1978.S75
1978.S6                           Soldiers
                                      For war songs concerning specific U. S. wars see
                                          M1631+
1978.S63                          Space
                                  Sports
1978.S7                             General
1978.S705                           Archery
1978.S707                           Automobile racing
1978.S713                           Baseball
1978.S714                           Basketball
1978.S715                           Bowling
1978.S716                           Boxing
1978.S7165                          Cycling
1978.S718                           Football
                                    Football, Rugby see M1978.S7265
1978.S72                            Golf
1978.S722                           Horsemanship
1978.S723                           Horse racing
1978.S726                           Rodeos
1978.S7265                          Rugby football
1978.S727                           Skiing
1978.S73                            Skydiving
1978.S75                            Soccer
                                  Spring see M1978.S417
                                  Summer see M1978.S418
1978.T25                          Tailors. Tailoring
1978.T3                           Taxation
                                  Television see M1978.R2
1978.T55                          Titanic (Steamship)
```

	Vocal music
	Secular vocal music
	Songs of specific groups or on specific topics
	By topic, A-Z
	Separate works -- Continued
1978.T6	Toleration
	Tramps see M1978.H6
1978.T8	Travel
1978.T87	Truck drivers
(1978.T9)	Turners
	see M1978.G9
1978.T97	Typing (Writing)
	Valentine's Day see M1978.S25
1978.V4	Vegetarianism
1978.V5	Voting
	For United States campaign songs see M1659.7+
1978.W3	Waiters
	Wandervogel see M1978.B6
1978.W38	Weather
	Cf. M1978.S4+ Seasons
1978.W4	Weddings
1978.W54	Wine
	Winter see M1978.S42
1978.W57	Witchcraft
1978.W64	Women
	Work see M1978.L3
1978.Z6	Zodiac
(1980)	Latin and other songs, primarily U.S. imprints, not elsewhere classified
	see the topic
1985	Musical games
	For action songs, drill songs, and musical games for children see M1993
	Secular vocal music for children
	Preschool and school music
1990	Kindergarten
	Primary and secondary schools
1992	Miscellaneous collections
1993	Action songs. Drill songs. Musical games
	Cf. M1985 Musical games
1994	School songbooks
	Class here collections of vocal music for use in schools
	Songs of particular schools. By school, A-Z
1994.5.A-Z	Collections
1994.6.A-Z	Separate works
	Forms and types
1995	Dramatic music

Vocal music
Secular vocal music
Secular vocal music for children
Forms and types -- Continued
1996   Cantatas

Other vocal music
    Including choruses, songs, etc.
    For choruses for children's voices with
        accompaniment of orchestra or other ensemble
        primarily for concert performance see M1546.5
1997   Collections
    For Boy Scouts of America, Girl Scouts of the
        United States of America, etc. see M1977.B6
1998   Separate works
    For Boy Scouts of America, Girl Scouts of the
        United States of America, etc. see M1978.B6
Sacred vocal music
1999   Collections
    Class here collections by two or more composers too varied
        to assign to a more specific class
Dramatic music
    Class here oratorios, liturgical dramas, rappresentazioni
        sacre, sacred musicals, etc.
    For secular oratorios see M1530+
Complete works
2000   Scores. Parts
    Class here works with accompaniment other than one or
        two keyboard instruments
2002   Vocal and chorus scores without accompaniment
2003   Vocal scores with keyboard instrument(s)
    Class here works with original or arranged
        accompaniment for one or two keyboard instruments
Excerpts
2004   Original accompaniment
    Class here works with accompaniment other than one or
        two keyboard instruments
Arranged accompaniment
    Class here works with accompaniment other than one or
        two keyboard instruments
2005   Orchestra or other ensemble
Vocal scores with keyboard instrument(s)
    Class here works with original or arranged
        accompaniment for one or two keyboard
        instruments
2006   Collections
2007   Separate works

Vocal music
  Sacred vocal music -- Continued
    Choral services, etc.
      Class here cyclical choral works composed to liturgical or
        other texts whether or not for use within the church or
        other religious sanctuary
      For individual parts of liturgical (e. g. Credo) or nonliturgical
        services set as separate compositions see M2020-
        M2102.5 and M2114.8
      For officially prescribed service music see M2147+
    Roman Catholic
      Masses
        Settings of the Ordinary. Requiems
          Complete works

2010	Accompaniment of orchestra or other ensemble
2011	Vocal and chorus scores without accompaniment. Unaccompanied works
2013	Accompaniment of organ, piano, or other instrument

            Including vocal scores with organ or piano
              accompaniment of works with original
              accompaniment of orchestra, etc.

2013.5	Unison voices
2014	Excerpts
2014.5	Settings of Propers

         Class here settings with or without the Ordinary
         For requiems see M2010+

2014.6	Offices and other services
2015	Orthodox
	Anglican
2016	Collections
	Separate works
2016.2	Morning and Evening service

        Including works with or without Communion service

2016.3	Morning service
2016.4	Evening service

        For sets of vesper prayers, hymns, etc., see
          M2079.x96, M2099.x96, and M2114.x96

2016.5	Communion service
2016.6	Chant settings

        Including services with or without accompaniment

2016.7	Unaccompanied services
2016.8	Special services

        Including Office of the Dead, Burial service,
          Benediction service, etc.

2017	Lutheran
2017.2	Other Protestant

Vocal music

  Sacred vocal music

    Choral services, etc. -- Continued

2017.6	Jewish

        Class here works accompanied by two or more instruments

        For works accompanied by keyboard instrument see M2079.5

        For unaccompanied works see M2099.5

        For officially prescribed worship services solely for use inside the synagogue see M2186+

(2017.7)	Unaccompanied services for cantor

      see M2186-M2187

(2017.9)	Other special

  Two or more solo voices

    Accompaniment of orchestra or other ensemble, or electronics

2018	Scores. Parts
2019	Vocal scores with keyboard instrument

    Accompaniment of one or two keyboard instruments, of one instrument other than keyboard, or unaccompanied

        Class here works whose performance by solo voices is specifically indicated

        For part songs, motets, etc., that may be performed by either solo voices or chorus see M2060+

      Duets

2019.2	Collections
2019.3	Separate works

      Trios, quartets, etc.

2019.4	Collections
2019.5	Separate works

  Choruses

      Class here choruses, anthems, cantatas, etc., with or without accompaniment

      For oratorios see M2000+

      For choral services, etc. see M2010+

    Accompaniment of orchestra, other ensemble of two or more instruments, or electronics

      Class here choruses, anthems, cantatas, etc., with or without solo voices

      For accompaniment originally for two keyboard instruments see M2061+

    Mixed voices

      Complete works

        Scores. Parts

          Orchestral accompaniment

            Class here original works and arrangements

	Vocal music
	Sacred vocal music
	Choruses
	Accompaniment of orchestra, other ensemble of two or more instruments, or electronics
	Mixed voices
	Complete works
	Scores. Parts
	Orchestral accompaniment -- Continued
2020	General
2020.3	With recitation
2021	Other accompaniment
	Class here works with accompaniment of string orchestra, band, other ensemble of two or more instruments, or electronics
	For original accompaniment of one or two keyboard instruments see M2061+
2022	Vocal and chorus scores without accompaniment
	Vocal and chorus scores with keyboard instrument(s)
	Class here accompaniment arranged for one or two keyboard instruments
2023	General
2023.3	With recitation
	Excerpts
2025	Original accompaniment
	For original accompaniment of one or two keyboard instruments see M2061+
2025.5	Vocal and chorus scores without accompaniment
	Arranged accompaniment
2026	Orchestra, etc.
	Vocal scores with keyboard instrument(s)
	Class here accompaniment arranged for one or two keyboard instruments
2027	Collections
2028	Separate works
	Men's voices
	Complete works
2029	Scores. Parts
2029.5	Vocal and chorus scores without accompaniment
2030	Vocal scores with keyboard instrument(s)
	Class here accompaniment arranged for one or two keyboard instruments
	For original accompaniment of one or two keyboard instruments see M2061+
	Excerpts

M

Vocal music
 Sacred vocal music
  Choruses
   Accompaniment of orchestra, other ensemble of two or
    more instruments, or electronics
    Men's voices
     Excerpts -- Continued

2031	Accompaniment of two or more instruments except two keyboard instruments, or electronics
2032	Vocal scores with keyboard instrument(s)

      Class here accompaniment arranged for one or two
       keyboard instruments
      For original accompaniment of one or two
       keyboard instruments see M2061+

    Treble voices
     Complete works

2033	Scores. Parts
2033.5	Vocal and chorus scores without accompaniment
2034	Vocal scores with keyboard instrument(s)

      Class here accompaniment arranged for one or two
       keyboard instruments
      For original accompaniment of one or two
       keyboard instruments see M2061+

     Excerpts

2035	Accompaniment of two or more instruments except two keyboard instruments, or electronics
2036	Vocal scores with keyboard instrument(s)

      Class here accompaniment arranged for one or two
       keyboard instruments
      For original accompaniment of one or two
       keyboard instruments see M2061+

(2037)	Unison voices

    see M2101.5

(2038-2058)	Anthems

    For obsolete numbers formerly used in this span see
     Table MZ10
    see M2020+

Vocal music
Sacred vocal music
Choruses -- Continued
Accompaniment of one instrument, two keyboard
instruments, or unaccompanied
Class here choruses with or without solo voices, and part
songs, anthems, motets, etc., that may be performed
by either chorus or solo voices
Class works in the following priority unless otherwise noted:
1) by type or absence of accompaniment, 2) by text, 3)
by season or occasion, 4) by type of chorus
For works in larger vocal forms originally with keyboard
accompaniment classified before 1985, see M2023,
M2024, M2028, M2030, M2032, M2034, and M2036
For works whose performance by solo voices is
specifically indicated see M2019.2+

2060	Collections of accompanied and unaccompanied works

Accompaniment of keyboard instrument(s)
Class here works accompanied by one or two keyboard
instruments
Collections
Including collections that contain some works with
accompaniment of other solo instrument

2061	Two or more types of chorus

For two or more types of chorus for treble
voices see M2064

2062	Mixed voices

For obsolete decimal subdivisions formerly used for
number of vocal parts see Table MZ3

2063	Men's voices

For obsolete decimal subdivisions formerly used for
number of vocal parts see Table MZ3

2064	Treble voices

For obsolete decimal subdivisions formerly used for
number of vocal parts see Table MZ3
Special seasons and occasions

2065	Christmas
2066	Easter
2067	Thanksgiving. Harvest
2068.A-Z	Other, A-Z
2068.A4	Advent
2068.A5	All Saints Day
2068.A6	Ascension Day
2068.C2	Candlemas
2068.C75	Corpus Christi Festival
2068.E5	Epiphany
2068.F3	Father's Day

	Vocal music
	Sacred vocal music
	Choruses
	Accompaniment of one instrument, two keyboard instruments, or unaccompanied
	Accompaniment of keyboard instrument(s)
	Collections
	Special seasons and occasions
	Other, A-Z -- Continued
2068.G5	Good Friday
2068.H56	Holy Saturday
	Holy Thursday see M2068.M35
2068.H58	Holy Week
2068.H6	Holy Year
2068.L5	Lent. Passiontide
2068.M33	Marian feasts
2068.M35	Maundy Thursday
2068.M6	Mother's Day
2068.N5	New Year
2068.P4	Palm Sunday
	Passiontide see M2068.L5
	Pentecost Festival see M2068.W4
2068.R3	Reformation Festival
2068.T5	Trinity Sunday
2068.W4	Whitsuntide. Pentecost Festival
	Other religions or denominations
2069	Catholic
	Islamic see M2079.3
	Orthodox see M2080
	Protestant see M2060+
	Jewish see M2079.5
(2070)	Protestant
	see M2061+
(2071.A-Z)	Other
	Separate works
2072	Mixed voices
	For obsolete decimal subdivisions formerly used for number of vocal parts see Table MZ3
2073	Men's voices
	For obsolete decimal subdivisions formerly used for number of vocal parts see Table MZ3
2074	Treble voices
	For obsolete decimal subdivisions formerly used for number of vocal parts see Table MZ3
	Special seasons and occasions
2075	Christmas
2076	Easter

	Vocal music
	Sacred vocal music
	Choruses
	Accompaniment of one instrument, two keyboard instruments, or unaccompanied
	Accompaniment of keyboard instrument(s)
	Separate works
	Special seasons and occasions -- Continued
2077	Thanksgiving. Harvest
2078.A-Z	Other, A-Z
2078.A4	Advent
2078.A5	All Saints Day
2078.A6	Ascension Day
2078.C2	Candlemas
2078.C75	Corpus Christi Festival
2078.E5	Epiphany
2078.F3	Father's Day
2078.G5	Good Friday
2078.H56	Holy Saturday
	Holy Thursday see M2078.M35
2078.H58	Holy Week
2078.H6	Holy Year
2078.L5	Lent. Passiontide
2078.M33	Marian feasts
2078.M35	Maundy Thursday
2078.M6	Mother's Day
2078.N5	New Year
2078.P4	Palm Sunday
	Passiontide see M2078.L5
	Pentecost Festival see M2078.W4
2078.R3	Reformation Festival
2078.T5	Trinity Sunday
2078.W4	Whitsuntide. Pentecost Festival
2079.A-Z	Special texts. By language, A-Z
	Subarrange each language by Table M6
	Including special parts of a liturgical text set as separate compositions
	For special texts not listed in Table M6 see the medium of performance, e.g., M2072 for Domine probasti me (Psalm 139) for mixed chorus with keyboard accompaniment
	Other religions or denominations
2079.3	Islamic
	Class here collections and separate works

Vocal music

Sacred vocal music

Choruses

Accompaniment of one instrument, two keyboard
instruments, or unaccompanied

Accompaniment of keyboard instrument(s)

Other religions or denominations -- Continued

2079.5 Jewish

Class here collections and separate works

For cyclical choral services and other larger
vocal works that may be sung outside the
synagogue see M2017.6

For officially prescribed worship services solely
for use inside the synagogue see M2186+

2080 Orthodox

Class here collections and separate works

Accompaniment of one instrument other than keyboard
instrument

For works for special seasons and occasions see
M2065+

For works with special texts see M2079.A+

2080.4 Two or more types of chorus

Class here collections only

2080.5 Mixed voices

2080.6 Men's voices

2080.7 Treble voices

Unaccompanied

Collections

2081 Two or more types of chorus

For collections of works for two or more types of
treble chorus see M2084

2082 Mixed voices

For obsolete decimal subdivisions formerly used for
number of vocal parts see Table MZ3

2083 Men's voices

For obsolete decimal subdivisions formerly used for
number of vocal parts see Table MZ3

2084 Treble voices

For obsolete decimal subdivisions formerly used for
number of vocal parts see Table MZ3

Special seasons and occasions

2085 Christmas

2086 Easter

2087 Thanksgiving. Harvest

2088.A-Z Other, A-Z

2088.A4 Advent

2088.A5 All Saints Day

	Vocal music
	Sacred vocal music
	Choruses
	Accompaniment of one instrument, two keyboard instruments, or unaccompanied
	Unaccompanied
	Collections
	Special seasons and occasions
	Other, A-Z -- Continued
2088.A6	Ascension Day
2088.C2	Candlemas
2088.C75	Corpus Christi Festival
2088.E5	Epiphany
2088.F3	Father's Day
2088.G5	Good Friday
2088.H56	Holy Saturday
	Holy Thursday see M2088.M35
2088.H58	Holy Week
2088.H6	Holy Year
2088.L5	Lent. Passiontide
2088.M33	Marian feasts
2088.M35	Maundy Thursday
2088.M6	Mother's Day
2088.N5	New Year
2088.P4	Palm Sunday
	Passiontide see M2088.L5
	Pentecost Festival see M2088.W4
2088.R3	Reformation Festival
2088.T5	Trinity Sunday
2088.W4	Whitsuntide. Pentecost Festival
	Other religions or denominations
2089	Catholic
2090	Protestant
	Islamic see M2099.3
	Jewish see M2099.5
	Orthodox see M2100
(2091)	Other
	see the religion or denomination
	Separate works
2092	Mixed voices
	For obsolete decimal subdivisions formerly used for number of vocal parts see Table MZ3
2093	Men's voices
	For obsolete decimal subdivisions formerly used for number of vocal parts see Table MZ3

Vocal music
Sacred vocal music
Choruses
Accompaniment of one instrument, two keyboard
instruments, or unaccompanied
Unaccompanied
Separate works -- Continued
2094 Treble voices
For obsolete decimal subdivisions formerly used for
number of vocal parts see Table MZ3
Special seasons and occasions
2095 Christmas
2096 Easter
2097 Thanksgiving. Harvest
2098.A-Z Other, A-Z
2098.A4 Advent
2098.A5 All Saints Day
2098.A6 Ascension Day
2098.C2 Candlemas
2098.C75 Corpus Christi Festival
2098.E5 Epiphany
2098.F3 Father's Day
2098.G5 Good Friday
2098.H56 Holy Saturday
Holy Thursday see M2098.M35
2098.H58 Holy Week
2098.H6 Holy Year
2098.L5 Lent. Passiontide
2098.M33 Marian feasts
2098.M35 Maundy Thursday
2098.M6 Mother's Day
2098.N5 New Year
2098.P4 Palm Sunday
Passiontide see M2098.L5
Pentecost Festival see M2098.W4
2098.R3 Reformation Festival
2098.T5 Trinity Sunday
2098.W4 Whitsuntide. Pentecost Festival
2099.A-Z Special texts. By language, A-Z
Subarrange each language by Table M6
Including special parts of a liturgical text set as
separate compositions
For special texts not listed in Table M6 see the
medium of performance, e.g., M2092 for Domine
probasti me (Psalm 139) for unaccompanied
chorus
Other religions or denominations

Vocal music
Sacred vocal music
Choruses
Accompaniment of one instrument, two keyboard
instruments, or unaccompanied
Unaccompanied
Other religions or denominations -- Continued

2099.3	Islamic
	Class here collections and separate works
2099.5	Jewish
	Class here collections and separate works
	For cyclical choral services and other larger vocal works that may be sung outside the synagogue see M2017.6
	For officially prescribed worship services solely for use inside the synagogue see M2186+
	Orthodox
	For obsolete subdivisions formerly used under this number see Table MZ11
	Class here choruses in all languages
2100	Collections
2100.2	Separate works
2101	Choruses, etc., in tonic sol-fa notation
2101.5	Unison choruses
	For Masses for unison chorus see M2013.5
	One solo voice
	Class here songs, arias, solo cantatas, etc.
	Including works with obligato chorus
	Accompaniment of orchestra, other ensemble of two or more instruments, or electronics
	For continuo accompaniment see M2110+
	Original compositions
2102	Collections
	Including collections containing both original works and arrangements
	Separate works
	Scores. Parts
2103	Orchestral accompaniment
2103.3	Other accompaniment
	Class here works with accompaniment of two or more instruments except keyboard instrument and one other instrument, or continuo
	For original accompaniment of keyboard instrument and one other instrument, or continuo see M2113.3
2104	Vocal scores with keyboard instrument
	Arrangements

	Vocal music
	Sacred vocal music
	One solo voice
	Accompaniment of orchestra, other ensemble of two or more instruments, or electronics
	Arrangements -- Continued
	Collections
2105	Scores. Parts
2106	Vocal scores with keyboard instrument
	Separate works
2107	Scores. Parts
2108	Vocal scores with keyboard instrument
	Accompaniment of one instrument, keyboard instrument and one other instrument, or unaccompanied
	Including continuo
	Collections
	For individual religions or denominations see M2114.1+
2110	Two or more composers
2112	One composer
	Separate works
	For obsolete numbers formerly used for voice range see Table MZ12
2113	Accompaniment of one instrument
2113.2	Unaccompanied
2113.3	Accompaniment of keyboard instrument and one other instrument
	Including continuo
2113.4	Song cycles
2114.A-Z	By language and text, A-Z
	Subarrange each language by Table M6
	Including individual parts of liturgical texts set as separate compositions
	For texts not listed in Table M6 see the medium of performance, e.g., M2113 for Domine probasti me (Psalm 139) for solo voice with keyboard accompaniment
	By religion or denomination
2114.1.A-Z	Protestant. By denomination, A-Z
	Class here collections and separate works
	For works not differentiated by denomination, see M2110-M2114
2114.1.B36	Baptist
2114.1.C5	Christian Science
(2114.1.M6)	Mormon
	see M2114.4.M67
2114.1.M6	Seventh-Day Adventist

	Vocal music
	Sacred vocal music
	One solo voice
	Accompaniment of one instrument, keyboard instrument
	and chordal instrument, or unaccompanied
	Separate works
	By religion or denomination -- Continued
2114.2	Orthodox
	Class here collections and separate works
2114.3	Jewish
	Class here collections and separate works
	For officially prescribed worship services solely
	for use inside the synagogue see M2186+
2114.4.A-Z	Other religions or denominations, A-Z
	Class here collections and separate works
	Islamic see M2114.4.M88
2114.4.M67	Mormon
2114.4.M88	Muslim. Islamic
	Special seasons and occasions
2114.5	Christmas
2114.6	Easter
2114.7	Thanksgiving. Harvest
	Other, A-Z
2114.8.A4	Advent
2114.8.A5	All Saints Day
2114.8.A6	Ascension Day
2114.8.C2	Candlemas
2114.8.C75	Corpus Christi Festival
2114.8.E5	Epiphany
2114.8.F3	Father's Day
2114.8.G5	Good Friday
2114.8.H56	Holy Saturday
	Holy Thursday see M2114.8.M35
2114.8.H58	Holy Week
2114.8.H6	Holy Year
2114.8.L5	Lent. Passiontide
2114.8.M33	Marian feasts
2114.8.M35	Maundy Thursday
2114.8.M6	Mother's Day
2114.8.N5	New Year
2114.8.P4	Palm Sunday
	Passiontide see M2114.8.L5
	Pentecost Festival see M2114.8.W4
2114.8.R3	Reformation Festival
2114.8.T5	Trinity Sunday
2114.8.W4	Whitsuntide. Pentecost Festival

	Vocal music
	Sacred vocal music -- Continued
	Hymnals. Hymn collections
	Including hymnals with music but without words
	For hymnals with words only, including those with tunes indicated see BV1+
2115	General
	Including collections of hymns of Christian and other religions
2115.5	Descant collections, with or without their hymns
	Christian
	Published in the United States
2116	Through 1820
	1821-
2117	General
	Class here multi-denominational and non-denominational hymnals in English or mainly in English
	For multi-denominational and non-denominational hymnals entirely or mainly in languages other than English see M2132.A+
	By denomination
	Including hymnals in languages other than English
2119	Catholic
2120	Orthodox
2122-2132	Protestant
	General see M2117
2122	Baptist
2123	Congregational
	For United Church of Christ see M2131.U62
2124.A-Z	Dutch and other Reformed
	For United Church of Christ see M2131.U62
2124.C55	Christian Reformed Church
2124.D7	Dutch Reformed (Reformed Church in the United States)
2124.G3	German Reformed (Reformed Church in the United States)
2125	Episcopal
2126	Lutheran
2127	Methodist
(2127.E7)	Epworth League
	see M2127
2128	Moravian
2129	Mormon
2130	Presbyterian
2131.A-Z	Other, A-Z

Vocal music
  Sacred vocal music
    Hymnals. Hymn collections
      Christian
        Published in the United States
          1821-
            By denomination
              Protestant
                Other, A-Z -- Continued

2131.A15	Aaronic Order
(2131.A3)	Adventist see M2131.S3
	African American Spiritual churches see M2131.S5
2131.A4	Amish
2131.A45	Anabaptist
2131.A5	Apostolic Christian Church
(2131.A7)	Avesta see M2131.M2

2131.B6	Brethren in Christ Church
	    For Church of the Brethren see
	        M2131.C65

(2131.B7)	Buddhist see M2145.B8
	Bruderhof Communities see M2131.H87
	Bruderhof Foundation see M2131.H87
2131.C29	Celestial Church of Christ
2131.C33	Církev československá husitská.
2131.C35	Christian and Missionary Alliance
2131.C43	Christian Catholic Apostolic Church in Zion. Dowieites
2131.C5	Christian Science. Church of Christ, Scientist
2131.C53	Christ's Church of the Golden Rule
2131.C54	Church of Christ (Holiness) U.S.A.
2131.C55	Church of Divine Man
2131.C57	Church of God (Anderson, Ind.)
2131.C6	Church of God, Holiness
2131.C63	Church of God General Conference
2131.C64	Church of God, the Eternal

2131.C65	Church of the Brethren
	    For Brethren in Christ Church see
	        M2131.B6

2131.C68	Church of the Nazarene
	Church of the Social Revolution see M2131.S44
	Church of the United Brethren in Christ see M2131.U6

M

	Vocal music
	Sacred vocal music
	Hymnals. Hymn collections
	Christian
	Published in the United States
	1821-
	By denomination
	Protestant
	Other, A-Z -- Continued
2131.D4	Disciples of Christ
2131.D5	Divine Science Church (U.S.)
	Dowieites see M2131.C43
	Ephrata Cloister see M2116
2131.E8	Evangelical Mission Covenant Church of America
2131.F8	Free Methodist Church of North America
	For Methodist see M2127
2131.F9	Society of Friends (Quakers)
	General Convention of the New Jerusalem in the United States of America see M2131.S8
	Holiness (Church of Christ) see M2131.C54
	Holiness (Church of God) see M2131.C6
2131.H87	Hutterian Brethren. Bruderhof Communities
2131.I2	I AM Religious Activity
2131.I55	International Churches of Christ
2131.I57	Intervarsity Christian Fellowship of the United States of America
2131.J4	Jehova's Witnesses
2131.J49	Jews for Jesus
2131.M2	Mazdaznan. Avesta
2131.M4	Mennonite Church USA
	For Amish see M2131.A4
2131.M6	Monism
2131.M7	Moral Re-armament (Organization)
(2131.N4)	National Spiritual Assembly of the Bahá'is of the United States
	see M2145.B34
	New Jerusalem Church see M2131.S8
2131.P4	Pentecostal Holiness Church
2131.P5	Pillar of Fire
	Quakers see M2131.F9
	Radio Church of God see M2131.W67
2131.R3	International Association of Religious Science Churches
2131.S3	Seventh-Day Adventist Church
2131.S4	Shakers

Vocal music
Sacred vocal music
Hymnals. Hymn collections
Christian
Published in the United States
1821-
By denomination
Protestant
Other, A-Z -- Continued

2131.S44	Church of the Social Revolution
2131.S5	African American Spiritual churches
2131.S8	Swedenborgian. General Convention of the New Jerusalem in the United States of America
2131.T78	True Jesus Church, U.S.A.
2131.U5	Unitarian churches. Unitarian Universalist Association
	For Universalist Church see M2131.U67
2131.U6	United Brethren in Christ, Church of the
2131.U62	United Church of Christ
	For Congregational see M2123
	For Dutch and other Reformed see M2124.A+
2131.U63	United Church of Religious Science
2131.U65	Unity School of Christianity
2131.U67	Universalist Church
	For Unitarian churches and Unitarian Universalist Association see M2131.U5
2131.W67	Worldwide Church of God
2132.A-Z	Multi- and non-denominational hymnals. By language, A-Z
	For obsolete numbers for language formerly used under this span see Table MZ13
2132.A35	Afrikaans
2132.A5	Albanian
2132.A57	Arabic
2132.A6	Armenian
2132.B46	Bengali
2132.C35	Cherokee
2132.C46	Cheyenne
2132.C5	Chinese
2132.C6	Croatian
2132.C9	Czech
2132.D3	Danish
2132.D7	Dutch
2132.E85	Eskimo languages

	Vocal music
	Sacred vocal music
	Hymnals. Hymn collections
	Christian
	United States
	1821-
	Multi and non-denominational hymnals. By language, A-Z -- Continued
2132.F3	Finnish
2132.F5	French
2132.G3	German
2132.G5	Greek
2132.H3	Hawaiian
2132.H8	Hungarian
2132.I2	Icelandic
2132.I55	Irish
2132.I6	Italian
	Latvian see M2132.L3
(2132.L24)	Lebanese
	see M2132.A57
2132.L3	Lettish. Latvian
2132.L4	Lithuanian
2132.N5	Norwegian
2132.P5	Polish
2132.P6	Portuguese
2132.R7	Russian
2132.S3	Slovak
2132.S5	Spanish
2132.S8	Swedish
2132.T2	Tagalog
2132.U7	Ukrainian
2132.W3	Welsh
2133	Published in other North American countries (not A-Z)
2134.A-Z	Published in Central and South America. By language, A-Z
	Published in Europe. By language, A-Z
	For obsolete numbers for language formerly used under this span see Table MZ13
2135	Dutch
2136	English
2137	French
2138	German
2139	Russian
2140.A-Z	Scandinavian languages
2140.D3	Danish
2140.N6	Norwegian
2140.S8	Swedish

	Vocal music
	Sacred vocal music
	Hymnals. Hymn collections
	Christian
	Europe. By language, A-Z -- Continued
2142.A-Z	Other, A-Z
2142.A42	Albanian
2142.A6	Armenian
2142.B38	Basque
2142.B8	Bulgarian
	Croatian see M2142.S35
2142.C9	Czech
2142.F4	Finnish
2142.F7	Frisian
2142.G3	Galician
2142.G7	Greek
2142.H9	Hungarian
2142.I2	Icelandic
2142.I5	Irish
2142.I6	Italian
(2142.L17)	Lapp
	see M2142.S26
2142.L2	Latin
(2142.L23)	Latvian
	see M2132.L3
2142.L5	Lithuanian
2142.P5	Polish
2142.R6	Romanian
2142.S26	Sami
2142.S35	Serbo-Croatian
2142.S4	Slovak
2142.S47	Sorbian languages
2142.S5	Spanish
(2142.S7)	Sami
	see M2142.S26
2142.U7	Ukrainian
2142.W3	Welsh
2143	Published in other regions and countries (not A-Z)
2144	Jewish
2145.A-Z	Other religions, A-Z
2145.B34	Bahai Faith
	Including National Spiritual Assembly of the Bahá'ís of
	the United States
2145.B8	Buddhist
2145.C56	Ch'ŏndogyo
(2145.D47)	Dervish
	see M2188.S8

	Vocal music
	Sacred vocal music
	Hymnals. Hymn collections
	Other religions, A-Z -- Continued
2145.D78	Druid
2145.H55	Hindu
2145.S57	Sikh
2145.Y6	Yoga
2146	Separate hymns

                              Including proof sheets of individual hymns published in collections

                  Liturgy and ritual

                      Class here officially prescribed service music

                      Arrange chronologically unless otherwise stated

                      For other church music composed to sacred texts for use in church services, class as provided in the schedule, e.g., M2016 a Protestant Episcopal choral service by one or more composers; M2020 a Te Deum with orchestral accompaniment; M2079.L3 a Credo with organ accompaniment and Latin text; M2079.E3 with English text; M2099.E6 a Magnificat in English for men's and boys' voices unaccompanied (English text), M2115-M2146 hymnals, etc.; M2 historical publications

                      For manuscripts and publications mainly rubrical, with the music merely one of the liturgical functions, see BL1+

                  Roman Catholic Church

2147	Copyists' manuscripts and their facsimiles

                      Arrange by century in Roman numerals followed by M with accession number, e.g., M2147 XII M13

                    Printed music

                      For liturgical music of individual dioceses see M2154.2.A+

                      For liturgical music of individual orders and congregations see M2154.4.A+

                      For liturgical music of other western rites see M2154.6.A+

2148.A-Z	Graduals. By language, A-Z

                      Subdivide each language by Table M16

                  Propers

2148.2.A-Z	Collections. By compiler or publisher, A-Z

                      Subdivide each compiler or publisher by Table M16

                      Arrange by title if compiler or publisher is unknown

2148.23.A-Z	Praefationes particulares. By language, A-Z

                      Subdivide each language by Table M16

2148.3.A-Z	Separate works. By feast day or person to whom the mass was dedicated, A-Z, and date

                      Advent

Vocal music
  Sacred vocal music
    Liturgy and ritual
      Roman Catholic Church
        Printed music
          Graduals. By language, A-Z, and date
            Propers
              Separate works. By feast day, or person to whom
                  the mass was dedicated, A-Z, and date
                Advent -- Continued

2148.3.A31	First Sunday of Advent
2148.3.A32	Second Sunday of Advent
2148.3.A88	Assumption of the Blessed Virgin Mary
2148.3.B59	Mary, Blessed Virgin, Saint
	Christmas
2148.3.C5	Christmas Eve
2148.3.C55	Christmas Day
	Specific masses
2148.3.C551	1st Mass
2148.3.C552	2nd Mass
2148.3.C553	3rd Mass
2148.3.C6	Circumcision. Octave Day of Christmas
2148.3.C65	Mass, Common, of a confessor not a bishop
2148.3.C67	Corpus Christi Festival
2148.3.D4	Mass on the day of death or burial
2148.3.E2	Easter Sunday
2148.3.E6	Epiphany
	Sundays after Epiphany
2148.3.E61	1st Sunday
2148.3.E62	2nd Sunday
2148.3.E63	3rd Sunday
2148.3.H64	Holy Thursday
2148.3.I46	Immaculate Heart of Mary
2148.3.J35	James, the Greater, Saint
2148.3.J4	Joan, of Arc, Saint
2148.3.M3	Feasts of the Blessed Virgin Mary throughout the year
	For individual feasts, see .A88, .B59, etc.
	Octave Day of Christmas see M2148.3.C6
2148.3.P3	Passion Sunday
2148.3.P45	Pentecost Festival
	Sundays after Pentecost Festival
2148.3.P4501	1st Sunday
2148.3.P4502	2nd Sunday
2148.3.P4503	3rd Sunday
2148.3.P4516	16th Sunday
2148.3.P66	Mass, Common, of one or more Popes

Vocal music
Sacred vocal music
Liturgy and ritual
Roman Catholic Church
Printed music
Graduals. By language, A-Z, and date
Propers
Separate works. By feast day, or person to whom
the mass was dedicated, A-Z, and date --
Continued

2148.3.T48	Teresa, of Avila, Saint
	Ordinaries
2148.4.A-Z	Kyriales. Collections of ordinaries. By language, A-Z
	Subdivide each language by Table M16
2148.5.A-Z	Single ordinaries
2148.5.A11-.A28	Numbered masses. By number, 1-18, and date
2148.5.A5-Z	Masses for special events. By event, A-Z, and date
	Antiphonaries
2149.A-Z	General. By language, A-Z
	Subdivide each language by Table M16
2149.2.A-Z	Special sections, A-Z
	Subarrange by language and add date
2149.2.B5	Benedictions
2149.2.C6	Compline
2149.2.H9	Hymnary
2149.2.L35	Lauds
2149.2.L4	Lectionary
2149.2.M4	Matins
2149.2.O2	O antiphons
2149.2.P8	Psalters and collections of psalms
2149.2.V4	Vesperals and collections of vespers
2149.3.A-Z	Collections of offices. By compiler or publisher, A-Z
	Subdivide each compiler or publisher by Table M16
	Subarrange by title if compiler or publisher is unknown
	Holy Week rite
2149.4.A1A-.A1Z	Collections. By language, A-Z
	Subdivide each language by Table M16
2149.4.A5-Z	Individual services. By service, A-Z
	Subdivide each language by Table M16
	Subarrange by language
2149.4.C35	Cantus Passionis
2149.4.C353	Cantus Passionis. Passio Secundum Joannem
2149.4.C356	Cantus Passionis. Passio Secundum Matthaeum

	Vocal music
	Sacred vocal music
	Liturgy and ritual
	Roman Catholic Church
	Printed music
	Antiphonaries
	Holy Week rite
	Individual services. By service, A-Z -- Continued
2149.4.E25	Easter preconium
2149.4.G7	Good Friday
2149.4.H68	Holy Saturday
2149.4.H69	Holy Thursday
2149.4.P34	Palm Sunday
2149.42.A-Z	Holy Week offices. By language, A-Z
	Subdivide each language by Table M16
2149.5.A-Z	Single offices, A-Z
	Subarrange by date
2149.5.A26	Achacius, of Mount Ararat, Saint
2149.5.A3	Adalbert, Saint, Bishop of Prague, ca. 956-997
2149.5.A4	Afra, Saint, of Augsburg, d. ca. 304
2149.5.A6	Anthony of Egypt, Saint, ca. 250-355 or 6
	Christmas
2149.5.C5	General
	Vespers see M2149.5.V525
	Office for the dead
2149.5.D4	General
2149.5.D44	Matins
2149.5.D48	Vespers
2149.5.D56	Dionysius, the Areopagite, Saint, 1st cent.
2149.5.E74	Erhard, Saint, d. 686?
2149.5.L52	Little office of the Blessed Virgin Mary
2149.5.M36	Martha, Saint
2149.5.M37	Martin, Saint, Bishop of Tours, ca. 316-397
2149.5.N5	Nikolaus, von der Flüe, Saint, 1417-1487
2149.5.P74	Presentation of the Blessed Virgin Mary
2149.5.Q57	Quirinus, Saint, d. 130?
2149.5.S56	Simpert, Saint, Bishop of Augsburg, 778-807
2149.5.V5-.V58	Vespers
2149.5.V5	General
2149.5.V52	Ascension
2149.5.V525	Christmas. 2d Vespers
2149.5.V53	Corpus Christi Festival
2149.5.V54	Easter
2149.5.V545	Joseph, Saint
2149.5.V55	Marian feasts
2149.5.V56	Pentecost Festival
2149.5.V57	Solemnity of the Most Holy Rosary

	Vocal music
	Sacred vocal music
	Liturgy and ritual
	Roman Catholic Church
	Printed music
	Antiphonaries
	Single offices, A-Z
	Vespers -- Continued
2149.5.V575	Sunday
2149.5.V58	Trinity
2149.5.W64	Wolfgang, Saint, 924?-994
2149.6	Processionals
	Subarrange by date
	Special ceremonies and occasions
2150	General
2150.2.A-Z	Collections of chants. By compiler or publisher, A-Z
	Subdivide each compiler or publisher by Table M16
2150.3.A-Z	Particular ceremonies, A-Z
	Subdivide each ceremony by Table M16
2150.3.B46-.B462	Benediction of the Blessed Sacrament
2150.3.B6-.B62	Blessing of a church organ
2150.3.B87-.B872	Burial rite
2150.3.C58-.C582	Confirmation
	Consecration of a church see M2150.3.D42+
2150.3.D42-.D422	Dedication of a church
2150.3.F57-.F572	First communion
2150.3.F67-.F672	Forty hours of adoration
2150.4.A-Z	Particular occasions, A-Z
	Subdivide each occasion by Table M16
2150.4.C35-.C352	Candlemas
2150.4.C5-.C52	Christmas
2151.A-Z	Liber usualis. By language, A-Z
	Subdivide each language by Table M16
(2152)	Directories and manuals for choirs
	see MT88
	Miscellaneous collections of liturgical music for general use
2153	General
2153.2.A-Z	Collections of chants. By compiler or title, A-Z
	Special Roman liturgies and rituals
2154.2.A-Z	Diocesan, A-Z
	e.g.
2154.2.C64	Cologne
2154.2.L4	Leavenworth
2154.2.L9	Luxemburg
2154.2.M4	Meissen
2154.2.M83	Münster

	Vocal music
	Sacred vocal music
	Liturgy and ritual
	Roman Catholic Church
	Printed music
	Special Roman liturgies and rituals
	Diocesan, A-Z -- Continued
2154.2.P6	Pittsburgh
2154.2.Q4	Québec
2154.2.S34	Salzburg
2154.2.S4	Sées
2154.4.A-Z	Orders and congregations, A-Z
2154.4.A9	Augustinian
2154.4.B45	Benedictine
2154.4.C34	Camaldolite
2154.4.C36	Capuchin
2154.4.C37	Carmelite
2154.4.C6	Cistercian
2154.4.D63	Discalced Trinitarian
2154.4.D65	Dominican
2154.4.F7	Franciscan
2154.4.H5	Hieronymite
2154.4.M5	Mercedarian
2154.4.P4	Passionist
2154.4.P74	Premonstratensian
2154.4.S58	Sisters of Charity of Saint Vincent de Paul
2154.4.S6	Sisters of the Good Shepherd
2154.4.U8	Ursuline
2154.6.A-Z	Non-Roman liturgies and rituals, A-Z
	Subarrange by uniform title and add date
2154.6.A45	Ambrosian
2154.6.A76	Armenian
2154.6.M7	Mozarabic
	Modern schisms from the Roman Catholic Church
2155.5	Old Catholic Church
2155.6	Polish Catholic Church
	Orthodox churches
2156	Copyists' manuscripts and their facsimiles
	Arrange by century in Roman numerals followed by M
	with accession number, e.g., M2156 XIII M1
	Printed music. By denomination, ethnic group, or
	language
2157	Greek
2158	Russian
2159.1	Bulgarian
2159.2	Czechoslovak
2159.3	Serbian

	Vocal music
	Sacred vocal music
	Liturgy and ritual
	Orthodox churches
	Printed music. By denomination, ethnic group, or language -- Continued
2159.5	Romanian
2160.2	Armenian
2160.3	Chaldean (i. e. Nestorian)
2160.4	Coptic
2160.5	Ethiopian
2160.6	Georgian
2160.65	Syrian
2160.67.A-Z	Other vernacular or ethnic groups, A-Z
2160.67.E5	English
2160.67.M27	Macedonian
2160.67.U4	Ukrainian
	Orthodox churches in communion with Rome (Uniat)
2160.7	General
	Byzantine rite
2160.71	General
2160.72	Bulgarian
2160.73	Greek
2160.74	Italo-Albanian
2160.75	Melchite
2160.76	Romanian
2160.77	Russian
2160.78	Ukrainian
	Other Eastern rites
2160.8	General
	Armenian see M2154.6.A76
2160.82	Chaldean. Nestorian
2160.83	Coptic
2160.84	Ethiopian
2160.85	Malabaric
2160.86	Maronite
	Nestorian see M2160.82
2160.87	Syrian
	Protestant churches
	Class here manuscripts and printed music
2161	General
2162	Baptist
2163	Congregational
2164	Dutch and other Reformed
(2166)	Irish Church
	Anglican Communion
	Church of England

	Vocal music
	Sacred vocal music
	Liturgy and ritual
	Protestant Churches
	Anglican Communion
	Church of England -- Continued
2167	Book of Common Prayer
	Including its immediate precursors
2168.2	Morning service
2168.3	Evening service
2168.4	Order of the Communion
2168.5	Other offices
2168.6	Chants
	Class here miscellaneous and special collections
(2168.7)	Directories, manuals, handbooks, etc.
	see MT88
2168.9	Other
	Protestant Episcopal Church in the U.S.A.
2169	Book of Common Prayer
	Including its immediate precursors
2170.2	Morning service
2170.3	Evening service
2170.4	Order of the Communion
2170.5	Other offices
2170.6	Chants
	Class here miscellaneous and special collections
(2170.7)	Directories, manuals, handbooks, etc.
	see MT88
2170.9	Other
2171.A-Z	Other. By country, A-Z
2171.C3	Anglican Church of Canada
	Lutheran
2172	European publications
2173	American publications
2175	Methodist
2177	Moravian
2179	Mormon
2181	Presbyterian
2183.A-Z	Other denominations, A-Z
2183.G4	General Church of the New Jerusalem.
	Swedenborgians
2183.S4	Svenska kyrkan
	Swedenborgians see M2183.G4
2184.A-Z	Other Christian churches, A-Z
2184.C5	Church of South India. Ten Intiyat Tiruccapai
2184.L52	Liberal Catholic Church

	Vocal music
	Sacred vocal music
	Liturgy and ritual
	Other Christian churches, A-Z -- Continued
(2184.T28)	Ten Intiyat Tiruccapai
	see M2184.C5
	Jewish
	Class here officially prescribed worship services solely for use inside the synagogue
	Including services with originally composed music for cantor without accompaniment and collections containing both traditional and originally composed music
	For cyclical choral services and other larger vocal works that may be sung outside the synagogue see M2017.6
2186	Collections
2187	Individual services
	Class here complete services and portions of services
2188.A-Z	Other non-Christian religions, A-Z
2188.B8	Buddhist
2188.H5	Hindu
2188.I74	Islam
2188.S5	Shinto
2188.S8	Sufi
2188.V35	Vaishnava
	Sacred vocal music for children
	For children's picture books illustrating the lyrics of single songs, with or without the music see PZ4.2+
	Dramatic music. Choruses
2190	General
2191.A-Z	Special seasons and occasions, A-Z
2191.A4	Advent
2191.C4	Children's Day
2191.C5	Christmas
2191.E2	Easter
2191.E6	Epiphany
2191.F38	Father's Day
	Harvest see M2191.T5
2191.H6	Holy Week
2191.L5	Lent. Passiontide
2191.M6	Mother's Day
2191.P3	Palm Sunday
	Passiontide see M2191.L5
2191.R2	Rally Day
2191.T5	Thanksgiving. Harvest

Vocal music
  Sacred vocal music
    Sacred vocal music for children -- Continued
    Solo voices
      Class here works for one or more solo singers
      Collections

2193	General

        Class here Sunday School or Bible School songbooks,
          etc. not differentiated by Christian denomination or
          other religion
      By religion or denomination

2194	Roman Catholic
2194.3	Jewish
2196	Separate works

    Popular religious and devotional music
      Class here gospel, revival, and temperance songs,
        contemporary Christian music, etc.

2198	Collections
2199	Separate works
5000	Unidentified compositions

      Including excerpts, fragments, etc., published or in manuscript

Literature on music
    Including individual performance ensembles
    Periodicals. Serials
        Class here general periodicals in the field of music
        Class periodicals consisting entirely of music in subclass M
        Class periodicals on specific topics with the topic, e.g.,
            Contemporary Christian music in ML3187.5, orchestral
            program notes in MT125

1	United States
	Foreign
4	Through 1800
5	1801-
	Directories. Almanacs
12	International
	United States
13	General works
14.A-Z	By region or state, A-Z (Table M1)
15.A-Z	By city, A-Z
17	Professions
18	Music trade
19	Other (not A-Z)
21.A-Z	Other regions or countries, A-Z

Societies and other organizations
    Including documents of performance organizations and individual
        performance ensembles associated with a particular city
    For works about individual performance ensembles that are
        mainly biographical see ML421.A+

25	General works
26.A-Z	International. By society or organization, A-Z
	Subdivide individual societies or organizations by Table M20
27.A-Z	National. By country A-Z
	Under each country, subdivide by society or organization
	Subdivide individual societies or organizations by Table M20
28.A-Z	Local. By city, A-Z
	Under each city, subdivide by society or organization
	Subdivide individual societies or organizations by Table M20

Special collections
    Class here unique collections. The Library of Congress uses
        ML29+ as shown
    Endowed collections

29	Elizabeth Sprague Coolidge Foundation (Table M13)
30	Other (Table M14)
31	Other special collections (Table M15)
	Institutions
32.A-Z	National. By country, A-Z
	Under each country, subdivide by institution
	Subdivide individual institutions by Table M20

	Institutions -- Continued
33.A-Z	Local. By city, A-Z
	Under each city, subdivide by institution
	Subdivide individual institutions by Table M20
	Festivals. Congresses
	Including performance festivals
	For congresses on specific topics, see the topic, e.g., Wind instruments, ML929.5
	For competitions see ML75.5+
35	General
36.A-Z	International. By festival or congress, A-Z
	Subdivide individual festivals or congresses by Table M11
37.A-Z	National. By country, A-Z
	Under each country, subdivide by festival or congress
	Subdivide individual festivals or congresses by Table M11
38.A-Z	Local. By city, A-Z
	Under each city, subdivide by festival or congress
	Subdivide individual festivals or congresses by Table M11
	Programs
	Class here programs not classed in ML25+ or MT4+
	For programs containing extensive analytical notes see MT90+
	Operas
40.A1-.A39	Collections. By compiler or title
40.A4-Z	Individual programs. By city, A-Z
	Subdivide each city by institution
42.A-Z	Concerts
42.A1-.A39	Collections. By compiler or title
42.A4-Z	Individual programs. By city, A-Z
	Subdivide each city by institution
44.A-Z	Other
44.A1-.A39	Collections. By compiler or title
44.A4-Z	Individual programs. By city, A-Z
	Subdivide each city by institution
45	Circulars and advertisements
	Class here miscellaneous circulars and advertisements not classed in ML25+ , ML140+ , or MT4+
46	Scrapbooks
	Librettos. Texts. Scenarios
	For works about librettos see ML2110
47	Miscellaneous collections
	Operas
	Including operettas, musicals, Singspiele, sacred operas, etc.
	Collections
48	Two or more composers or authors
49	One composer or author
	Separate works

Librettos. Texts. Scenarios
    Operas
        Separate works. By title -- Continued
50   Non-U.S. imprints, 1801- . U.S. imprints, 1851- . By
                    composer
                    Subarrange by title
                    Use .Z99 for librettos by three or more composers, librettos
                        for which the music is not originally composed but
                        compiled from various sources, and librettos for which
                        no composer is identified
50.2   Non-U.S. imprints through 1800. By title
                    Subarrange by composer or author
50.6   U.S. imprints through 1850. By title
                    Subarrange by composer or author
50.7   Ballad operas. By title
50.9   Parodies
        Ballets, masques, pantomimes, etc.
51   Collections
        Separate works
52   Non-U.S. imprints, 1801- . U.S. imprints, 1851- . By
                    composer
                    Subarrange by title
                    Use .Z99 for librettos by three or more composers, librettos
                        for which the music is not originally composed but
                        compiled from various sources, and librettos for which
                        no composer is identified
52.2   Non-U.S. imprints through 1800. By title
                    Subarrange by composer or author
52.6   U.S. imprints through 1850. By title
                    Subarrange by composer or author
        Film operas
            Including operettas, musicals, Singspiele, sacred operas, etc.
52.65   Collections
52.7   Separate works. By composer
                Subarrange by title
                Use .Z99 for works by three or more composers, works for
                    which the music is not originally composed but compiled
                    from various sources, or works for which no composer is
                    identified
52.75-.8   Radio operas
            Including operettas, musicals, Singspiele, sacred operas, etc.
52.75   Collections

Librettos. Texts. Scenarios
  Radio operas -- Continued
52.8   Separate works. By composer
      Subarrange by title
      Use .Z99 for works by three or more composers, works for
          which the music is not originally composed but compiled
          from various sources, or works for which no composer is
          identified
  Oratorios
52.85   Collections
    Separate works
53   Non-U.S. imprints, 1801- . U.S. imprints, 1851- . By
        composer
      Subarrange by title
      Use .Z99 for librettos by three or more composers, librettos
          for which the music is not originally composed but
          compiled from various sources, and librettos for which
          no composer is identified
53.2   Non-U.S. imprints through 1800. By title
      Subarrange by composer or author
53.6   U.S. imprints through 1850. By title
      Subarrange by composer or author
53.8-54.2   Other choral works
    For oratorios see ML52.85+
53.8   Collections
    Separate works
54   1801- imprints. By composer
      Subarrange by title
      Use .Z99 for librettos by three or more composers, librettos
          for which the music is not originally composed but
          compiled from various sources, and librettos for which
          no composer is identified
54.2   Imprints through 1800. By title
      Subarrange by composer or author
      Use .Z99 for librettos by three or more composers, librettos
          for which the music is not originally composed but
          compiled from various sources, and librettos for which
          no composer is identified
  Solo vocal works
    Including works for one or more solo singers or speakers and
      lyrics of popular songs
    For collections of folk-song texts published as poetry, see class
      P
    For collections of folk-song texts published without the
      music but intended for use in singing, e.g., songsters
      see M1627+
54.6   1801- imprints

Librettos. Texts. Scenarios
Solo vocal works -- Continued

54.7   Imprints through 1800
54.8   Other

Aspects of the field of music as a whole
Collections of essays, articles, etc. (nonserial)
Class here collections on several topics
Class collections on a specific topic with the topic
For collections of anecdotes, humor, etc. see ML65

55   Several authors
Including Festschriften, arranged by honoree

60   One author
e.g.

60.L24   Lanier, Sidney, 1842-1881

62   Grants and scholarships
For governmental and municipal subvention of music see
ML3916+

(63)   Topics not elsewhere provided for

(64)   Poems and other belles lettres about music
see class P

65   Anecdotes, humor, etc.
Class here historical works
For collections of creative literary works see
PN6231.M85

(66)   Quotations, maxims, etc., and birthday books
see subclass PN

(67)   Music in the home
For social aspects of music, see ML3916+

68   Radio, television, etc., and music
For works about music videos see PN1992.8.M87
Cf. ML3849 Relations between music and other arts

(71)   Registration of musicians, examination by government
boards, standardization, etc.
For music as a profession see ML3795
For examinations and exercises see MT9

Construction of concert halls, opera houses, etc., see
TH4711

Computers and music
Class here general works on the use of computers in the field of
music
For computers as musical instruments see ML1093
For works on computer music see ML1379+
For techniques of composing computer music see MT56
For works on computer sound processing see MT723

73   Periodicals. Societies. Serials
73.5   Congresses
74   General works

	Aspects of the field of music as a whole
	Computers and music -- Continued
	Computer software
	For software catalogs see ML158.8
74.3	General works
74.4.A-Z	Individual programs and systems, A-Z
74.7	Computer network resources
	Prizes, competitions, etc.
75.5	General works
76.A-Z	Individual prizes, competitions, etc., A-Z
	e.g.
76.G7	Grammy Awards
	Literary authors and music
	For philosophical works on the relationships between music and other arts see ML3849
79	Two or more authors
80.A-Z	Individual authors, A-Z
	e.g.
80.C25	Camões, Luiz de, 1524?-1580
80.S5	Shakespeare, William, 1564-1616
81	Musical prodigies
	For children and music see ML83
82	Women and music
83	Children and music
	For musical prodigies see ML81
	Visual and pictorial topics
85	Music in art. Musical instruments in art
	For relations between music and other arts see ML3849
86	Music on coins. Music on ceramics
	For music on postage stamps and postmarks see HE6183.M85
	Pictorial works
	Musicians
	Class here portraits, caricatures, etc., and pictorial materials about musicians
87.A-Z	Collections, two or more musicians
87.A1-.A39	Of miscellaneous individual items
87.A4-Z	In book form
88.A-Z	Individual musicians, A-Z
89	Other
	Class here general works, e.g. illustrated histories of music or of musical instruments
	For pictorial works on specific topics, see the topic, e.g., Jazz, see ML3505.8+
	For illustrated title pages see ML112.5

Aspects of the field of music as a whole -- Continued
(90)   Writings of musicians
For works on a specific topic see the topic
For collections of correspondence see ML385+ and ML410+
For collections of essays, articles, etc., on several topics
see ML55+
Manuscript studies and manuscripts
Cf. ML135 Bibliographies of manuscripts
93   Manuscript studies
Manuscripts
For manuscripts assigned to special collections in the Music
Division, Library of Congress see Table M13 , Table M14 ,
and Table M15
Class here works completely or partly in autograph manuscript,
manuscript copies of particular importance, printed works
with manuscript emendations, and facsimiles of such works
Miscellaneous collections
Class here collections containing both musical compositions
and textual works by one or more individuals
94   Manuscripts
94.5   Facsimiles
Textual works
Class here correspondence and miscellaneous items
For manuscripts of historical works see the topic, e.g.
theoretical works to 1601, ML171 ; theoretical works
written after 1600, MT5.5
95   Manuscripts
95.5   Facsimiles
Musical compositions
Including sketches and arrangements
For copyists' manuscripts intended as performing editions,
see subclass M
For historical collections, including facsimiles, of
autograph and copyists' manuscripts see M2+
For collections of scholarly historical sources see M2.1
For copyists' manuscripts and their facsimiles of
Roman Catholic liturgical music see M2147
For copyists' manuscripts and their facsimiles of
Orthodox liturgical music see M2156

	Manuscript studies and manuscripts
	Manuscripts
	Musical compositions -- Continued
96	Manuscripts
	Including individual works and sketches, and collections by one or more composers
	Arrange manuscripts in a single hand by writer of the manuscript
	Arrange manuscripts in more than one hand by composer or title
	Class copyists' manuscripts intended as performance editions with printed music
	Facsimiles
	Class facsimiles of autograph manuscripts intended as performance editions with printed music
	Including fascimiles accompanied by transcriptions
	Arrange fascimiles of manuscripts in a single hand by the writer of the manuscript
	Arrange fascimiles of manuscripts in more than one hand by composer or title
	For published collections of musical sources that include facsimiles of manuscripts see M2+
96.4	Collections
	Class here collections of works and sketches by one or more composers
96.5	Separate works
(97)	Catalogs of collectors, dealers, etc.
	see ML135+
	Dictionaries. Encyclopedias
100	General works
101.A-Z	By region or country, A-Z
102.A-Z	By topic, A-Z
102.A2	Accordion
102.B35	Bands
102.B5	Big bands
	Including jazz bands
102.B6	Blues
102.B63	Blues rock music
102.B7	Brass instruments
	Class here general works
	Carnatic music see ML102.K37
102.C3	Carols
102.C45	Gregorian chants
	Choral music see ML102.V6

Dictionaries. Encyclopedias

By topic, A-Z -- Continued

102.C5	Church music

        Class here general works

        For individual types of church music see the type, e.g.

            ML102.C45 Gregorian chants

102.C6	Computer music. Computers and music
102.C7	Country music
	Dance bands see ML102.B5
102.D57	Disc jockeys
102.D85	Dulcimer
102.E4	Electronic music
102.F55	Flamenco
102.F58	Flute
102.F66	Folk music
	Form, Musical see ML102.M87
102.G2	Gagaku
102.G6	Gospel music
	Gregorian chants see ML102.C45
102.G8	Guitar
102.H37	Harmonica
102.H38	Harp
102.H385	Harpsichord
102.H4	Hát bội
102.H56	Hindustani music
102.H95	Hymns
102.I5	Instruments

        Class here general works

        For individual instruments, families of instruments, or types of

            ensembles see the instrument, family, or type of

            ensemble, e.g. ML102.G8 Guitar; ML102.K5 Keyboard

            instruments, ML102.O66 , Orchestra

102.J3	Jazz
	Jazz bands see ML102.B5
102.J4	Jewish music and musicians
102.K37	Carnatic music
102.K5	Keyboard instruments

        Class here general works

        For individual keyboard instruments see the instrument, e.g.

            ML102.O7 Organ

102.M53	Microtonal music
102.M56	Military music
102.M68	Motion picture music
102.M83	Music therapy
102.M85	Music trade
	Musicals see ML102.M88
102.M87	Musical form

Dictionaries. Encyclopedias

By topic, A-Z -- Continued

102.M875	Musical theater
	For musicals and revues see ML102.M88
102.M88	Musicals. Revues
	For musical theater see ML102.M875
102.N49	New Age music
102.N5	New Wave music
102.O6	Opera
102.O66	Orchestra
102.O7	Organ
102.P4	Percussion instruments
102.P5	Piano
	Plainchant see ML102.C45
102.P66	Popular music
	Class here general works
	For forms and types of popular music see the form or type, e.g. ML102.R6 Rock music
102.R2	Raga
102.R27	Rap
	Revues see ML102.M88
102.R4	Rhythm
102.R6	Rock music
102.S25	Salsa
102.S6	Songs
102.S65	Soul music
102.S67	Sound recordings
102.S74	Steel bands
102.S77	Stringed instruments
	Class here general works
	For individual stringed instruments see the instrument, e.g. ML102.V4 Violin
102.T3	Tala
102.T35	Tangos
102.T43	Techno music
102.T45	Tejano music
(102.T5)	Themes, motives
	For thematic catalogs by period, place, publisher, etc., see the period, place, publisher, etc.
	For thematic catalogs by medium of performance see ML128.A+
	For thematic catalogs of individual composers see ML134.A+
102.T58	Titles of musical works
102.U53	Underground dance music
102.V4	Violin
102.V45	Violin and keyboard instrument

	Dictionaries. Encyclopedias
	By topic, A-Z -- Continued
102.V6	Vocal music
	Class here general works
	For individual types of vocal music see the type, e.g. ML102.C3 Carols
102.W56	Wind instruments
	Class here general works
	For individual families or instruments see the family or instrument, e.g., ML102.B7 , Brass instruments
102.W67	World music
102.Z37	Zarzuela
	Bio-bibliographical
	For dictionaries and encyclopedias on specific topics see ML102.A+
105	International
106.A-Z	National. By region or country, A-Z
106.A4	Algeria
106.A7	Argentina
(106.A74)	Argentina
	see ML106.A7
106.A93	Australia
106.A95	Austria
106.A98	Azerbaijan
106.B4	Belgium
106.B6	Bolivia
106.B7	Brazil
106.B8	Bulgaria
106.C3	Canada
106.C48	Chile
106.C5	China
106.C8	Cuba
(106.C9)	Czech Republic. Czechoslovakia
	see ML106.C95
106.C95	Czech Republic. Czechoslovakia
106.D65	Dominican Republic
106.E2	Ecuador
106.E3	Egypt
	England see ML106.G7
106.E8	Estonia
106.E85	Europe
106.F6	Finland
106.F8	France
106.G3	Germany
106.G7	Great Britain
	Including England, Scotland, and Wales

	Dictionaries. Encyclopedias
	Bio-bibliographical
	National. By region or country, A-Z -- Continued
106.G8	Greece
	Including ancient Greece and Rome
106.H8	Honduras
106.H85	Hungary
106.I2	Iceland
106.I73	Ireland
106.I75	Israel
106.I8	Italy
106.J33	Japan
106.K6	Korea
106.L38	Latvia
106.L58	Lithuania
106.M6	Mexico
106.M629	Moldova
106.N4	Netherlands
(106.N458)	Netherlands
	see ML106.N4
106.P6	Philippines
106.P7	Poland
(106.P787)	Poland
	see ML106.P7
106.P8	Portugal
(106.P85)	Portugal
	see ML106.P8
106.P9	Puerto Rico
106.R77	Romania
106.R8	Russia. Soviet Union. Russia (Federation)
106.S3	Silesia
(106.S36)	Scotland
	see ML106.G7
106.S45	Seychelles
106.S56	Slovakia
106.S66	South Africa
(106.S68)	Soviet Union
	see ML106.R8
106.S7	Spain
106.S8	Sweden
106.S9	Switzerland
106.T28	Taiwan
106.T8	Tunisia
106.T87	Turkey
106.U26	Ukraine
	United States
106.U3	General works

	Dictionaries. Encyclopedias
	Bio-bibliographical
	National. By region or country, A-Z
	United States
106.U4A-.U4Z	By region or state, A-Z (Table M1)
106.U8	Uruguay
106.V4	Venezuela
106.V5	Vietnam
	Wales see ML106.G7
(106.Y8)	Yugoslavia
107.A-Z	Local, A-Z
	For regions and states of the United States see ML106.U4A+
108	Terminological
109	Pronouncing
	Music librarianship
	Including cataloging, classification, etc.
	For cataloging of sound recordings in general see Z695.715
110	Periodicals. Societies. Serials
111	General works
111.5	Sound recordings
	Including discography and collecting
	Music printing and publishing
112	General works
112.5	Music title pages
	Including illustrated title pages
	Bibliography
	Class here bibliographies of music and bibliographies of works about music
112.8	Theory, practice, history
	International
113	General works
	By period
114	Through 1600
115	1601-1700
116	1701-1800
117	1801-1900
118	1901-2000
119	2001-
120.A-Z	By region or country, A-Z
120.A35	Africa (General)
120.A7	Arab countries (General)
120.A74	Argentina
120.A75	Armenia
120.A78	Asia (General)
120.A8	East Asia (General)

Bibliography
   By region or country, A-Z -- Continued

120.A86	Australia
120.A9	Austria
120.B28	Belarus
120.B3	Belgium
120.B6	Bolivia
120.B7	Brazil
120.B84	Bulgaria
120.C2	Canada
120.C25	Caribbean Area (General)
120.C45	Chile
120.C5	China
120.C7	Colombia
120.C85	Cuba
120.C87	Cypress
120.C9	Czech Republic. Czechoslovakia
120.D3	Denmark
	East Asia see ML120.A8
120.E5	England
	Cf. ML120.G7 Great Britain
120.E8	Estonia
120.F5	Finland
120.F7	France
120.G3	Germany
(120.G67)	Gorno-Altay, Russia
	see ML120.R8
120.G7	Great Britain
	Cf. ML120.E5 England
120.H9	Hungary
120.I5	India
120.I53	Indonesia
120.I64	Iran
120.I65	Iraq
120.I7	Ireland
120.I745	Islands of the Pacific
120.I75	Israel
120.I8	Italy
120.J3	Japan
120.J35	Jamaica
(120.J4)	Jewish music
	see ML128.J4
120.K7	Korea
(120.L4)	Latin America
	see ML120.S7
120.L6	Lithuania
120.M43	Malta

Bibliography
By region or country, A-Z -- Continued

120.M5	Mexico
	Montenegro see ML120.S47
(120.M53)	Muslim countries
	see ML128.A7
(120.N49)	Negro music, United States
	see ML128.B45
120.N5	Netherlands
120.N53	New Zealand
120.N6	Norway
120.P3	Pakistan
120.P36	Papua New Guinea
120.P6	Poland
120.P7	Portugal
120.R64	Romania
120.R8	Russia. Soviet Union
120.S34	Scandinavian countries (General)
120.S47	Serbia. Montenegro. Yugoslavia
120.S49	Silesia
120.S51	Slovakia
120.S52	Slovenia
120.S58	South Africa
(120.S59)	Soviet Union
	see ML120.R8
120.S6	Spain
120.S7	South America. Latin America (General)
120.S73	Southeast Asia (General)
120.S78	Sudan
120.S8	Sweden
120.S84	Switzerland
120.T8	Turkey
(120.T85)	Turkey
	see ML120.T8
120.U39	Ukraine
120.U5	United States
120.U7	Uruguay
120.V4	Venezuela
(120.W5)	White Russia
	see ML120.B28
(120.Y8)	Yugoslavia
	see ML120.S47
125.A-Z	Local, A-Z
128.A-Z	By topic, A-Z
128.A2	Ability, Musical
128.A3	Accordion
	African American music see ML128.B45

Bibliography

    By topic, A-Z -- Continued

        African American spirituals see ML128.S4

128.A45	Alleluia
128.A54	American political music
	Cf. ML128.P66 Presidents. Presidential candidates
	Analysis see ML128.A7
128.A67	Appalachian dulcimer
128.A7	Appreciation. Analysis
128.B17	Bagpipe
128.B2	Ballets
128.B23	Band music
128.B235	Bandora
128.B24	Baritone. Euphonium
128.B26	Bassoon
128.B29	Big band music
128.B3	Biography
128.B45	Black music. African American music
128.B47	Music for the blind
128.B49	Blues
	Braille music see ML128.B47
128.B73	Brass instruments
	Class here general works
	For individual brass instruments see the instrument, e.g.
	ML128.C86 Cornett
128.C13	Campaign songs
128.C15	Cantatas
	Carnatic music see ML128.K37
128.C2	Catholic Church music
(128.C37)	Central America
	see ML128.S7
128.C4	Chamber music
	Children's music see ML128.J8
128.C46	Chorales
128.C48	Choruses
128.C5	Christian Science church music
128.C54	Church music
	Class here general bibliographies of literature about music for
	Christian worship and of music for Christian worship
	For church music of individual denominations see the
	denomination, e.g. ML128.C2 Catholic church music
	For specific types of church music see the type, e.g.
	ML128.L2 Lenten and Easter music
	For general works on sacred music see ML128.S17
128.C58	Clarinet
128.C59	Community music
	Competitions see ML128.P68

Bibliography
By topic, A-Z -- Continued

128.C62	Computer music. Computers and music
	For electronic music see ML128.E4
128.C8	Concertina
128.C82	Conducting. Conductors.
	Conference proceedings see ML128.M8
128.C84	Concerto
	Class here works about the concerto
	For concertos for specific instruments, see the instrument,
	e.g., ML128.T76 , Trombone
128.C86	Cornett
128.D3	Dance music
	Including folk dance music
128.D5	Music dictionaries
128.D56	Discographies
	Class here bibliographies of discographies
	For discographies see ML155.5+
	Dissertations
	For ethnomusicology see ML128.E8
	For musicology see ML128.M8
	Doctoral dissertations
	For ethnomusicology see ML128.E8
	For musicology see M128.M8
128.D58	Dömbra
128.D6	Double bass
	Easter music see ML128.L2
128.E38	Misteri d'Elx
128.E4	Electronic music
	For computer music see ML128.C62
	English horn see ML128.O2
128.E8	Ethnomusicology
	For musicology see ML128.M8
	Euphonium see ML128.B24
128.E9	Expatriate musicians
	Festa de Elche see ML128.E38
128.F47	Festivals
	Festschriften see ML128.M8
	Film music for music education see ML128.M7
128.F7	Flute
128.F74	Folk music
	For folk dance music see ML128.D3
	For folk songs see ML128.F75
128.F75	Folk songs
128.F8	Funeral music
128.G6	Goigs

	Bibliography
	By topic, A-Z -- Continued
(128.G74)	Ground bass
	see ML128.O7
128.G8	Guitar
128.H2	Harmonium. Reed organ
128.H3	Harp
128.H35	Harpsichord
128.H6	History of music
128.H67	Horn
128.H75	Humor
128.H8	Hymns
128.I6	Incidental music
128.I625	Indians of North America
128.I64	Instruction and study
128.I65	Instrumental music

Class here general works

For individual forms and types of instrumental music, see the form or type, e. g. ML128.C4 , Chamber music ; ML128.M25 , Marches

| 128.I66 | Instruments |

Class here general works

For individual instruments and families of instruments see the instrument or family, e.g. ML128.D6 Double bass; ML128.P23 Percussion instruments

| 128.J3 | Jazz |
| 128.J4 | Jewish music |

Including sacred and secular music, music by Jewish composers, etc.

| 128.J8 | Juvenile music |

Class here music for children to perform or listen to

128.K37	Carnatic music
(128.K4)	Kindergarten music
	see ML128.S25
128.K5	Keyboard instruments

Class here general works

For individual keyboard instruments, see the instrument, e.g. ML128.P3 Piano

128.K8	Ku Klux Klan in music
128.L2	Lenten music. Easter music
128.L28	Abraham Lincoln sheet music
(128.L3)	Literature of music
	see specific types of literature in ML128.A+
128.L5	Librettos
128.L88	Lute
128.M2	Madrigals

For part songs in general see ML128.P13

Bibliography
By topic, A-Z -- Continued

128.M23	Mandolin
128.M25	Marches
128.M27	Medical and physiological aspects of music
	For music therapy see ML128.M77
128.M3	Medieval music
128.M4	Military music
	Misteri d'Elx see ML128.E38
128.M67	Motets
128.M7	Motion picture music
	Music and society see ML128.S298
(128.M74)	Music competitions
	see ML128.P68
	Music for the blind see ML128.B47
	Music theory see ML128.T5
128.M77	Music therapy
	Musical ability see ML128.A2
128.M78	Musicals. Revues
128.M8	Musicology
	Including conference proceedings, Festschriften, theses, and dissertations
	For ethnomusicology see ML128.E8
128.N3	National music. Patriotic music
(128.N4)	Negro spirituals
	see ML128.S4
128.N7	Notation
128.O2	Oboe. English horn. Oboe d'amore
	Oboe d'amore see ML128.O2
128.O4	Opera. Operas
128.O45	Oratorios
128.O5	Orchestra. Orchestral music
128.O6	Organ
128.O7	Ostinato. Ground bass
(128.O8)	Oriental music
	see the region or country in ML120.A+
128.P13	Part songs
	Class here general works
	For madrigals see ML128.M2
128.P15	Pastoral music (Secular)
	Patriotic music see ML128.N3
128.P23	Percussion instruments
128.P235	Performance practice
128.P24	Periodicals
128.P26	Peru in music
	Physiological aspects of music see ML128.M27
128.P3	Piano

	Bibliography
	By topic, A-Z -- Continued
	Political songs, American see ML128.A54
128.P6	Polonaises
128.P63	Popular music
128.P66	Presidents. Presidential candidates
128.P68	Prizes, competitions, etc.
128.P69	Program music
128.P7	Protestant church music
128.P8	Psychological aspects of music
128.Q56	Qin music
128.R25	Ragas
128.R28	Rap
128.R31	Recorder
	Reed organ see ML128.H2
	Revues see ML128.M78
128.R6	Rock music
128.R65	Rockabilly music
128.S17	Sacred music
128.S2	Sacred vocal music
128.S24	Salsa
128.S247	Saxophone
128.S25	School music
128.S29	Scores
128.S295	Singers
128.S298	Sociology of music. Social aspects of music. Music and society
128.S3	Songs
	For students' songs see ML128.S75
	Cf. ML128.M78 Musicals. Revues
	Cf. ML128.P63 Popular music
	Sound recordings
	see ML156+
	For bibliographies of discographies see ML128.D56
128.S4	Spirituals
128.S6	Star-spangled banner
128.S68	String quartets
128.S7	Stringed instruments
	Class here general works
	For individual stringed instruments, see the instrument, e.g. ML128.D6 Double bass
128.S75	Students' songs
128.S9	Symphonies
128.T3	Tabla
128.T36	Tambura (Fretted lute)
128.T4	Television music
128.T48	Thematic catalogs

Bibliography
By topic, A-Z -- Continued
128.T5	Music theory
	Theses
	For ethnomusicology see ML128.E8
	For musicology see ML128.M8
128.T746	Trio sonatas
128.T75	Trios
128.T76	Trombone
128.T78	Trumpet
128.T8	Tuba
128.T9	Twelve-tone system
128.V35	Viola da gamba. Viols
128.V36	Viola
128.V38	Viola d'amore
128.V4	Violin
128.V5	Violoncello
128.V7	Vocal music
128.W16	Waltzes
128.W2	War
128.W4	Wedding music
128.W5	Wind instruments
	Class here general works
	For individual wind instruments see the instrument, e.g.
	ML128.B24 Baritone. Euphonium
128.W7	Women in music
128.Z8	Zither
132.A-Z	Graded lists. By medium
132.A2	General works
132.B3	Band music
132.C4	Chamber music
132.C5	Choral music
132.F58	Flute music
132.H27	Handbell music
132.H3	Harp music
132.O68	Orchestral music
132.O7	Organ music
132.P3	Piano music
132.S6	Songs
132.S8	String orchestra music
132.T76	Trombone music
132.T83	Tuba music
132.V36	Viola music
132.V4	Violin music
132.V7	Vocal music
	Individuals. Individual performance groups

	Bibliography
	Individuals. Individual performance groups -- Continued
134.A-Z	Composers, A-Z
	Subdivide individual composers by Table M12
134.5.A-Z	Others, A-Z
	Including individual performance groups
	e.g.
134.5.B42	Beatles
134.5.B74	Brecht, Bertolt, l898-1956
134.5.J4	Joan, of Arc, Saint, 1412-1431
134.5.L45	Lenin, Vladimir Il'ich, 1870-1924
135	Manuscripts
	For manuscripts in catalogs of public and institutional libraries see ML136.A+
	For manuscripts in catalogs of private collections see ML138.A+
	For manuscripts in catalogs of secondhand dealers see ML152
	Catalogs
	Libraries
	Public and institutional
	Including descriptive literature on libraries
136.A1	General
	Including union catalogs
136.A11-Z	Individual libraries and collections. By place, A11-Z
	Subarrange by library, institution, person featured, etc.
138.A-Z	Private. By name of collection, A-Z
139	Circulating
140	Art
	Including dealers' catalogs
	Class here catalogs of portraits, etc., of musical interest
	For iconography see ML85
	For catalogs of exhibitions see ML141.A+
141.A-Z	Exhibitions. By city, A-Z
	Subarrange by featured artist or name of exhibiting institution
	For catalogs of exhibits of musical instruments see ML462.A+
	Publishers. Dealers
	Class here trade catalogs of publications, instruments, accessories, etc.
	Publishers
144	General works
145.A-Z	Individual publishers, A-Z
	Subarrange catalogs of individual publishers by Table M17
	Dealers
150	General works

Bibliography
  Catalogs
    Publishers. Dealers
      Dealers -- Continued
152   Secondhand dealers
155   Instruments and accessories
                For descriptive catalogs of musical instruments,
                  instrument collections, or exhibitions see
                  ML461+
      Discography
                Class here discographies of musical sound recordings in any
                  audio format or medium, and reviews, indexes, etc., of
                  musical sound recordings
                For discographies of non-music sound recordings on specific
                  topics, see the topic in classes B-L and N-Z
                For bibliographies of discographies see ML128.D56
                For discographies of non-music sound recordings not
                  limited to a topic see ZA4750
(155.5)   General trade catalogs
                  see ML156
(155.52)   By compiler, A-Z
                  see ML156.2
(155.54)   By topic, A-Z
                  see ML156.4.A-Z
(155.55)   Individual composers. By composer, A-Z
                  see ML156.5.A-Z
(155.57)   Individual performers and performance groups. By
                  performer or group, A-Z
                  see ML156.7.A+
(155.59)   Reviews, indexes, etc.
                  see ML156.9
        By source, collection, etc.
156   General trade catalogs
156.2   Other
                Class here catalogs of individual record companies,
                  catalogs of sound recordings in individual libraries,
                  collectors' catalogs, etc.
156.4.A-Z   By topic, A-Z
             American Indian music see ML156.4.I5
156.4.B3   Band music
156.4.B36   Banjo music
156.4.B5   Big band music
             Bluegrass music see ML156.4.C7
156.4.B6   Blues. Rhythm and blues
156.4.C34   Carnatic music

Bibliography
  Discography
    By topic, A-Z -- Continued

156.4.C4	Chamber music
	Class here general works
	For individual instruments see the instrument, e.g.,
	ML156.4.F43 Flute music
156.4.C5	Children's music
156.4.C54	Christmas music
	Church music see ML156.4.R4
156.4.C6	Clarinet music
156.4.C65	Computer music
156.4.C7	Country music. Bluegrass music
156.4.D3	Dance music
156.4.E4	Electronic music
156.4.E5	Environmental music
156.4.F35	Faust legend in music
156.4.F4	Flamenco
156.4.F43	Flute music
156.4.F45	Folk dance music
156.4.F5	Folk music
156.4.F6	Folk songs
156.4.G4	Gay music
156.4.G8	Guitar music
156.4.H3	Harpsichord music
156.4.H7	Horn music
156.4.I5	Indian music (American Indian)
156.4.I58	Instrumental music
	Class here general works
	For music for individual instruments, families of
	instruments, and types of ensembles see the
	instrument, family, or type of ensemble, e.g.
	ML156.4.G8 Guitar music; ML156.4.P4 ; Percussion
	music; ML156.4.O5 Orchestral music
156.4.J3	Jazz
156.4.J4	Jewish music
	Including sacred and secular music, music by Jewish
	composers, etc.
156.4.L2	Labor songs
156.4.M5	Military music
156.4.M6	Motion picture music
156.4.M8	Musicals. Revues
156.4.N3	National music
156.4.N48	New Age music
156.4.O46	Operas
156.4.O5	Orchestral music
156.4.O6	Organ music

Bibliography
Discography
By topic, A-Z -- Continued

156.4.P27	Pasillos
156.4.P4	Percussion music
156.4.P5	Piano music
156.4.P6	Popular music

           Class here general works
           For particular forms, types, etc., of popular music see the
                form or type, etc., e. g. ML156.4.R45 Ragtime music

156.4.R25	Ragtime music
156.4.R27	Rap music
156.4.R34	Recorder music
156.4.R36	Reggae music
156.4.R4	Religious music. Sacred music
	Rhythm and blues see ML156.4.B6
	Revues see ML156.4.M8
156.4.R6	Rock music
	Sacred music see ML156.4.R4
156.4.S3	Saxophone music
156.4.S4	School music
156.4.S6	Soul music
156.4.S8	Steel band music
156.4.S87	Surf music
	Symphonic music see ML156.4.O5
156.4.T4	Television music
156.4.T7	Trombone music
156.4.T8	Trumpet music
156.4.V48	Viola music
156.4.V7	Vocal music
156.4.W4	Western swing
156.4.W6	Women musicians
156.4.W63	World music
156.4.W65	World War, 1939-1945
156.5.A-Z	Individual composers, A-Z
156.7.A-Z	Individual performers and performance groups, A-Z
156.9	Reviews, indexes, etc.
158	Other (not A-Z)

           Including player piano rolls

Moving image media
           Class here lists and catalogs of musical and music-related
                performances in any moving image format or medium

158.4	General works
158.6.A-Z	By topic, A-Z
158.6.A35	African American music
158.6.C66	Conductors
158.6.O6	Operas

Bibliography
Moving image media
By topic, A-Z -- Continued

158.6.P53	Piano music
158.6.S9	Swing
158.8	Computer software

For historiography and musicology see ML3797+
For ethnomusicology see ML3797.6+

History and criticism
General works

159	Published through 1800
160	Published 1801-
161	Outlines. Tables. Syllabi

By period
Ancient

162	General works

Including non-Western music

164	Mesopotamia and Egypt
166	Jews

Including literature on music in the Bible
Greece and Rome

167	Collections

Including sources, documents, essays
Individual authors
Class here texts with or without commentary

168	Ancient
169	Modern

Medieval. Renaissance
Including the 16th century

169.8	Periodicals. Societies. Serials
170	Collections (nonserial)
171	Written through 1600

Class here original works and commentaries
For works on music theory written before 1601 see
MT5.5
Secondary literature published after 1600

172	General works
174	Theory

Including notation
For history of notation see ML431

178	Sacred music
180	Secular music
182	Troubadours. Trouvères
183	Meistersinger. Minnesingers
188	Byzantine music
189	Arab music
190	Other (not A-Z)

	History and criticism
	By period -- Continued
	1601-
193	General works
194	1601-1700
195	1701-1800
196	1801-1900
197	1901-
	By region or country
	For works on a region or country in relation to a topic, see the topic, e.g. ML624+ the organ in France
	For works on a city in relation to a topic, see the topic, e.g. ML1711.8.P5 Opera in Philadelphia
	America
198-198.6	General works (Table M3)
199-199.6	Latin America (Table M3)
	North America
	For Indians of North America see ML3557
199.9	General works
199.91	Addresses, essays, lectures
	By period
199.92	Early to 1700
199.93	1701-1800
199.94	1801-1900
199.95	1901-2000
199.96	2001-
	United States
200	General works
200.1	Addresses, essays, lectures
	By period
200.2	Through 1700
200.3	1701-1800
200.4	1801-1900
	1901-2000
200.5	General works
200.6	World War I, 1914-1918
	Including works issued by government agencies
200.62	2001-
200.7.A-Z	By region, state, etc., A-Z (Table M1 modified)
(200.7.C15)	This number not used
200.7.C2	California
200.8.A-Z	By city, A-Z
	Class here general works
200.9	Other
205-205.9	Canada (Table M4)

	History and criticism
	By region or country
	America
	North America -- Continued
207.A-Z	West Indies. Caribbean Area
	For obsolete numbers formerly used under this span see Table MZ14
207.A1	General works
207.A2-Z	By West Indian island, country, etc., A-Z
207.C8-.C89	Cuba (Table M8)
207.C87-.C879	Curaçao (Table M8)
207.D6-.D69	Dominican Republic (Table M8)
207.H6-.H69	Haiti (Table M8)
207.J29-.J299	Jamaica (Table M8)
207.M43-.M439	Martinique (Table M8)
207.N48-.N489	Netherlands Antilles (Table M8)
207.P8-.P89	Puerto Rico (Table M8)
207.T59-.T599	Trinidad and Tobago (Table M8)
210-210.9	Mexico (Table M4)
	Central America
220-220.6	General works (Table M3)
221-221.9	Belize (Table M4)
222-222.9	Costa Rica (Table M4)
223-223.9	Guatemala (Table M4)
224-224.9	Honduras (Table M4)
225-225.9	Nicaragua (Table M4)
226-226.9	Panama (Table M4)
227-227.9	El Salvador (Table M4)
	South America
230-230.6	General works (Table M3)
231-231.9	Argentina (Table M4)
232-232.9	Brazil (Table M4)
233-233.9	Chile (Table M4)
234-234.9	Colombia (Table M4)
235-235.9	Ecuador (Table M4)
236-236.9	Peru (Table M4)
237-237.9	Uruguay (Table M4)
238-238.9	Venezuela (Table M4)
239.A-Z	Other, A-Z
239.B6-.B69	Bolivia (Table M8)
239.P3-.P39	Paraguay (Table M8)
239.S9-.S99	Suriname (Table M8)
	Europe
	For obsolete numbers formerly used under this span see Table MZ14
240-240.6	General works (Table M3)
246-246.9	Austria (Table M4)

History and criticism
  By region or country
    Europe -- Continued

247-247.9	Czechoslovakia. Czech Republic (Table M4)
248-248.9	Hungary (Table M4)
249-249.9	Slovakia (Table M4)
	Balkan Peninsula
250-250.6	General works (Table M3)
252-252.9	Bulgaria (Table M4)
254-254.9	Greece (Table M4)
256-256.9	Montenegro (Table M4)
	For Serbia and Montenegro see ML260+
258-258.9	Romania (Table M4)
260-260.9	Serbia. Yugoslavia. Serbia and Montenegro (Table M4)
	For Montenegro see ML256+
261-261.9	Slovenia (Table M4)
262-262.9	Croatia (Table M4)
	Prior to 1978 used for Turkey
263-263.9	Bosnia and Hercegovina (Table M4)
264-264.9	Macedonia (Republic) (Table M4)
265-265.9	Belgium (Table M4)
	Including Netherlands to about 1600
269-269.9	Finland (Table M4)
	Prior to 1978 Finland was classified in ML304
270-270.9	France (Table M4)
275-275.9	Germany (Table M4)
	Great Britain. Ireland
285-285.6	General works (Table M3)
286-286.9	England (Table M4)
287-287.9	Ireland. Northern Ireland (Table M4)
288-288.9	Scotland (Table M4)
289-289.9	Wales (Table M4)
290-290.9	Italy (Table M4)
295-295.9	Netherlands (Table M4)
	For Netherlands to about 1600 see ML265+
297-297.9	Poland (Table M4)
300-300.9	Russia. Soviet Union. Russia (Federation) (Table M4)
	For former Soviet republics in Asia see ML330+
	Baltic States
302-302.6	General works (Table M3)
303-303.9	Estonia (Table M4)
304-304.9	Latvia (Table M4)
	Prior to 1978 used for Finland
305-305.9	Lithuania (Table M4)
308-309.9	Ukraine (Table M4)
309.A-Z	Other former Soviet republics (Europe), A-Z
309.B4-.B49	Belarus (Table M8)

ML

History and criticism
  By region or country
    Europe
      Other former Soviet republics (Europe), A-Z -- Continued
309.M6-.M69   Moldova (Table M8)
                       Scandinavia
310-310.6   General works (Table M3)
311-311.9   Denmark (Table M4)
                         Prior to 1978, ML311.5 used for Iceland
312-312.9   Norway (Table M4)
313-313.9   Sweden (Table M4)
314-314.9   Iceland (Table M4)
                         Prior to 1978, Iceland was classified in ML311.5
315-315.9   Spain (Table M4)
317-317.9   Portugal (Table M4)
320-320.9   Switzerland (Table M4)
325.A-Z   Other European regions or countries, A-Z
                         Subdivide each region or country by Table M7 or M8
325.L5-.L59   Liechtenstein (Table M8)
325.M3-.M39   Malta (Table M8)
325.M6-.M69   Monaco (Table M8)
325.S2-.S29   San Marino (Table M8)
                     Asia
                       For obsolete numbers formerly used under this span, see
                         Table MZ14
330-330.6   General works (Table M3)
332-332.9   Saudi Arabia (Table M4)
334-334.9   Armenia (Table M4)
336-336.9   China (Table M4)
337-337.9   Taiwan (Table M4)
338-338.9   India (Table M4)
340-340.9   Japan (Table M4)
342-342.9   Korea (Table M4)
                         Including South Korea
343-343.9   Korea (North) (Table M4)
344-344.9   Iran (Table M4)
345.A-Z   Other Asian regions or countries, A-Z
                         Subdivide each region or country by Table M7 or M8
345.A35-.A359   Afghanistan (Table M8)
345.A98-.A989   Azerbaijan (Table M8)
345.B32-.B329   Bangladesh (Table M8)
345.B8-.B89   Burma. Myanmar (Table M8)
345.C3-.C39   Cambodia (Table M8)
345.C9-.C99   Cyprus (Table M8)
345.G28-.G289   Georgia (Table M8)
345.I43-.I439   India (Table M8)
345.I48-.I489   Indochina (Table M7)

History and criticism
  By region or country
    Asia
      Other Asian regions or countries, A-Z -- Continued

345.I5-.I59	Indonesia (Table M8)
345.I72-.I729	Iraq (Table M8)
345.I8-.I89	Israel (Table M8)
	For Palestine see ML345.P3+
345.K28-.K289	Kazakhstan (Table M8)
345.K8-.K89	Kuwait (Table M8)
345.K96-.K969	Kyrgyzstan (Table M8)
345.L42-.L429	Lebanon (Table M8)
345.M28-.M289	Malaysia (Table M8)
345.M65-.M659	Mongolia (Table M8)
	Myanmar see ML345.B8+
345.N46-.N469	Nepal (Table M8)
345.O5-.O59	Oman (Table M8)
345.P28-.P289	Pakistan (Table M8)
345.P3-.P39	Palestine (Table M8)
	For Israel see ML345.I8+
345.P52-.P529	Philippines (Table M8)
345.S7-.S79	Sri Lanka (Table M8)
345.S97-.S979	Syria (Table M8)
345.T3-.T39	Tajikistan (Table M8)
345.T5-.T59	Thailand (Table M8)
345.T8-.T89	Turkey (Table M8)
	Prior to 1978 Turkey was classified in ML262
345.T93-.T939	Turkmenistan (Table M8)
345.U95-.U959	Uzbekistan (Table M8)
345.V5-.V59	Vietnam (Table M8)
345.Y4-.Y49	Yemen (Table M8)
348-348.6	Arab countries (Table M3)

    Class here general works
    For individual Arab regions and countries in Asia see
      ML330+
    For individual Arab regions and countries in Africa see
      ML355.A+
    For works about Arab music written to 1601 see ML189
  Africa

350-350.6	General (Table M3)
355.A-Z	By region or country, A-Z
	Subdivide each region or country by Table M7 or M8
355.C3-.C39	Cape Verde (Table M8)
355.E3-.E39	Egypt (Table M8)
	For music of ancient Egypt see ML164
355.L75-.L759	Libya (Table M8)
355.M8-.M89	Morocco (Table M8)

History and criticism
  By region or country
    Africa
      By region or country, A-Z -- Continued

355.N6-.N69	Nigeria (Table M8)
355.S7-.S79	Sub-Saharan Africa (Table M7)
355.S8-.S89	Sudan (Table M8)
355.T8-.T89	Tunisia (Table M8)
360-360.6	Australia, Oceania, etc. (Table M3)

Biography
  Collective
    Including correspondence

385	General works
390	Composers. Arrangers

Performers
  Including collective works about performing groups
  For individual performing groups see ML421.A+

394	General works

Instrumentalists

395	General works
396	Organists
397	Pianists
398	Stringed instrument players

  Including string quartets, etc.

399	Other instruments
400	Singers
402	Conductors
403	Theoreticians, historians, critics, etc.

  Including librettists, lyricists, etc.
  For works on writers of hymn texts, see BV

404	Manufacturers of instruments

  Including works about corporate bodies

405	Music publishers, printers, dealers

  Including works about corporate bodies

406	Others

  Including collectors, managers, etc.

Individual. By subject of the biography, A-Z
  If a person is known in more than one area of musical activity,
    choose as the sole class for the person the class for the
    area in which he or she is best known. Where no area
    clearly predominates and the person is a composer, e.g.
    Leonard Bernstein, classify in ML410.A-Z

History and criticism
Biography
Individual. By subject of the biography, A-Z -- Continued

410.A-Z	Composers

Including discussions of a composer's compositions from a historical or biographical perspective
Names listed below are given as examples
For works consisting primarily of analysis of musical compositions see MT90+

410.A796	Harut'yunyan, Alek'sandr Grigori, 1920-
410.A798	Asenjo y Barbieri, Francisco, 1823-1894
	Bach, Johann Sebastian, 1685-1750
410.B1	General works
410.B13	Critical works
410.B14	Family of Johann Sebastian Bach

Class here general works about the family. For works about individual family members, see separate classes, e.g., ML410.B16 Carl Philipp Emanuel Bach.

Barbieri, Francisco Asenjo, 1823-1894 see ML410.A798
Beethoven, Ludwig van, 1770-1827

410.B4	General works
410.B42	Biographical-critical works

For purely critical or analytical works see MT

(410.B43)	Other

see ML410.B4

410.B698	Bond, Carrie Jacobs, 1862-1946
410.C4	Chaĭkovskiĭ, Petr Il'ich, 1840-1893
410.C8	Cornelius, Peter, 1824-1874

Harut'yunyan, Alek'sandr Grigori, 1920- see ML410.A796
Jacobs Bond, Carrie, 1862-1946 see ML410.B698

410.R19	Rama Varma Kulasekhara Perumal, Maharaja of Travancore, 1813-1846
410.R85	Rouget de Lisle, Claude Joseph, 1760-1836
410.S15	Saint-Saëns, Camille, 1835-1921

Svātitirunāḷ, 1813-1846 see ML410.R19
Tchaikovsky, Peter Ilich, 1840-1893 see ML410.C4

410.W1-.W2	Wagner, Richard, 1813-1883 (Table M18)
	Performers
	Instrumentalists
	Keyboard players
416.A-Z	Organists

History and criticism
  Biography
    Individual. By subject of the biography, A-Z
      Performers
        Instrumentalists
          Keyboard players
            Organists -- Continued

416.S33	Schweitzer, Albert
	Cf. B2430.S37+ Schweitzer as philosopher
	Cf. BX4827.S35 Schweitzer as theologian
	Cf. CT1018.S45+ Schweitzer (General biography)
	Cf. R722.32.S35 Schweitzer as medical missionary
417.A-Z	Other
	Class here pianists, harpsichordists, performers on several keyboard instruments, etc.
418.A-Z	Stringed instrument players
419.A-Z	Other
420.A-Z	Singers
421.A-Z	Performing groups
	Class here works that are mainly biographical
	Names listed below are given as examples
	For documents of performance organizations and individual performance ensembles associated with a particular city see ML25+
421.A44	Amadeus String Quartet
421.B4	The Beatles
421.P6	Pink Floyd
421.R64	Rolling Stones
422.A-Z	Conductors, A-Z
423.A-Z	Theoreticians, historians, critics, etc.
424.A-Z	Manufacturers of instruments
427.A-Z	Music publishers, printers, dealers
429.A-Z	Others
	Including managers

Composition and performance
  Composition

430	General works
430.5	Style
430.7	Improvisation
	Notation
	For early works to 1601 see ML171
431	General works
432	Reform proposals
437	Rhythm
440	Melody

	History and criticism
	Composition and performance
	Composition -- Continued
442	Continuo
444	Harmony
446	Counterpoint
448	Musical form

Class here works not limited to a specific medium of
performance

455	Instrumentation
457	Interpretation. Performance practice
458	Conducting
	Instruments and instrumental music
459	Periodicals. Societies. Serials
460	General works
	Descriptive catalogs of musical instruments, instrument collections, and exhibitions

For trade catalogs see ML155

461	General works
462.A-Z	Individual collections and exhibitions. By city, A-Z

Subarrange by name of institution

	By period
465	Through 1600

For ancient periods see ML162+

467	1601-1750
469	1751-1850
471	1851-
	By region or country
	America
475-475.6	General works (Table M3)
476-476.9	United States (Table M4)
478-478.9	Canada (Table M4)
480	West Indies. Caribbean Area

Including individual West Indian islands, countries, etc.
(not A-Z)

482-482.9	Mexico (Table M4)
	Central America
484-484.6	General works (Table M3)

Prior to 2007, also used for individual countries of
Central America (not A-Z)

485.A-Z	By region or country, A-Z

Subdivide each region or country by Table M7 or M8

486.A-Z	South America
486.A1-.A6	General works (Table M7)
486.A7-.A79	Argentina (Table M8)
486.B5-.B59	Bolivia (Table M8)
486.B7-.B79	Brazil (Table M8)

History and criticism
  Instruments and instrumental music
    By region or country
      America
        South America -- Continued

486.C5-.C59	Chile (Table M8)
486.C6-.C69	Colombia (Table M8)
486.E25-.E259	Ecuador (Table M8)
486.F74-.F749	French Guiana (Table M8)
486.P4-.P49	Peru (Table M8)
486.V45-.V459	Venezuela (Table M8)

      Europe
        For obsolete numbers formerly used uder this span see
          Table MZ15

489-489.6	General works (Table M3)
491-491.9	Austria (Table M4)
493-493.9	Czechoslovakia. Czech Republic (Table M4)
494-494.9	Hungary (Table M4)
495-495.9	Slovakia (Table M4)
496-496.9	Belgium (Table M4)
497-497.9	France (Table M4)
499	Germany (Table M4)
(500)	East Germany see ML499
501-501.9	Great Britain. England (Table M4) For Northern Ireland, Scotland, Wales, see ML501.7+
502-502.9	Ireland (Table M4)
503-503.9	Italy (Table M4)
505-505.9	Netherlands (Table M4)
507-507.9	Russia. Soviet Union. Russia (Federation) (Table M4)
508.A-Z	Baltic States
508.A1-.A16	General works (Table M7)
508.E8-.E89	Estonia (Table M8)
508.L4-.L49	Latvia (Table M8)
508.L6-.L69	Lithuania (Table M8)
511.A-Z	Other former Soviet republics (Europe), A-Z For Asian republics see ML541.A+
511.B4-.B49	Belarus (Table M8)
511.M6-.M69	Moldova (Table M8)
511.U38-.U389	Ukraine (Table M8)

        Scandinavia

513-513.6	General works (Table M3)
514-514.9	Denmark (Table M4)
515-515.9	Norway (Table M4)
516-516.9	Sweden (Table M4)
518-518.9	Spain (Table M4)
519-519.9	Portugal (Table M4)

History and criticism
   Instruments and instrumental music
      By region or country
         Europe -- Continued

520-520.9	Switzerland (Table M4)
522.A-Z	Other European regions or countries, A-Z
	Subdivide each region or country by Table M7 or M8
522.B84-.B849	Bulgaria (Table M8)
522.C87-.C879	Croatia (Table M8)
522.G74-.G749	Greece (Table M8)
522.H9-.H99	Hungary (Table M8)
522.P6-.P69	Poland (Table M8)
522.R8-.R89	Romania (Table M8)
522.S5-.S59	Serbia. Serbia and Montenegro. Yugoslavia (Table M8)
522.S57-.S579	Slovenia (Table M8)
	Asia
	For obsolete numbers formerly used under this span see Table MZ15
525-525.6	General works (Table M3)
527-527.9	Saudi Arabia (Table M4)
531-531.9	China (Table M4)
533-533.9	India (Table M4)
535-535.9	Japan (Table M4)
537-537.9	Korea (Table M4)
539-539.9	Iran (Table M4)
541.A-Z	Other Asian regions or countries, A-Z
	For obsolete numbers formerly used under this span see Table MZ15
	Subdivide each region or country by Table M7 or M8
(541.A785-.A7856)	Asia, Southeastern
	see ML541.S68+
541.A98-.A989	Azerbaijan (Table M8)
541.B79-.B799	Brunei (Table M8)
541.B93-.B939	Burma (Table M8)
541.C16-.C169	Cambodia (Table M8)
541.G28-.G289	Georgia (Table M8)
541.I7-.I79	Iraq (Table M8)
541.K3-.K39	Kazakhstan (Table M8)
541.K86-.K869	Kurdistan (Table M8)
541.K98-.K989	Kyrgyzstan (Table M8)
541.M35-.M359	Malaysia (Table M8)
	Middle East see ML541.N42+
541.M65-.M659	Mongolia (Table M8)
541.N42-.N426	Near East (Table M7)
541.N45-.N459	Nepal (Table M8)
541.O5-.O59	Oman (Table M8)

History and criticism
  Instruments and instrumental music
    By region or country
      Asia
        Other Asian regions or countries, A-Z -- Continued

541.P16-.P169	Pacific Area (Table M8)
541.P28-.P289	Pakistan (Table M8)
541.P3-.P39	Palestine (Table M8)
541.P6-.P69	Philippines (Table M8)
541.S68-.S686	Southeast Asia (General) (Table M7)
541.S72-.S729	Sri Lanka (Table M8)
541.T28-.T289	Taiwan (Table M8)
541.T5-.T59	Thailand (Table M8)
541.T78-.T789	Turkey (Table M8)
541.U9-.U99	Uzbekistan (Table M8)
541.V5-.V59	Vietnam (Table M8)
544	Africa
	Including individual regions and countries (not A-Z)
547	Australia, Oceania, etc.
	Including individual regions and countries (not A-Z)
548-548.6	Jews (Table M3)
	Class here general works
	For works about ancient music see ML166
	For works about sacred vocal music see ML3195
	For works about secular music see ML3776

  Instruments
    Keyboard instruments

549	General works
	Organ
549.8	Periodicals. Societies. Serials
549.9	Congresses
550	General works
	For tuning see MT165
	Construction and repair
552	General works
	By period
553	Through 1600
554	1601-1700
555	1701-1800
556	1801-1900
557	1901-
	By region or country
	North America
560-560.6	General works (Table M3)
561-561.9	United States (Table M4)
563-563.9	Canada (Table M4)

History and criticism
  Instruments and instrumental music
    Instruments
      Keyboard instruments
        Organ
          Construction and repair
            By region or country
              North America -- Continued

564	West Indies. Caribbean Area
	Including individual West Indian islands, countries, etc. (not A-Z)
565-565.9	Mexico (Table M4)
	Central America
566-566.6	General works (Table M3)
	For general works cataloged prior to 2007 see ML567.A+
567.A-Z	By region or country, A-Z
	Subdivide each region or country by Table M7 or M8
	Prior to 2007, also used for general works
	South America
568-568.6	General works (Table M3)
	Prior to 2007, also used for individual countries of South America (not A-Z)
569.A-Z	By region or country, A-Z
	Subdivide each region or country by Table M7 or M8
	Europe
570-570.6	General works (Table M3)
572-572.9	Austria (Table M4)
573-573.9	Belgium (Table M4)
574-574.9	France (Table M4)
576-576.9	Germany (Table M4)
578-578.9	Great Britain. England (Table M4)
	For Northern Ireland, Soctland, Wales, see ML578.7+
579-579.9	Ireland (Table M4)
580-580.9	Italy (Table M4)
582-582.9	Netherlands (Table M4)
584-584.9	Russia. Soviet Union. Russia (Federation) (Table M4)
586-586.9	Scandinavia
	Including individual countries (not A-Z)
588-588.9	Spain (Table M4)
589-589.9	Portugal (Table M4)
590-590.9	Switzerland (Table M4)

History and criticism
Instruments and instrumental music
Instruments
Keyboard instruments
Organ
Construction and repair
By region or country -- Continued

592.A-Z	Other regions or countries, A-Z
	For obsolete numbers formerly used under this span see Table MZ15
	Subdivide each region or country by Table M7 or M8
	Class here European and other regions or countries
592.A78-.A786	Asia (General) (Table M7)
592.A9-.A99	Australia (Table M8)
592.C63-.C636	Cape of Good Hope (Table M7)
592.C87-.C879	Croatia (Table M8)
592.C9-.C99	Czech Republic. Czechoslovakia (Table M8)
592.E9-.E99	Estonia (Table M8)
592.F5-.F59	Finland (Table M8)
592.H8-.H89	Hungary (Table M8)
592.L35-.L359	Latvia (Table M8)
592.L9-.L99	Luxembourg (Table M8)
592.N45-.N459	New Zealand (Table M8)
592.P6-.P69	Poland (Table M8)
592.R8-.R89	Romania (Table M8)
592.S4-.S49	Serbia. Serbia and Montenegro. Yugoslavia (Table M8)
592.S56-.S569	Slovakia (Table M8)
592.S57-.S579	Slovenia (Table M8)
592.S6-.S69	South Africa (Table M8)
	Individual organs
	Including history and specifications
594.A1	Collected works (nonserial)
594.A25-Z	By place, A-Z
595	Parts of the organ
597	Specific types of organ
	Including reed organ, electronic organ, etc.
	Music and playing
600	General works
	By period
603	Through 1600
604	1601-1700
605	1701-1800
606	1801-1900
607	1901-2000

History and criticism
Instruments and instrumental music
Instruments
Keyboard instruments
Organ
Music and playing
By period -- Continued

608	2001-
	By region or country
	North America
610-610.6	General works (Table M3)
611-611.9	United States (Table M4)
613-613.9	Canada (Table M4)
614	West Indies. Caribbean Area
	Including individual West Indian islands, countries, etc. (not A-Z)
615-615.9	Mexico (Table M4)
	Central America
616-616.6	General works (Table M3)
	For general works cataloged prior to 2007 see ML617.A+
617.A-Z	By region or country, A-Z
	Subdivide each region or country by Table M7 or M8
	Prior to 2007, also used for general works
	South America
618-618.6	General works (Table M3)
	Prior to 2007 also used for individual countries of South America (not A-Z)
619.A-Z	By region or country, A-Z
	Subdivide each region or country by Table M7 or M8
	Europe
620-620.6	General works (Table M3)
622-622.9	Austria (Table M4)
623-623.9	Belgium (Table M4)
624-624.9	France (Table M4)
626-626.9	Germany (Table M4)
628-628.9	Great Britain. England (Table M4)
	For Northern Ireland, Scotland, Wales, see ML628.7+
629-629.9	Ireland (Table M4)
630-630.9	Italy (Table M4)
632-632.9	Netherlands (Table M4)
634-623.9	Russia. Soviet Union. Russia (Federation) (Table M4)

History and criticism
Instruments and instrumental music
Instruments
Keyboard instruments
Organ
Music and playing
By region or country
Europe -- Continued

636	Scandinavia
	Including individual countries (not A-Z)
638-638.9	Spain (Table M4)
639-639.9	Portugal (Table M4)
640-640.9	Switzerland (Table M4)
642.A-Z	Other regions or countries, A-Z

Subdivide each region or country by Table M7 or M8
Class here European and other regions or countries
Forms and types

645	Sonata
646	Suite
647	Other (not A-Z)
649	Reed organ music

Piano, harpsichord, clavichord, etc.
Class here works about the piano or its predecessors

| 649.8 | Periodicals. Societies. Serials |
| 650 | Piano |

Including works also covering predecessors of the piano

| 651 | Harpsichord, clavichord, etc. |

Construction and repair

| 652 | General works |

By period

653	Through 1600
654	1601-1700
655	1701-1800
656	1801-1900
657	1901-2000
658	2001-

By region or country
North America

660-660.6	General works (Table M3)
661-661.9	United States (Table M4)
663-663.9	Canada (Table M4)
664	West Indies. Caribbean Area

Including individual West Indian islands, countries, etc. (not A-Z)

History and criticism
  Instruments and instrumental music
    Instruments
      Keyboard instruments
        Piano, harpsichord, clavichord, etc.
          Construction and repair
           By region or country

	North America -- Continued
665-665.9	Mexico (Table M4)
	Central America
666-666.6	General works (Table M3)
	For general works cataloged prior to 2007 see ML667.A+
667.A-Z	By region or country, A-Z
	Subdivide each region or country by Table M7 or M8
	Prior to 2007, also used for general works
	South America
668-668.6	General works (Table M3)
	Prior to 2007, also used for individual countries of South America (not A-Z)
669.A-Z	By region or country, A-Z
	Subdivide each region or country by Table M7 or M8
	Europe
670-670.6	General works (Table M3)
672-672.9	Austria (Table M4)
673- 673.9	Belgium (Table M4)
674-674.9	France (Table M4)
676-676.9	Germany (Table M4)
678-678.9	Great Britain. England (Table M4)
	For Northern Ireland, Scotland, Wales, see ML678.7+
679-679.9	Ireland (Table M4)
680-680.9	Italy (Table M4)
682-682.9	Netherlands (Table M4)
684-684.9	Russia. Soviet Union. Russia (Federation) (Table M4)
686	Scandinavia
	Including individual countries (not A-Z)
688-688.9	Spain (Table M4)
689-689.9	Portugal (Table M4)
690-690.9	Switzerland (Table M4)

History and criticism
 Instruments and instrumental music
  Instruments
   Keyboard instruments
    Piano, harpsichord, clavichord, etc.
     Construction and repair
      By region or country -- Continued

692.A-Z	Other regions or countries, A-Z

Subdivide each region or country by Table M7 or M8

Class here European and other regions or countries

694	Specific makes

Cf. ML424.A+ Individual manufacturers of instruments

695	Specific parts of the piano
697	Other kinds of pianos

Including new keyboards and electronic pianos

     Music and playing

700	General works

By period

703	Through 1600
704	1601-1700
705	1701-1800
706	1801-1900
707	1901-

By region or country
 North America

710-710.6	General works (Table M3)
711-711.9	United States (Table M4)
713-713.9	Canada (Table M4)
714	West Indies. Caribbean Area

Including individual West Indian islands, countries, etc. (not A-Z)

715-715.9	Mexico (Table M4)

Central America

716-716.6	General works (Table M3)

For general works cataloged prior to 2007 see ML717.A+

717.A-Z	By region or country, A-Z

Subdivide each region or country by Table M7 or M8

Prior to 2007, also used for general works

South America

718-718.6	General works (Table M3)

Prior to 2007, also used for individual countries of South America (not A-Z)

	History and criticism
	Instruments and instrumental music
	Instruments
	Keyboard instruments
	Piano, harpsichord, clavichord, etc.
	Music and playing
	By region or country
	South America -- Continued
719.A-Z	By region or country, A-Z
	Subdivide each region or country by Table M7 or M8
	Europe
720-720.6	General works (Table M3)
722-722.9	Austria (Table M4)
723-723.9	Belgium (Table M4)
724-724.9	France (Table M4)
726-726.9	Germany (Table M4)
728-728.9	Great Britain. England (Table M4)
	For Northern Ireland, Scotland, Wales, see ML728.7+
729-729.9	Ireland (Table M4)
730-730.9	Italy (Table M4)
732-732.9	Netherlands (Table M4)
734-734.9	Russia. Soviet Union. Russia (Federation) (Table M4)
736	Scandinavia
	Including individual countries (not A-Z)
738-738.9	Spain (Table M4)
739-739.9	Portugal (Table M4)
740-740.9	Switzerland (Table M4)
742.A-Z	Other regions or countries, A-Z
	Subdivide each region or country by Table M7 or M8
	Class here European and other regions or countries
742.E75-.E759	Estonia (Table M8)
742.F5-.F59	Finland (Table M8)
742.I2-.I29	Iceland (Table M8)
742.L78-.L789	Lithuania (Table M8)
742.P6-.P69	Poland (Table M8)
742.T93-.T939	Turkmenistan (Table M8)
742.U4-.U49	Ukraine (Table M8)
	Forms and types
745	Sonata
746	Suite
747	Other (not A-Z)

	History and criticism
	Instruments and instrumental music
	Instruments -- Continued
	Stringed instruments. Bowed stringed instruments
	Class here general works on instruments with strings that are bowed, hammered, or plucked, as well as works limited to bowed stringed instruments
	For stringed instruments with keyboards see ML549+
	For plucked instruments see ML999+
749.5	Periodicals. Societies. Serials
750	General works
755	Construction and repair
756	Music and playing
(760)	Early instruments
	see the instrument
	Violin
800	General works
	Construction and repair
802	General works
	By period
803	Through 1600
804	1601-1700
805	1701-1800
806	1801-1900
807	1901-
	By region or country
	North America
810-810.6	General works (Table M3)
811-811.9	United States (Table M4)
813-813.9	Canada (Table M4)
814	West Indies. Caribbean Area
	Including individual West Indian islands, countries, etc. (not A-Z)
815-815.9	Mexico (Table M4)
	Central America
816-816.6	General works (Table M3)
	For general works cataloged prior to 2007 see ML817.A+
817.A-Z	By region or country, A-Z
	Subdivide each region or country by Table M7 or M8
	Prior to 2007, also used for general works
	South America
818-818.6	General works (Table M3)
	Prior to 2007, also used for individual countries of South America (not A-Z)

History and criticism
Instruments and instrumental music
Instruments
Stringed instruments. Bowed stringed instruments
Violin
Construction and repair
By region or country
South America -- Continued
819.A-Z   By region or country, A-Z
Subdivide each region or country by Table M7 or M8
Europe
820-820.6   General works (Table M3)
822-822.9   Austria (Table M4)
823-823.9   Belgium (Table M4)
824-824.9   France (Table M4)
826-826.9   Germany (Table M4)
828-828.9   Great Britain. England (Table M4)
For Northern Ireland, Scotland, Wales, see ML828.7+
829-829.9   Ireland (Table M4)
830-830.9   Italy (Table M4)
832-832.9   Netherlands (Table M4)
834-834.9   Russia. Soviet Union. Russia (Federation) (Table M4)
836   Scandinavia
Including individual countries (not A-Z)
838-838.9   Spain (Table M4)
839-839.9   Portugal (Table M4)
840-840.9   Switzerland (Table M4)
842.A-Z   Other regions or countries, A-Z
For obsolete numbers formerly used under this span, see Table MZ15
Subdivide each region or country by Table M7 or M8
Class here European and other regions or countries
842.C89-.C899   Czech Republic. Czechoslovakia (Table M8)
842.H9-.H99   Hungary (Table M8)
845   Parts of the violin. Accessories
Including the bow
846   Other
Including prices
Music and playing
850   General works
By period
853   Through 1600

History and criticism
　Instruments and instrumental music
　　Instruments
　　　Stringed instruments. Bowed stringed instruments
　　　　Violin
　　　　　Music and playing
　　　　　　By period -- Continued
854	1601-1700
855	1701-1800
856	1801-1900
857	1901-

　　　　　　By region or country
　　　　　　　North America
860-860.6	General works (Table M3)
861-861.9	United States (Table M4)
863-863.9	Canada (Table M4)
864	West Indies. Caribbean Area

　　　　　　　　　Including individual West Indian islands,
　　　　　　　　　　countries, etc. (not A-Z)
865-865.9	Mexico (Table M4)

　　　　　　　Central America
866-866.6	General works (Table M3)

　　　　　　　　　For general works cataloged prior to 2007
　　　　　　　　　　see ML867.A+
867.A-Z	By region or country, A-Z

　　　　　　　　　Subdivide each region or country by Table M7 or
　　　　　　　　　　M8
　　　　　　　　　Prior to 2007, also used for general works
　　　　　　　South America
868-868.6	General works (Table M3)

　　　　　　　　　Prior to 2007, also used for individual countries
　　　　　　　　　　of South America (not A-Z)
869.A-Z	By region or country, A-Z

　　　　　　　　　Subdivide each region or country by Table M7 or
　　　　　　　　　　M8
　　　　　　　Europe
870-870.6	General works (Table M3)
872-872.9	Austria (Table M4)
873-873.9	Belgium (Table M4)
874-874.9	France (Table M4)
876-876.9	Germany (Table M4)
878-878.9	Great Britain. England (Table M4)

　　　　　　　　　For Northern Ireland, Scotland, Wales, see
　　　　　　　　　　ML878.7+
879-879.9	Ireland (Table M4)
880-880.9	Italy (Table M4)
882-882.9	Netherlands (Table M4)

	History and criticism
	Instruments and instrumental music
	Instruments
	Stringed instruments. Bowed stringed instruments
	Violin
	Music and playing
	By region or country
	Europe -- Continued
884-884.9	Russia. Soviet Union. Russia (Federation) (Table M4)
886	Scandinavia
	Including individual countries (not A-Z)
888-888.9	Spain (Table M4)
889-889.9	Portugal (Table M4)
890-890.9	Switzerland (Table M4)
892.A-Z	Other regions or countries, A-Z
	Subdivide each region or country by Table M7 or M8
	Class here European and other regions or countries
	Forms and types
895	Sonata
896	Suite
897	Other (not A-Z)
	Viola
900	General works
901	Construction and repair
905	Music and playing
	Violoncello
910	General works
911	Construction and repair
915	Music and playing
	Double bass
920	General works
921	Construction and repair
925	Music and playing
927.A-Z	Other bowed stringed instruments, A-Z
927.B37	Baryton
927.C36	Campanula
927.E7	Er hu
927.G83	Gŭdulka
927.H27	Hardanger fiddle
927.K49	Keyed fiddle
	Lira (Short-necked fiddle) see ML927.L9
927.L57	Lira da braccio
927.L59	Lirone
927.L9	Lyra. Lira (Short-necked fiddle)

History and criticism
Instruments and instrumental music
Instruments
Stringed instruments. Bowed stringed instruments
Other bowed stringed instruments, A-Z -- Continued

927.L97	Lyra viol
927.P75	Psalmodikon
927.R33	Rabāb
927.R35	Rabeca
927.S4	Sarangi
927.T7	Trumpet marine
927.V5	Viol family. Viols
927.V56	Viola d'amore
927.V6	Violo
927.V63	Violone

Wind instruments

929	Periodicals. Societies. Serials
929.5	Congresses
930	General works
931	Woodwind instruments (General)
933	Brass instruments (General)

Flute. Piccolo

935	General works
936	Construction and repair
937	Music and playing

Oboe

940	General works
941	Construction and repair
943	Music and playing

Clarinet

945	General works
946	Construction and repair
948	Music and playing

Bassoon

950	General works
951	Construction and repair
953	Music and playing

Horn

955	General works
956	Construction and repair
958	Music and playing

Trumpet. Keyed trumpet. Cornet. Bugle. Keyed bugle.
Flügelhorn

960	General works
961	Construction and repair
963	Music and playing

Trombone

	History and criticism
	Instruments and instrumental music
	Instruments
	Wind instruments
	Trombone -- Continued
965	General works
966	Construction and repair
968	Music and playing
	Tuba. Baritone, etc.
	Including low brass instruments common to the Western band and orchestra, e.g., euphonium, sousaphone.
970	General works
971	Construction and repair
973	Music and playing
	Saxophone
975	General works
976	Construction and repair
978	Music and playing
980	Bagpipes
990.A-Z	Other wind instruments, A-Z
	For obsolete numbers formerly used under this span see Table MZ16
990.A5	Alboka
990.A54	Alphorn
990.B32	Bānsurī
990.B35	Basset horn
990.B57	Birbynẹ
990.B66	Bone flute
990.C5	Chalumeau
990.C65	Cornett
(990.C68)	Courting flute
	see ML990.N37
990.C8	Crumhorn
990.C95	Csakan
990.D5	Di zi
990.D53	Didjeridu
990.D76	Duduk (Oboe)
990.D8	Dulzaina
990.F6	Flaviol
990.G83	Guan
990.H4	Heckelphone
(990.H75)	Hsiao
	see ML990.X53
990.K36	Kaval
990.L38	Launeddas
990.L54	Ligawka
990.L57	Liquimofono

History and criticism
  Instruments and instrumental music
    Instruments
      Wind instruments
        Other wind instruments, A-Z -- Continued

990.N37	Native American flute
990.N39	Nāy
990.O3	Ocarina
990.O7	Ophicleide
990.P3	Panpipes
990.P45	Penny whistle
990.P56	Pinkallu
990.P57	P'iri
990.P67	Post horn
990.Q46	Quena
990.R4	Recorder
990.R8	Russian horn
990.S3	Sackbut
990.S5	Shakuhachi
990.S515	Shawm
	Sheng see ML1089.S5
990.S55	Shofar
990.S58	Siku
990.S6	Siwa
990.S87	Šupeljka
990.T34	Taegŭm
990.T46	Tenora
990.T8	Tuba stentoro-phonica. Vamp-horn
	Vamp-horn see ML990.T8
990.W37	Washint
990.X53	Xiao
990.Z8	Zumari

     Plucked instruments

999	Periodicals. Societies. Serials
1000	General works
1001	Construction and repair
1003	Music and playing
	Harp
1005	General works
1006	Construction and repair
1008	Music and playing
	Lute
1010	General works
1011	Construction and repair
	Music and playing
1012	Literature to about 1650
	Including sources, documents, etc.

	History and criticism
	Instruments and instrumental music
	Instruments
	Plucked instruments
	Lute
	Music and playing -- Continued
1013	Literature after about 1650
1015.A-Z	Other plucked instruments, A-Z
	For obsolete numbers formerly used under this span, see Table MZ16
1015.A6	Appalachian dulcimer
1015.A9	Autoharp
1015.B23	Bağlama
1015.B24	Balalaika
1015.B25	Bandura
1015.B26	Bandurria
1015.B3	Banjo
1015.B35	Bass guitar
1015.B4	Berimbau
1015.B55	Biwa
1015.C3	Celtic harp
1015.C37	Charango
1015.C47	Cheng. Zheng
1015.C5	Ch'in. Qin
1015.C56	Chitarra battente
1015.C58	Cittern
1015.C83	Cuatro
1015.D35	Đàn bâù
1015.D36	Đàn tranh
1015.D66	Dömbra
	Dulcimer see ML1041
	Dulcimer, Appalachian see ML1015.A6
	Electric guitar see ML1015.G9
1015.G9	Guitar
1015.G93	Gusli
1015.I3	Ichigenkin
1015.K23	Kacapi (Lute)
1015.K24	Kacapi (Zither)
1015.K27	Kanklės
1015.K3	Kantele
1015.K6	Kobza
1015.K64	Kokle
1015.K65	Kŏmun'go
1015.K66	Kora
1015.K68	Koto
1015.L89	Lyre
1015.L9	Lyre-guitar

	History and criticism
	Instruments and instrumental music
	Instruments
	Plucked instruments
	Other plucked instruments, A-Z -- Continued
1015.M2	Mandolin
1015.M25	Mbira. Sanza
1015.O9	Oud
1015.P5	Pi pa
1015.P8	Psaltery
	Qin see ML1015.C5
1015.S3	San xian
(1015.S35)	Sanza
	see ML1015.M25
1015.S37	Sarod
1015.S39	Saúng-gauk
1015.S4	Saz
1015.S46	Setār
1015.S52	Shamisen
1015.S56	Simsimīyya
1015.S6	Sitar
1015.T3	Tambura (Fretted lute)
1015.T5	Tiple
1015.U5	Ukulele
1015.V5	Vina
1015.V56	Viola-de-cocho
1015.Y35	Yang qin
1015.Y83	Yue qin
	Zheng see ML1015.C47
1015.Z5	Zither
(1018.A-Z)	Music and playing, By instrument, A-Z
	see ML1015.A+
	Percussion instruments
	For obsolete numbers formerly used under this span see Table MZ16
1030	General works
	Drums
	Including drum set
1035	General works
1036	Timpani
1038.A-Z	Other, A-Z
1038.A7	Arará
1038.A8	Atabaque
1038.B38	Batá
1038.B63	Bodhrán
1038.B66	Bonkó
1038.B7	Bronze drum

History and criticism
Instruments and instrumental music
Instruments
Percussion instruments
Drums
Other, A-Z -- Continued

1038.C25	Cajón
1038.C28	Catá
1038.C4	Ceṇḍa
1038.D5	Dhimay
1038.D54	Djembe
1038.E35	Ekue
1038.F46	Fêli
1038.K7	Kotsuzumi
1038.M33	Mādal
1038.M74	Mridanga
1038.N4	Nāykhīm
1038.P38	Paṟai
1038.P85	Pung
1038.R43	Rebana
1038.S26	Santūr
1038.S65	Snare drum
1038.S74	Steel drum
1038.T3	Tabla
1038.T35	Taiko
1038.T83	Tumba
1038.T85	Tupan
1038.Y93	Yuka
1039	Bells. Carillons. Gongs. Chimes
	Including change ringing, peals, etc.
1041	Dulcimer
1048	Xylophone and similar instruments
	Including marimba, vibraphone, anklung, etc.
1049	Other percussion instruments (not A-Z)
	Mechanical instruments, devices, etc.
	For obsolete numbers formerly used under this span see Table MZ16
	For electronic instruments see ML1091.8+
1049.8	Periodicals. Societies. Serials
1050	General works
1055	Recording instruments
	Class here phonograph, sound recordings, music recorder, etc.
	For electronic instruments see ML1091.8+
1058	Barrel organ. Mechanical organs
	Music box
1065	Periodicals. Societies. Serials

	History and criticism
	Instruments and instrumental music
	Instruments
	Mechanical instruments, devices, etc.
	Music box
1066	General works
1067	Musical clocks
1070	Player piano and similar instruments
1080	Metronome
1081	Other (not A-Z)
	Other instruments
	For electronic instruments see ML1091.8+
1083	Accordion. Bandoneon. Concertina
1085	Glass harmonica
1086	Hurdy-gurdy
1087	Jew's harp
	Mouth organs
1088	Harmonica
1089.A-Z	Other, A-Z
1089.K24	Kaen
1089.M45	Melodica
1089.S5	Sheng
1089.S54	Shō
(1090)	Recording instruments
	see ML1055
1091	Other (not A-Z)
	Including parts of instruments or accessories common to more than one family of instruments
	Electronic instruments
1091.8	Periodicals. Societies. Serials
1092	General works
1093	Computers as musical instruments
	For general works on the use of computers in the field of music see ML74
	Ensembles
	Chamber music
1100	General works
	By period
1102	Through 1750
1104	1751-1900
1106	1901-
	By region or country
	North America
1110-1110.6	General works (Table M3)
1111-1111.9	United States (Table M4)
1113-1113.9	Canada (Table M4)

History and criticism
Instruments and instrumental music
Ensembles
Chamber music
By region or country
North America -- Continued

1114	West Indies. Caribbean Area
	Including individual West Indian islands, countries etc. (not A-Z)
1115-1115.9	Mexico (Table M4)
	Central America
1116-1116.6	General works (Table M3)
	For general works cataloged prior to 2007 see ML1117.A+
1117.A-Z	By region or country, A-Z
	Subdivide each region or country by Table M7 or M8
	Prior to 2007, also used for general works
	South America
1118-1118.6	General works (Table M3)
	Prior to 2007, also used for individual countries of South America (not A-Z)
1119.A-Z	By region or country, A-Z
	Subdivide each region or country by Table M7 or M8
	Europe
1120-1120.6	General works (Table M3)
1122-1122.9	Austria (Table M4)
1126-1126.9	Belgium (Table M4)
1127-1127.9	France (Table M4)
1129-1129.9	Germany (Table M4)
1131-1131.9	Great Britain. England (Table M4)
	For Northern Ireland, Scotland, Wales, see ML1131.7+
1132-1132.9	Ireland (Table M4)
1133-1133.9	Italy (Table M4)
1135-1135.9	Netherlands (Table M4)
1137-1137.9	Russia. Soviet Union. Russia (Federation) (Table M4)
1142	Scandinavia
	Including individual countries (not A-Z)
1147-1147.9	Spain (Table M4)
1148-1148.9	Portugal (Table M4)
1149-1149.9	Switzerland (Table M4)
1151.A-Z	Other regions or countries, A-Z
	Subdivide each region or country by Table M7 or M8
	Class here European and other regions or countries
1151.A7-.A79	Armenia (Table M8)
1151.C95-.C959	Czech Republic (Table M8)

                History and criticism
                  Instruments and instrumental music
                    Ensembles
                      Chamber music
                        By region or country
                          Other regions or countries, A-Z -- Continued

1151.I53-.I539	Indonesia (Table M8)
1151.I75-.I759	Israel (Table M8)
1151.J3-.J39	Japan (Table M8)
1151.S56-.S569	Slovakia (Table M8)
1151.T93-.T939	Turkmenistan (Table M8)
1151.U38-.U389	Ukraine (Table M8)

                      Forms and types

(1154)	General
	see the specific form or type
1156	Sonata
1158	Suite
1160	String quartet
1165	Other (not A-Z)

                    Orchestra
                      For dance orchestra music see ML3518

1200	General works
	By period
1202	Through 1750
1204	1751-1850
1206	1851-1950
1208	1951-

                    By region or country
                      North America

1210-1210.6	General works (Table M3)
1211-1211.9	United States (Table M4)
1213-1213.9	Canada (Table M4)
1214	West Indies. Caribbean Area
	Including individual West Indian countries, etc. (not A-Z)
1215-1215.9	Mexico (Table M4)

                    Central America
                        Prior to 2007, not subdivided between general works and works by region or country

1216.A1-.A6	General works (Table M7)
1216.A7-Z	By region or country, A-Z
	Subdivide each region or country by Table M7 or M8

                    South America

1217-1217.6	General works (Table M3)
	Prior to 2007, also used for individual countries of South America (not A-Z)

	History and criticism
	Instruments and instrumental music
	Ensembles
	Orchestra
	By region or country
	South America -- Continued
1218.A-Z	By region or country, A-Z
	Subdivide each region or country by Table M7 or M8
	Europe
1220-1220.6	General works (Table M3)
1222-1222.9	Austria (Table M4)
1226-1226.9	Belgium (Table M4)
1227-1227.9	France (Table M4)
1229-1229.9	Germany (Table M4)
1231-1231.9	Great Britain. England (Table M4)
	For Northern Ireland, Scotland, Wales, see ML1231.7+
1232-1232.9	Ireland (Table M4)
1233-1233.9	Italy (Table M4)
1235-1235.9	Netherlands (Table M4)
1237-1237.9	Russia. Soviet Union. Russia (Federation) (Table M4)
1242	Scandinavia
	Including individual countries (not A-Z)
1247-1247.9	Spain (Table M4)
1248-1248.9	Portugal (Table M4)
1249-1249.9	Switzerland (Table M4)
1251.A-Z	Other regions or countries, A-Z
	Subdivide individual regions by Table M7
	Subdivide individual countries by Table M8
	Class here European and other regions or countries
(1251.A8)	Asia, Southeastern (General)
	see ML1251.S66+
1251.A83-.A839	Australia (Table M8)
1251.B87-.B879	Burma (Table M8)
1251.C95-.C959	Czech Republic. Czechoslovakia (Table M8)
1251.G8-.G89	Greece (Table M8)
1251.H9-.H99	Hungary (Table M8)
1251.I53-.I539	Indonesia (Table M8)
1251.J35-.J359	Japan (Table M8)
(1251.J4)	Java
	see ML1251.I53+
1251.M4-.M49	Malaysia (Table M8)
1251.M54-.M546	Middle East (Table M7)
1251.N5-.N59	New Zealand (Table M8)
1251.P7-.P79	Poland (Table M8)
1251.S57-.S579	Slovenia (Table M8)

History and criticism
Instruments and instrumental music
Ensembles
Orchestra
By region or country
Other regions or countries, A-Z -- Continued

1251.S66-.S666	Southeast Asia (General) (Table M7)
1251.T3-.T39	Tajikistan (Table M8)
1251.T9-.T99	Turkey (Table M8)
1251.U38-.U389	Ukraine (Table M8)

Forms and types

1255	Symphony
1258	Suite
1261	Overture
1263	Concerto
(1270)	General
	see the specific form or type
1270.A-Z	Other forms and types, A-Z
1270.C68	Courante
1270.S9	Symphonic poem

Band
Including military music
For big band, jazz band, dance band, or dance
orchestra music see ML3518

1299	Periodicals. Societies. Serials
1300	General works

By period

1302	Through 1800
1304	1801-1900
1306	1901-

By region or country
North America

1310-1310.6	General works (Table M3)
1311-1311.9	United States (Table M4)
1313-1313.9	Canada (Table M4)
1314	West Indies. Caribbean Area
	Including individual West Indian islands, countries, etc. (not A-Z)
1315-1315.9	Mexico (Table M4)

Central America
Prior to 2007, not subdivided between general works
and works by region or country

1316.A1-.A6	General works (Table M7)
1316.A7-Z	By region or country, A-Z
	Subdivide each region or country by Table M7 or M8
1316.G8-.G89	Guatemala (Table M8)

History and criticism
  Instruments and instrumental music
    Ensembles
      Band
        By region or country -- Continued
          South America
            Prior to 2007, not subdivided between general works
              and works by region or country

1317.A1-.A6	General works (Table M7)
1317.A7-Z	By region or country, A-Z
	Subdivide each region or country by Table M7 or M8
1317.B7-.B79	Brazil (Table M8)
1317.C6-.C69	Colombia (Table M8)
	Europe
1320-1320.6	General works (Table M3)
1322-1322.9	Austria (Table M4)
1326-1326.9	Belgium (Table M4)
1327-1327.9	France (Table M4)
1329-1329.9	Germany (Table M4)
1331-1331.9	Great Britain. England (Table M4)
	For Northern Ireland, Scotland, Wales, see ML1331.7+
1332-1332.9	Ireland (Table M4)
1333-1333.9	Italy (Table M4)
1335-1335.9	Netherlands (Table M4)
1337-1337.9	Russia. Soviet Union. Russia (Federation) (Table M4)
1342	Scandinavia
	Including individual countries (not A-Z)
1347-1347.9	Spain (Table M4)
1348-1348.9	Portugal (Table M4)
1349-1349.9	Switzerland (Table M4)
1351.A-Z	Other regions or countries, A-Z
	Subdivide each region or country by Table M7 or M8
	Class here European and other regions or countries
1351.B9-.B99	Bulgaria (Table M8)
1351.C5-.C59	China (Table M8)
1351.C92-.C929	Czech Republic (Table M8)
1351.F5-.F59	Finland (Table M8)
1351.G7-.G79	Greece (Table M8)
1351.H9-.H99	Hungary (Table M8)
1351.I7-.I79	Iran (Table M8)
1351.J3-.J39	Japan (Table M8)
1351.N4-.N49	New Zealand (Table M8)
1351.R6-.R69	Romania (Table M8)
1351.T8-.T89	Turkey (Table M8)
1351.U47-.U479	Ukraine (Table M8)

	History and criticism
	Instruments and instrumental music
	Ensembles
	Band -- Continued
1354	Forms and types
	Electronic music. Computer music
	For general works on the use of computers in the field of music see ML74
1379	Periodicals. Societies. Serials
1380	General works
	Vocal music
1400	General works
	By period
1402	Through 1600
1403	1601-1700
1404	1701-1800
1405	1801-1900
1406	1901-
	By region or country
	North America
1410-1410.6	General works (Table M3)
1411-1411.9	United States (Table M4)
1413-1413.9	Canada (Table M4)
1414	West Indies. Caribbean Area
	Including individual West Indian islands, countries, etc. (not A-Z)
1415-1415.9	Mexico (Table M4)
	Central America
	Prior to 2007, not subdivided between general works and works by region or country
1416.A1-.A6	General works (Table M7)
1416.A7-Z	By region or country, A-Z
	Subdivide each region or country by Table M7 or M8
	South America
1417-1417.6	General works (Table M3)
	Prior to 2007, also used for individual countries of South America (not A-Z)
1418.A-Z	By region or country, A-Z
	Subdivide each region or country by Table M7 or M8
	Europe
1420-1420.6	General (Table M3)
1422-1422.9	Austria (Table M4)
1424-1424.9	Czechoslovakia. Czech Republic (Table M4)
1425-1425.9	Hungary (Table M4)
1426-1426.9	Belgium (Table M4)
1427-1427.9	France (Table M4)
1429-1429.9	Germany (Table M4)

	History and criticism
	Vocal music
	By region or country
	Europe -- Continued
1431-1431.9	Great Britain. England (Table M4)
	For Northern Ireland, Scotland, Wales, see ML1431.7+
1432-1432.9	Ireland (Table M4)
1433-1433.9	Italy (Table M4)
1435-1435.9	Netherlands (Table M4)
1437-1437.9	Russia. Soviet Union. Russia (Federation) (Table M4)
1440-1440.9	Poland (Table M4)
1442	Scandinavia
	Including individual countries (not A-Z)
1446-1446.9	Slovakia (Table M4)
1447-1447.9	Spain (Table M4)
1448-1448.9	Portugal (Table M4)
1449-1449.9	Switzerland (Table M4)
1451.A-Z	Other regions or countries, A-Z
	Subdivide each region or country by Table M7 or M8
	Class here European and other regions or countries
1451.A73-.A736	Arab countries (Table M7)
1451.B425-.B4256	Benelux countries (General) (Table M7)
1451.B5-.B59	Bolivia (Table M8)
1451.B9-.B99	Bulgaria (Table M8)
1451.C5-.C59	China (Table M8)
1451.C93-.C939	Cyprus (Table M8)
1451.E75-.E759	Estonia (Table M8)
1451.G8-.G89	Greece (Table M8)
1451.I5-.I59	India (Table M8)
1451.J3-.J39	Japan (Table M8)
1451.K6-.K69	Korea (Table M8)
1451.T5-.T59	Thailand (Table M8)
1451.T95-.T959	Turkmenistan (Table M8)
1460	Vocal technique
	Including history of the teaching of singing
	Choral music
	Including sacred and secular music
1499	Periodicals. Societies. Serials
1500	General works
	By period
1502	Through 1600
1503	1601-1700
1504	1701-1800
1505	1801-1900
1506	1901-
	By region or country
	North America

	History and criticism
	Vocal music
	Choral music
	By region or country
	North America -- Continued
1510-1510.6	General works (Table M3)
1511-1511.9	United States (Table M4)
1513-1513.9	Canada (Table M4)
1514	West Indies. Caribbean Area
	Including individual West Indian islands, countries, etc. (not A-Z)
1515-1515.9	Mexico (Table M4)
	Central America
1516-1516.6	General works (Table M3)
	Prior to 2007, also used for individual countries of Central America (not A-Z)
1517.A-Z	By region or country, A-Z
	Subdivide each region or country by Table M7 or M8
	Prior to 2007, used for South America
	South America
	For works about South America cataloged prior to 2007 see ML1517.A+
1518-1518.6	General works (Table M3)
1519.A-Z	By region or country, A-Z
	Subdivide each region or country by Table M7 or M8
	Europe
1520-1520.6	General works (Table M3)
1522-1522.9	Austria (Table M4)
1526-1526.9	Belgium (Table M4)
1527-1527.9	France (Table M4)
1528-1528.9	Germany (Table M4)
1531-1531.9	Great Britain. England (Table M4)
	For Northern Ireland, Scotland, Wales, see ML1531.7+
1532-1532.9	Ireland (Table M4)
1533-1533.9	Italy (Table M4)
1535-1535.9	Netherlands (Table M4)
1537-1537.9	Russia. Soviet Union. Russia (Federation) (Table M4)
1542	Scandinavia
	Including individual countries (not A-Z)
1547-1547.9	Spain (Table M4)
1548-1548.9	Portugal (Table M4)
1549-1549.9	Switzerland (Table M4)
1551.A-Z	Other regions or countries, A-Z
	For obsolete numbers formerly used under this span see Table MZ17
	Subdivide each region or country by Table M7 or M8
	Class here European and other regions or countries

History and criticism
  Vocal music
    Choral music
      By region or country
        Other regions or countries, A-Z -- Continued

1551.B8-.B89	Bulgaria (Table M8)
1551.C74-.C749	Congo (Democratic Republic). Belgian Congo (Table M8)
1551.C9-.C99	Czech Republic. Czechoslovakia (Table M8)
1551.E8-.E89	Estonia (Table M8)
1551.F5-.F59	Finland (Table M8)
1551.H85-.H859	Hungary (Table M8)
1551.I4-.I49	India (Table M8)
1551.I75-.I759	Israel (Table M8)
1551.L35-.L359	Latvia (Table M8)
1551.L78-.L789	Lithuania (Table M8)
1551.M65-.M659	Montenegro (Table M8)
1551.P64-.P649	Poland (Table M8)
1551.R84-.R849	Romania (Table M8)
1551.S4-.S49	Serbia. Serbia and Montenegro (Table M8)
1551.S52-.S526	Silesia (General) (Table M7)
1551.S55-.S559	Slovakia (Table M8)
1551.S6-.S69	South Africa (Table M8)
1551.T9-.T99	Turkey (Table M8)
1551.U4-.U49	Ukraine (Table M8)
1554	Forms and types

        Class here works about both sacred and secular music
  Secular vocal music

1600	General works
	By period
1602	Through 1600
1603	1601-1700
1604	1701-1800
1605	1801-1900
1606	1901-

    By region or country
      North America

1610-1610.6	General works (Table M3)
1611-1611.9	United States (Table M4)
1613-1613.9	Canada (Table M4)
1614	West Indies. Caribbean Area

        Including individual West Indian islands, countries, etc. (not A-Z)

1615-1615.9	Mexico (Table M4)
	Central America

	History and criticism
	Vocal music
	Secular vocal music
	By region or country
	Central America -- Continued
1616-1616.6	General works (Table M3)
	Prior to 2007, also used for individual countries of Central America (not A-Z)
1617.A-Z	By region or country, A-Z
	Subdivide each region or country by Table M7 or M8
	Prior to 2007, used for South America
	South America
	For works about South America cataloged prior to 2007 see ML1617.A+
1618-1618.6	General works (Table M3)
1619.A-Z	By region or country, A-Z
	Subdivide each region or country by Table M7 or M8
	Europe
1620-1620.6	General works (Table M3)
1622-1622.9	Austria
1626-1626.9	Belgium (Table M4)
1627-1627.9	France (Table M4)
1629-1629.9	Germany (Table M4)
1631-1631.9	Great Britain. England (Table M4)
	For Northern Ireland, Scotland, Wales, see ML1631.7+
1632-1632.9	Ireland (Table M4)
1633-1633.9	Italy (Table M4)
1635-1635.9	Netherlands (Table M4)
1637-1637.9	Russia. Soviet Union. Russia (Federation) (Table M4)
1642	Scandinavia
	Including individual countries (not A-Z)
1647-1647.9	Spain (Table M4)
1648-1648.9	Portugal (Table M4)
1649-1649.9	Switzerland (Table M4)
1651.A-Z	Other regions or countries, A-Z
	Subdivide each region or country by Table M7 or M8
	Class here European and other regions or countries
	Forms and types
	Dramatic music
	Class here works about opera, incidental music, melodrama, etc.
	For works about ballet, pantomime, etc., music see ML3460
1699	Periodicals. Societies. Serials
1700	General works
1700.1	Addresses, essays, lectures
	By period

	History and criticism
	Vocal music
	Secular vocal music
	Forms and types
	Dramatic music
	By period -- Continued
1702	Through 1650
1703	1651-1750
1704	1751-1850
1705	1851-1950
1706	1951-
	By region or country
	North America
1710-1710.6	General works (Table M3)
1711-1711.9	United States (Table M4)
1713-1713.9	Canada (Table M4)
1714	West Indies. Caribbean Area
	Including individual West Indian islands, countries, etc. (not A-Z)
1715-1715.9	Mexico (Table M4)
	Central America
	Prior to 2007, not subdivided between general works and works by region or country
1716.A1-.A6	General works (Table M7)
1716.A7-Z	By region or country, A-Z
	Subdivide each region or country by Table M7 or M8
	South America
	Prior to 2007, individual regions and countries sometimes classifed together with general works
1717.A1-.A6	General works (Table M7)
1717.A7-Z	By region or country, A-Z
	Subdivide each region or country by Table M7 or M8
1717.A7-.A79	Argentina (Table M8)
1717.B6-.B69	Bolivia (Table M8)
1717.B8-.B89	Brazil (Table M8)
1717.C5-.C59	Chile (Table M8)
1717.C6-.C69	Colombia (Table M8)
	Europe
	For obsolete numbers formerly used under this span see Table MZ17
1720-1720.6	General works (Table M3)
1723-1723.9	Austria (Table M4)
1724-1724.9	Czechoslovakia. Czech Republic (Table M4)
1725-1725.9	Hungary (Table M4)
1726-1726.9	Belgium (Table M4)

History and criticism
  Vocal music
    Secular vocal music
      Forms and types
        Dramatic music
          By region or country
            Europe -- Continued
              France (Table M4 modified)
                By period
                  1701-1800

1727.3	General works
1727.33	Guerre des bouffons
	Class sources here
1727.35	Gluck-Piccinni controversy
	Class sources here
1729-1729.9	Germany (Table M4)
1731-1731.9	Great Britain. England (Table M4)
	For Northern Ireland, Scotland, Wales, see
	ML1731.7+
1732-1732.9	Ireland (Table M4)
1733-1733.9	Italy (Table M4)
1735-1735.9	Netherlands (Table M4)
1736-1736.9	Poland (Table M4)
1737-1737.9	Russia. Soviet Union. Russia (Federation) (Table M4)
1738.A-Z	Baltic States
1738.A1-.A16	General works (Table M7)
1738.E8-.E89	Estonia (Table M8)
1738.L4-.L49	Latvia (Table M8)
1738.L5-.L59	Lithuania (Table M8)
1741.A-Z	Other former Soviet republics (Europe), A-Z
	For Asian republics see ML1751.A+
1741.B4-.B49	Belarus (Table M8)
1741.M6-.M69	Moldova (Table M8)
1741.U78-.U789	Ukraine (Table M8)
	Scandinavia
1742-1742.6	General works (Table M3)
1743-1743.9	Denmark (Table M4)
1744-1744.9	Norway (Table M4)
1745-1745.9	Sweden (Table M4)
1746-1746.9	Slovakia (Table M4)
1747-1747.9	Spain (Table M4)
1748-1748.9	Portugal (Table M4)
1749-1749.9	Switzerland (Table M4)

History and criticism
 Vocal music
  Secular vocal music
   Forms and types
    Dramatic music
     By region or country -- Continued

1751.A-Z	Other regions or countries, A-Z
	For obsolete numbers formerly used under this span see Table MZ17
	Subdivide each region or country by Table M7 or M8
	Class here European and other regions or countries
1751.A38-.A389	Albania (Table M8)
1751.A7-.A79	Armenia (Table M8)
1751.A92-.A929	Australia (Table M8)
1751.A98-.A989	Azerbaijan (Table M8)
1751.B8-.B89	Bulgaria (Table M8)
1751.C5-.C59	China (Table M8)
1751.F5-.F59	Finland (Table M8)
1751.G26-.G269	Georgia (Table M8)
1751.G8-.G89	Greece (Table M8)
1751.H85-.H859	Hungary (Table M8)
1751.I5-.I59	India (Table M8)
1751.I75-.I759	Israel (Table M8)
1751.J3-.J39	Japan (Table M8)
1751.K3-.K39	Kazakhstan (Table M8)
1751.K7-.K79	Korea (Table M8)
1751.K8-.K89	Korea (North) (Table M8)
1751.M43-.M439	Malta (Table M8)
1751.M66-.M669	Monaco (Table M8)
1751.N4-.N46	Near East (General) (Table M7)
1751.N5-.N59	New Zealand (Table M8)
1751.R8-.R89	Romania (Table M8)
1751.S29-.S296	Savoy (Table M7)
1751.S4-.S49	Serbia and Montenegro (Table M8)
1751.S5-.S59	Singapore (Table M8)
1751.S71-.S719	South Africa (Table M8)
1751.S72-.S729	Sri Lanka (Table M8)
1751.T25-.T259	Taiwan (Table M8)
1751.U9-.U99	Uzbekistan (Table M8)
1751.V53-.V539	Vietnam (Table M8)
	Forms and types
	For works on a particular form or type in a particular country, see the country
1800	Serious opera
1850	Comic opera
1900	Operetta

History and criticism
　Vocal music
　　Secular vocal music
　　　Forms and types
　　　　Dramatic music
　　　　　Forms and types -- Continued

1950	Other types with spoken dialogue
	Class here general works about individual types, e.g., ballad opera, Singspiel, zarzuela
2000	Incidental music
2050	Melodrama
2054	Musicals. Revues
	Motion picture music
	For works about musical films see PN1995.9.M86
2074	Periodicals. Societies. Serials
2075	General works
2080	Television music
	For works about music videos see PN1992.8.M87
2100	Other (not A-Z)
2110	Libretto
	Including writing, translating, etc., of librettos
2400	Cantata
	Class here works on cantatas in which the chorus predominates
	For works on the solo cantata see ML2800+
	Solo voice(s)
	Class here works covering music for one or more solo voices
	For works entirely on music for two or more solo voices, including part songs see ML2600+
	For works entirely on music for one solo voice see ML2800+
2500	General works
	By period
2502	Through 1600
2503	1601-1700
2504	1701-1800
2505	1801-1900
2506	1901-
	By region or country
	North America
2510-2510.6	General works (Table M3)
2511-2511.9	United States (Table M4)
2513-2513.9	Canada (Table M4)

History and criticism
  Vocal music
    Secular vocal music
      Forms and types
        Solo voice(s)
          By region or country
            North America -- Continued

2514	West Indies. Caribbean Area
	Including individual West Indian islands, countries, etc. (not A-Z)
2515-2515.9	Mexico (Table M4)
	Central America
	Prior to 2007, not subdivided between general works and works by region or country
2516.A1-.A6	General works (Table M7)
2516.A7-Z	By region or country, A-Z
	Subdivide each region or country by Table M7 or M8
	South America
	Prior to 2007, not subdivided between general works and works by region or country
2517.A1-.A6	General works (Table M7)
2517.A7-Z	By region or country, A-Z
	Subdivide each region or country by Table M7 or Table M8
	Europe
2520-2520.6	General works (Table M3)
2522-2522.9	Austria (Table M4)
2526-2526.9	Belgium (Table M4)
2527-2527.9	France (Table M4)
2529-2529.9	Germany (Table M4)
2531-2531.9	Great Britain. England (Table M4)
	For Northern Ireland, Scotland, Wales, see ML2531.7+
2532-2532.9	Ireland (Table M4)
2533-2533.9	Italy (Table M4)
2535-2535.9	Netherlands (Table M4)
2537-2537.9	Russia. Soviet Union. Russia (Federation) (Table M4)
2542	Scandinavia
	Including individual countries (not A-Z)
2547-2547.9	Spain (Table M4)
2548-2548.9	Portugal (Table M4)
2549-2549.9	Switzerland (Table M4)

ML

History and criticism
Vocal music
Secular vocal music
Forms and types
Solo voice(s)
By region or country -- Continued

2551.A-Z	Other regions or countries, A-Z

For obsolete numbers formerly used under this span
see Table MZ17
Subdivide each region or country by Table M7 or M8
Class here European and other regions or countries

2551.C5-.C59	China (Table M8)
2551.H9-.H99	Hungary (Table M8)
2551.I5-.I59	India (Table M8)
2551.J36-.J369	Japan (Table M8)
2551.K67-.K679	Korea (Table M8)
2551.P6-.P69	Poland (Table M8)
2551.S67-.S679	Sri Lanka (Table M8)
2551.S73-.S739	Sudan (Table M8)
2551.T37-.T379	Tanzania (Table M8)
2551.U38-.U389	Ukraine (Table M8)

Two or more solo voices
Including part songs

2600	General works

By period

2602	Through 1600
2603	1601-1700
2604	1701-1800
2605	1801-1900
2606	1901-

By region or country
North America

2610-2610.6	General works (Table M3)
2611-2611.9	United States (Table M4)
2613-2613.9	Canada (Table M4)
2614	West Indies. Caribbean Area

Including individual West Indian islands,
countries, etc. (not A-Z)

2615-2615.9	Mexico (Table M4)

Central America

2616-2616.6	General works (Table M3)

Prior to 2007, also used for individual countries
of Central America (not A-Z)

2617.A-Z	By region or country, A-Z (Table M3)

Subdivide each region or country by Table M7 or
M8
Prior to 2007, used for South America

	History and criticism
	Vocal music
	Secular vocal music
	Forms and types
	Solo voice(s)
	Two or more solo voices
	By region or country -- Continued
	South America
	For works about South American cataloged prior to 2007 see ML2617.A+
2618-2618.6	General works (Table M3)
2619.A-Z	By region or country, A-Z
	Subdivide each region or country by Table M7 or M8
	Europe
2620-2520.6	General works (Table M3)
2622-2622.9	Austria (Table M4)
2626-2626.9	Belgium (Table M4)
2627-2627.9	France (Table M4)
2629-2629.9	Germany (Table M4)
2631-2631.9	Great Britain. England (Table M4)
	For Northern Ireland, Scotland, Wales, see ML2631.7+
2632-2632.9	Ireland (Table M4)
2633-2633.9	Italy (Table M4)
2635-2635.9	Netherlands (Table M4)
2637-2637.9	Russia. Soviet Union. Russia (Federation) (Table M4)
2642	Scandinavia
	Including individual countries (not A-Z)
2647-2647.9	Spain (Table M4)
2648-2648.9	Portugal (Table M4)
2649-2649.9	Switzerland (Table M4)
2651.A-Z	Other regions or countries, A-Z
	Subdivide each region or country by Table M7 or M8
	Class here European and other regions or countries
	Forms and types
(2654)	General
	see the specific form or type
2660	Men's voices
2665	Treble voices
2670	Glees, catches, etc.
	One solo voice
	Class here works about lied, chanson, romance, solo cantata, ballad, aria, etc.

	History and criticism
	Vocal music
	Secular vocal music
	Forms and types
	Solo voice(s)
	One solo voice -- Continued
2800	General works
	By period
2802	Through 1600
2803	1601-1750
2804	1751-1800
2805	1801-1850
2806	1851-1900
2807	1901-
	By region or country
	North America
2810-2810.6	General works (Table M3)
2811-2811.9	United States (Table M4)
2813-2813.9	Canada (Table M4)
2814	West Indies. Caribbean Areea
	Including individual West Indian islands, countries, etc. (not A-Z)
2815-2815.9	Mexico (Table M4)
	Central America
	Prior to 2007, not subdivided between general works and works by region or country
2816.A1-.A6	General works (Table M7)
2816.A7-Z	By region or country, A-Z
	Subdivide each region or country by Table M7 or M8
	South America
	Prior to 2007, individual regions and countries sometimes classifed together with general works
2817.A1-.A6	General works (Table M7)
2817.A7-Z	By region or country, A-Z
	Subdivide each region or country by Table M7 or M8
2817.B65-.B659	Bolivia (Table M8)
2817.B7-.B79	Brazil (Table M8)
	Europe
2820-2820.6	General works (Table M3)
2822-2822.9	Austria (Table M4)
2826-2826.9	Belgium (Table M4)
2827-2827.9	France (Table M4)
2829-2829.9	Germany (Table M4)

History and criticism
　　Vocal music
　　　Secular vocal music
　　　　Forms and types
　　　　　Solo voice(s)
　　　　　　One solo voice
　　　　　　　By region or country
　　　　　　　　Europe -- Continued

2831-2831.9	Great Britain. England (Table M4)
	For Northern Ireland, Scotland, Wales, see ML2831.7+
2832-2832.9	Ireland (Table M4)
2833-2833.9	Italy (Table M4)
2835-2835.9	Netherlands (Table M4)
2837-2837.9	Russia. Soviet Union. Russia (Federation) (Table M4)
2842	Scandinavia
	Including individual countries (not A-Z)
2847-2847.9	Spain (Table M4)
2848-2848.9	Portugal (Table M4)
2849-2849.9	Switzerland (Table M4)
2851.A-Z	Other regions or countries, A-Z
	For obsolete numbers formerly used under this span see Table MZ17
	Subdivide each region or country by Table M7 or M8
	Class here European and other regions or countries
2851.A8-.A89	Australia (Table M8)
2851.C6-.C69	China (Table M8)
2851.E3-.E39	Egypt (Table M8)
2851.I5-.I59	Indonesia (Table M8)
2851.J36-.J369	Japan (Table M8)
2851.K67-.K679	Korea. South Korea (Table M8)
2851.K68-.K689	Korea (North) (Table M8)
2851.P6-.P69	Poland (Table M8)
2851.R6-.R69	Romania (Table M8)
2851.S47-.S479	Serbia. Serbia and Montenegro (Table M8)
	South Africa see ML2851.U45+
2851.U45-.U459	Union of South Africa. South Africa (Table M8)
2851.V5-.V59	Vietnam (Table M8)
2854	Forms and types
(2860)	Art ballad
	see ML2854
(2862)	Other
	see ML2854
2870	Minstrel music

	History and criticism
	Vocal music
	Secular vocal music
	Forms and types -- Continued
	Christmas carols
2880	General works
2881.A-Z	By region or country, A-Z

For obsolete numbers formerly used under this span
see Table MZ17

Subdivide each region or country by Table M7 or M8

2881.A9-.A99	Austria (Table M8)
2881.C2-.C29	Canada (Table M8)
2881.E3-.E36	Europe, Eastern (Table M7)
2881.E5-.E59	England (Table M8)
2881.F4-.F49	France (Table M8)
2881.G3-.G39	Germany (Table M8)
2881.G74-.G749	Greece (Table M8)
2881.P7-.P79	Poland (Table M8)
2881.R6-.R69	Romania (Table M8)
2881.S4-.S49	Serbia. Serbia and Montenegro (Table M8)
2881.U6-.U69	United States (Table M8)
	Sacred vocal music

Class here works about musical compositions
For religious aspects of music see ML3921+

2900	General works
	By period
2902	Through 1600
2903	1601-1700
2904	1701-1800
2905	1801-1900
2906	1901-
	By region or country
	North America
2910-2910.6	General works (Table M3)
2911-2911.9	United States (Table M4)
2913-2913.9	Canada (Table M4)
2914	West Indies. Caribbean Area

Including individual West Indian islands, countries, etc.
(not A-Z)

2915-2915.9	Mexico (Table M4)
	Central America
2916-2916.6	General works (Table M3)

Prior to 2007, also used for individual countries of
Central America (not A-Z)

2917.A-Z	By region or country, A-Z

Subdivide each region or country by Table M7 or M8
Prior to 2007, used for South America

	History and criticism
	Vocal music
	Sacred vocal music
	By region or country -- Continued
	South America
	For works about South America cataloged prior to 2007 see ML2917.A+
2918-2918.6	General works (Table M3)
2919.A-Z	By region or country, A-Z
	Subdivide each region or country by Table M7 or M8
	Europe
2920-2920.6	General works (Table M3)
2922-2922.9	Austria (Table M4)
2926-2926.9	Belgium (Table M4)
2927-2927.9	France (Table M4)
2929-2929.9	Germany (Table M4)
2931-2931.9	Great Britain. England (Table M4)
2932-2932.9	Ireland (Table M4)
2933-2933.9	Italy (Table M4)
2935-3935.9	Netherlands (Table M4)
2937-2937.9	Russia. Soviet Union. Russia (Federation) (Table M4)
2942	Scandinavia
	Including individual countries (not A-Z)
2947-2947.9	Spain (Table M4)
2948-2948.9	Portugal (Table M4)
2949-2949.9	Switzerland (Table M4)
2951.A-Z	Other regions or countries, A-Z
	Subdivide each region or country by Table M7 or M8
	Class here European and other regions or countries
2951.A33-.A336	Africa (General) (Table M7)
2951.C64-.C649	China (Table M8)
2951.C9-.C99	Czech Republic. Czechoslovakia (Table M8)
2951.E3-.E39	Ethiopia (Table M8)
2951.H8-.H89	Hungary (Table M8)
2951.K45-.K459	Kenya (Table M8)
2951.M43-.M436	Mediterranean Region (Table M7)
2951.P6-.P69	Poland (Table M8)
2951.R6-.R69	Romania (Table M8)
2951.S53-.S536	Silesia (General) (Table M7)
2951.S95-.S959	Syria (Table M8)
2951.T3-.T39	Tanzania (Table M8)
2951.U3-.U39	Ukraine (Table M8)
	By religion or denomination
2999	Periodicals. Societies. Serials
	Christian
3000	General works

	History and criticism
	Vocal music
	Sacred vocal music
	By religion or denomination
	Christian -- Continued
3001	Music in the church
	Cf. BV290 Theology
	Catholic
	Roman Catholic
3002	General works
	By period
3003	Through 1600
3004	1601-1700
3005	1701-1800
3006	1801-1900
3007	1901-
	By region or country
	North America
3010-3010.6	General works (Table M3)
3011-3011.9	United States (Table M4)
3013-3013.9	Canada (Table M4)
3014	West Indies. Caribbean Area
	Including individual West Indian islands, countries, etc. (not A-Z)
3015-3015.9	Mexico (Table M4)
	Central America
	Prior to 2007, not subdivided between general works and works by region or country
3016.A1-.A6	General works (Table M7)
3016.A7-Z	By region or country, A-Z
	Subdivide each region or country by Table M7 or M8
	South America
	Prior to 2007, individual regions and countries sometimes classifed together with general works
3017.A1-.A6	General works (Table M7)
3017.A7-Z	By region or country, A-Z
	Subdivide each region or country by Table M7 or M8
3017.B7-.B79	Brazil (Table M8)
3017.C5-.C59	Chile (Table M8)
3017.E2-.E29	Ecuador (Table M8)
3017.P47-.P479	Peru (Table M8)
	Europe
3020-3020.6	General works (Table M3)
3022-3022.9	Austria (Table M4)

History and criticism
 Vocal music
  Sacred vocal music
   By religion or denomination
    Christian
     Catholic
      Roman Catholic
       By region or country
        Europe -- Continued

3026-3026.9	Belgium (Table M4)
3027-3027.9	France (Table M4)
3029-3029.9	Germany (Table M4)
3031-3031.9	Great Britain. England (Table M4)
	For Northern Ireland, Scotland, Wales, see ML3031.7+
3032-3032.9	Ireland (Table M4)
3033-3033.9	Italy (Table M4)
3036-3036.9	Netherlands (Table M4)
3037-3037.9	Russia. Soviet Union. Russia (Federation) (Table M4)
3042	Scandinavia
	Including individual countries (not A-Z)
3047-3047.9	Spain (Table M4)
3048-3048.9	Portugal (Table M4)
3049-3049.9	Switzerland (Table M4)
3051.A-Z	Other regions or countries, A-Z
	For obsolete numbers formerly used under this span see Table MZ17
	Subdivide each region or country by Table M7 or M8
	Class here European and other regions or countries
3051.B65-.B659	Bosnia and Hercegovina (Table M8)
3051.C74-.C749	Congo (Democratic Republic). Zaire (Table M8)
3051.C9-.C99	Czech Republic. Czechoslovakia (Table M8)
3051.E34-.E349	Egypt (Table M8)
3051.E352-.E3526	Europe, Eastern (General) (Table M7)
3051.F5-.F59	Finland (Table M8)
3051.G4-.G49	Ghana (Table M8)
3051.H9-.H99	Hungary (Table M8)
3051.I4-.I49	India (Table M8)
3051.J3-.J39	Japan (Table M8)
3051.L36-.L366	Lapland (Table M7)
3051.L89-.L899	Luxembourg (Table M8)
3051.M33-.M339	Macedonia (Table M8)
3051.M43-.M439	Malta (Table M8)

History and criticism
  Vocal music
    Sacred vocal music
      By religion or denomination
        Christian
          Protestant
            By region or country -- Continued
              Central America
                Prior to 2007, not subdivided between general works and works by region or country

3116.A1-.A6	General works (Table M7)
3116.A7-Z	By region or country, A-Z
	Subdivide each region or country by Table M7 or M8

              South America
                Prior to 2007, individual regions and countries sometimes classifed together with general works

3117.A1-.A6	General works (Table M7)
3117.A7-Z	By region or country, A-Z
	Subdivide each region or country by Table M7 or M8
3117.B7	Brazil (Table M8)

              Europe

3120-3120.6	General works (Table M3)
3122-3122.9	Austria (Table M4)
3126-3126.9	Belgium (Table M4)
3127-3127.9	France (Table M4)
3129-3129.9	Germany (Table M4)
3131-3131.9	Great Britain. England (Table M4)
	For Northern Ireland, Scotland, Wales, see ML3131.7+
3132-3132.9	Ireland (Table M4)
3133-3133.9	Italy (Table M4)
3135-3135.9	Netherlands (Table M4)
3137-3137.9	Finland (Table M4)
3142	Scandinavia
	Including individual countries (not A-Z)
3147-3147.9	Spain (Table M4)
3148-3148.9	Portugal (Table M4)
3149-3149.9	Switzerland (Table M4)
3151.A-Z	Other regions or countries, A-Z
	Subdivide each region or country by Table M7 or M8
	Class here European and other regions or countries
3151.H9-.H99	Hungary (Table M8)

History and criticism
  Vocal music
    Sacred vocal music
      By religion or denomination
       Christian
        Protestant
         By region or country
          Other regions or countries, A-Z -- Continued

3151.K6-.K69	Korea. South Korea (Table M8)
3151.T26-.T269	Taiwan (Table M8)
	By denomination
3160	Baptist
	Christian Reformed Church see ML3164
3161	Church of the Brethren
	Cf. ML3178.B7 Brethren churches
(3161.5)	Church of Christ, Scientist. Christian Science see ML3178.C55
	Church of Jesus Christ of Latter-day Saints see ML3174
3162	Congregational
3164	Dutch and other Reformed. Christian Reformed Church
3166	Anglican Communion
3167	Evangelical and Reformed Church
(3167.5)	Society of Friends (Quakers) see ML3178.F7
3168	Lutheran
3169	Mennonite
3170	Methodist
3172	Moravian
3174	Mormon. Church of Jesus Christ of Latter-day Saints
3176	Presbyterian
3178.A-Z	Other, A-Z
(3178.A76)	Armenian Church see ML3190
3178.B7	Brethren churches
	Cf. ML3161 Church of the Brethren
3178.C55	Christian Science
3178.F7	Society of Friends (Quakers)
(3178.M4)	Mennonite Church see ML3169
3178.N4	Church of the Nazarene
3178.P4	Pentecostal churches
	Quakers see ML3178.F7
3178.S39	Schwenkfelders
3178.S5	Shakers

History and criticism
  Vocal music
    Sacred vocal music
      By religion or denomination
        Christian
          Protestant
            By denomination
              Other, A-Z -- Continued

3178.S9	Svenska missionsförbundet
3178.U46	United Church of Christ

            Forms and types

(3180)	General
	see the specific form or type
3182	Liturgy and ritual
3184	Chorale
3186	Psalmody, hymnology, etc.
	For works about texts or the origin and meaning of
	hymns, see BV

            Gospel music

3186.8	Periodicals. Societies. Serials
3187	General works
3187.5	Contemporary Christian music
	Including Christian rock music
3188	Other (not A-Z)
3190	Other Christian denominations
3195	Jewish
3197	Other religions (not A-Z)
	Including Islamic

      Forms and types

(3200)	General
	see the specific form or type

        Oratorio

3201	General works

          By period

3203	Through 1600
3204	1601-1700
3205	1701-1800
3206	1801-1900
3207	1901-

          By region or country
            North America

3210-3210.6	General works (Table M3)
3211-3211.9	United States (Table M4)
3213-3213.9	Canada (Table M4)
3214	West Indies. Caribbean Area
	Including individual West Indian islands, countries,
	etc. (not A-Z)

ML

History and criticism
  Vocal music
    Sacred vocal music
      Forms and types
        Oratorio
          By region or country
            North America -- Continued

3215-3215.9	Mexico (Table M4)
	Central America
3216-3216.6	General works (Table M3)
	Prior to 2007, also used for individual countries of Central America (not A-Z)
3217.A-Z	By region or country, A-Z
	Subdivide each region or country by Table M7 or M8
	Prior to 2007, used for South America
	South America
	For works about South America cataloged prior to 2007 see ML3217.A+
3218-3218.6	General works (Table M3)
3219.A-Z	By region or country, A-Z
	Subdivide each region or country by Table M7 or M8
	Europe
3220-3220.6	General works (Table M3)
3222-3222.9	Austria (Table M4)
3226-3226.9	Belgium (Table M4)
3227-3227.9	France (Table M4)
3229-3229.9	Germany (Table M4)
3231-3231.9	Great Britain. England (Table M4)
	For Northern Ireland, Scotland, Wales, see ML3231.7+
3232-3232.9	Ireland (Table M4)
3233-3233.9	Italy (Table M4)
3235-3235.9	Netherlands (Table M4)
3237-3237.9	Russia. Soviet Union. Russia (Federation) (Table M4)
3242	Scandinavia
	Including individual countries (not A-Z)
3247-3247.9	Spain (Table M4)
3248-3248.9	Portugal (Table M4)
3249-3249.9	Switzerland (Table M4)
3251.A-Z	Other regions or countries, A-Z
	Subdivide each region or country by Table M7 or M8
	Class here European and other regions or countries
3251.P6-.P69	Poland (Table M8)

History and criticism
Vocal music
Sacred vocal music
Forms and types -- Continued

3260	Other choral forms generally in several movements
	Including cantatas
3265	Chorales
	Class here works not treated from a denominational standpoint
3270	Psalmody. Hymns and hymn singing
	Class here works not written from a denominational standpoint
3275	Other (not A-Z)

Program music

3300	General works

By period

3302	Through 1800
3303	1801-1900
3304	1901-

By region or country
North America

3310-3310.6	General works (Table M3)
3311-3311.9	United States (Table M4)
3313-3313.9	Canada (Table M4)
3314	West Indies. Caribbean Area
	Including individual West Indian islands, countries (not A-Z)
3315-3315.9	Mexico (Table M4)

Central America

3316-3316.6	General works (Table M3)
	Prior to 2007, also used for individual countries of Central America (not A-Z)
3317.A-Z	By region or country, A-Z
	Subdivide each region or country by Table M7 or M8
	Prior to 2007, used for South America

South America
For works about South American classified prior to 2007 see ML3317.A+

3318-3318.6	General works (Table M3)
3319.A-Z	By region or country, A-Z
	Subdivide each region or country by Table M7 or M8

Europe

3320-3320.6	General works (Table M3)
3322-3322.9	Austria (Table M4)
3326-3326.9	Belgium (Table M4)
3327-3327.9	France (Table M4)
3329-3329.9	Germany (Table M4)

	History and criticism
	Program music
	By region or country
	Europe -- Continued
3331-3331.9	Great Britain. England (Table M4)
	For Northern Ireland, Scotland, Wales, see ML3331.7+
3332-3332.9	Ireland (Table M4)
3333-3333.9	Italy (Table M4)
3335-3335.9	Netherlands (Table M4)
3337-3337.9	Russia. Soviet Union. Russia (Federation) (Table M4)
3342	Scandinavia
	Including individual countries (not A-Z)
3347-3347.9	Spain (Table M4)
3348-3348.9	Portugal (Table M4)
3349-3349.9	Switzerland (Table M4)
3351.A-Z	Other regions or countries, A-Z
	Subdivide each region or country by Table M7 or M8
	Class here European and other regions or countries
3351.I75-.I759	Israel (Table M8)
(3354.A-Z)	Forms and types. By form or type, A-Z
	Dance music
	For history of dancing see GV1580+
3400	General works
	By period
3402	Through 1600
3403	1601-1700
3404	1701-1800
3405	1801-1900
3406	1901-
	By region or country
	North America
3410-3410.6	General works (Table M3)
3411-3411.9	United States (Table M4)
3413-3413.9	Canada (Table M4)
3414	West Indies. Caribbean Area
	Including individual West Indian islands, countries, etc. (not A-Z)
3415-3415.9	Mexico (Table M4)
	Central America
	Prior to 2007, not subdivided between general works and works by region or country
3416.A1-.A6	General works (Table M7)
3416.A7-Z	By region or country, A-Z
	Subdivide each region or country by Table M7 or M8
	South America
	Prior to 2007, not subdivided between general works and works by region or country

	History and criticism
	Dance music
	By region or country
	South America -- Continued
3417.A1-.A6	General works (Table M7)
3417.A7-Z	By region or country, A-Z
	Subdivide each region or country by Table M7 or M8
	Europe
3420-3420.6	General works (Table M3)
3422-3422.9	Austria (Table M4)
3426-3426.9	Belgium (Table M4)
3427-3427.9	France (Table M4)
3429-3429.9	Germany (Table M4)
3431-3431.9	Great Britain. England (Table M4)
	For Northern Ireland, Scotland, Wales, see ML3431.7+
3433-3433.9	Italy (Table M4)
3435-3435.9	Netherlands (Table M4)
3437-3437.9	Russia. Soviet Union. Russia (Federation) (Table M4)
3442	Scandinavia
	Including individual countries (not A-Z)
3447-3447.9	Spain (Table M4)
	Including works about Portugal cataloged before 1975
3448-3448.9	Portugal (Table M4)
3449-3449.9	Switzerland (Table M4)
3451.A-Z	Other regions or countries, A-Z
	Subdivide each region or country by Table M7 or M8
	Class here European and other regions or countries
3451.G8-.G89	Greece (Table M8)
3451.H9-.H99	Hungary (Table M8)
3451.I4-.I49	India (Table M8)
3451.I5-.I59	Indonesia (Table M8)
	Forms and types
(3454)	General
	see ML3460+
3460	Ballet, pantomime, etc.
3465	Other (not A-Z)
	Class here works about polka, waltz, two-step, etc.
	Popular music
	For works on music videos see PN1992.8.M87
3469	Periodicals. Societies. Serials
3470	General works
	By region or country
	Class here general works on popular music in a particular region or country
	For works about a particular kind or style of popular music, e.g., jazz, rock music see ML3505.8+

	History and criticism
	Popular music
	By region or country -- Continued
	America
	Including Latin America
3475	General works
	North America
3476	General works
	United States
3476.8	Periodicals. Societies. Serials
3477	General works
3477.1	Addresses, essays, lectures
3477.7.A-Z	By region or state, A-Z (Table M1)
3477.8.A-Z	By city, A-Z
	African American music
3478	Periodicals. Societies. Serials
3479	General works
3481	Hispanic American music
3484-3484.8	Canada (Table M9)
3485-3485.8	Mexico (Table M9)
3486	West Indies. Carribean Area
3486.A1	General works
3486.A2-Z	By West Indian island or country, etc., A-Z
3486.B35-.B358	Barbados (Table M10)
3486.C82-.C828	Cuba (Table M10)
3486.C87-.C878	Curaçao (Table M10)
3486.D65-.D658	Dominican Republic (Table M10)
3486.G8-.G88	Guadeloupe (Table M10)
3486.H3-.H38	Haiti (Table M10)
3486.J3-.J38	Jamaica (Table M10)
3486.P8-.P88	Puerto Rico (Table M10)
3486.S25-.S258	Saint Martin (Table M10)
3486.T7-.T78	Trinidad (Table M10)
3487.A-Z	Central and South America
3487.A1	General works
3487.A7-3847.Z	By region or country, A-Z
	Subdivide each country by Table M10
3487.A7-.A78	Argentina (Table M10)
3487.B5-.B58	Bolivia (Table M10)
3487.B7-.B78	Brazil (Table M10)
3487.C55-.C558	Chile (Table M10)
3487.C7-.C78	Colombia (Table M10)
3487.C8-.C88	Costa Rica (Table M10)
3487.E2-.E28	Ecuador (Table M10)
3487.G9-.G98	Guatemala (Table M10)
3487.N5-.N58	Nicaragua (Table M10)
3487.P37-.P378	Paraguay (Table M10)

History and criticism
  Popular music
    By region or country
      America
        Central and South America
          By region or country, A-Z -- Continued

3487.P4-.P48	Peru (Table M10)
3487.U8-.U88	Uruguay (Table M10)
3487.V4-.V48	Venezuela (Table M10)
3488-3499	Europe

          For obsolete numbers formerly used under this span see
            Table MZ18

3488	General works
3489-3489.8	France (Table M9)
3490-3490.8	Germany (Table M9)
3492-3492.8	Great Britain. England (Table M9)

          For Northern Ireland, Scotland, Wales, see ML3492.7+

3493-3493.8	Ireland (Table M9)
3494-3494.8	Italy (Table M9)
3495-3495.8	Netherlands (Table M9)
3496-3496.8	Poland (Table M9)
3497-3497.8	Russia. Soviet Union. Russia (Federation) (Table M9)
3498-3498.8	Spain (Table M9)
3499.A-Z	Other regions or countries, A-Z

          For obsolete numbers formerly used under this span see
            Table MZ18
          Subdivide each country by Table M10

3499.A9-.A98	Austria (Table M10)
3499.B38-.B388	Belarus (Table M10)
3499.B4-.B48	Belgium (Table M10)
3499.B8-.B88	Bulgaria (Table M10)
3499.C9-.C98	Czech Republic. Czechoslovakia (Table M10)
3499.D4-.D48	Denmark (Table M10)
3499.E75-.E758	Estonia (Table M10)
3499.F5-.F58	Finland (Table M10)
3499.F6	Flanders
3499.G8-.G88	Greece (Table M10)
3499.H85-.H858	Hungary (Table M10)
3499.M33-.M338	Macedonia (Table M10)
3499.N7-.N78	Norway (Table M10)
3499.P8-.P88	Portugal (Table M10)
3499.R6-.R68	Romania (Table M10)
3499.S42-.S428	Serbia. Serbia and Montenegro (Table M10)
3499.S48-.S488	Slovakia (Table M10)
3499.S5-.S58	Slovenia (Table M10)
3499.S91-.S918	Sweden (Table M10)
3499.S92-.S928	Switzerland (Table M10)

	History and criticism
	Popular music
	By region or country -- Continued
	Asia
3500	General works
	For obsolete use of this number see Table MZ21
	Prior to 1993, used for pageants, folk festivals, and community music
3501-3501.8	Japan (Table M9)
3502.A-Z	Other regions or countries, A-Z
	For obsolete numbers formerly used under this span see Table MZ18
	Subdivide each country by Table M10
3502.A75	Asia, East (General)
3502.A785	Asia, Southeastern (General)
3502.C5-.C58	China (Table M10)
	East Asia (General) see ML3502.A75
3502.I4-.I48	India (Table M10)
3502.I5-.I58	Indonesia (Table M10)
3502.I75-.I758	Israel (Table M10)
3502.K6-.K68	Korea (South) (Table M10)
3502.K7-.K78	Korea (Table M10)
3502.M4-.M48	Malaysia (Table M10)
3502.P26-.P268	Papua New Guinea (Table M10)
3502.P5-.P58	Philippines (Table M10)
	Southeast Asia (General) see ML3502.A785
3502.T26-.T268	Taiwan (Table M10)
3502.T5-.T58	Thailand (Table M10)
3502.T9-.T98	Turkey (Table M10)
3502.V5-.V58	Vietnam (Table M10)
	Africa
3502.5	General works
3503.A-Z	By region or country, A-Z
	For obsolete numbers formerly used under this span see Table MZ18
	Subdivide each country by Table M10
3503.A4-.A48	Algeria (Table M10)
3503.A5-.A58	Angola (Table M10)
3503.C66-.C668	Congo (Brazzaville) (Table M10)
3503.C68-.C688	Congo (Democratic Republic). Zaire (Table M10)
3503.G4-.G48	Ghana (Table M10)
3503.K46-.K468	Kenya (Table M10)
3503.N6-.N68	Nigeria (Table M10)
3503.S6-.S68	South Africa (Table M10)
3503.T34-.T348	Tanzania (Table M10)
	Zaire see ML3503.C68+
3503.Z55-.Z558	Zimbabwe (Table M10)

	History and criticism
	Popular music
	By region or country -- Continued
3504-3504.8	Australia (Table M9)
3505.A-Z	Other regions or countries, A-Z
	Subdivide each country by Table M10
3505.N45-.N458	New Zealand (Table M10)
3505.P16	Pacific Area (General)
	Types and styles
	Jazz
3505.8	Periodicals. Societies. Serials
3505.9	Congresses
3506	General works
3507	Addresses, essays, lectures
	By region or country
3508-3508.8	United States (Table M9)
3509.A-Z	Other regions or countries, A-Z
	For obsolete numbers formerly used under this span see Table MZ18
	Subdivide each country by Table M10
3509.A7-.A78	Argentina (Table M10)
3509.A9-.A98	Austria (Table M10)
3509.B42-.B428	Belgium (Table M10)
3509.B46-.B468	Bermuda (Table M10)
3509.B7-.B78	Brazil (Table M10)
3509.C2-.C28	Canada (Table M10)
3509.C76-.C768	Croatia (Table M10)
3509.C88-.C888	Cuba (Table M10)
3509.C9-.C98	Czech Republic. Czechoslovakia (Table M10)
3509.D45-.D458	Denmark (Table M10)
3509.E5-.E58	England (Table M10)
	For Great Britain see ML3509.G7
3509.E9	Europe (General)
3509.F5-.F58	Finland (Table M10)
3509.F7-.F78	France (Table M10)
3509.G3-.G38	Germany (Table M10)
3509.G7	Great Britain (General)
	For England see ML3509.E5+
3509.I5-.I58	Indonesia (Table M10)
3509.I82-.I828	Israel (Table M10)
3509.I85-.I858	Italy (Table M10)
3509.J3-.J38	Japan (Table M10)
3509.M47	Mediterranean Region
3509.M6-.M68	Mexico (Table M10)
3509.N4-.N48	Netherlands (Table M10)
3509.N6-.N68	Nigeria (Table M10)
3509.N8-.N88	Norway (Table M10)

History and criticism
　Popular music
　　Types and styles
　　　Jazz
　　　　By region or country
　　　　　Other regions or countries, A-Z -- Continued

3509.P7-.P78	Poland (Table M10)
3509.P84-.P848	Portugal (Table M10)
3509.R8-.R88	Russia. Soviet Union. Russia (Federation) (Table M10)
3509.S34	Scandinavian countries (General)
3509.S6-.S68	South Africa (Table M10)
3509.S8-.S88	Sweden (Table M10)
3509.S9-.S98	Switzerland (Table M10)
3509.T97-.T978	Turkey (Table M10)
3509.V4-.V48	Venezuela (Table M10)
3516	Barbershop quartets. Barbershop choruses
3518	Big band music. Jazz band music. Dance band music. Dance orchestra music
	Bluegrass music
3519	Periodicals. Societies. Serials
3520	General works
	Blues. Rhythm and blues
	Including traditional blues
3520.8	Periodicals. Societies. Serials
3521	General works
3522	Celtic music
	Country music
	Including country rock music
3523	Periodicals. Societies. Serials
3524	General works
3526	Disco music
3527	Doo-wop
3527.8	Funk
3527.84	Go-go music
3528	Honky-tonk music
3528.5	House music
3528.7	Industrial music
3528.8	Klezmer music
3529	New Age music
3529.5	Novelty songs
3530	Ragtime music
3531	Rap music
3532	Reggae music
3532.5	Reggaetón music

History and criticism
  Popular music
    Types and styles -- Continued
      Rock music
           Including specific types of rock music, e.g. punk rock,
              heavy metal
           For works on Christian rock music see ML3187.5
           For works on country rock music see ML3523+
           For works on doo-wop see ML3527
           For works on rockabilly music see ML3535
           For works on rock music videos see PN1992.8.M87

3533.8	Periodicals. Societies. Serials
3534	General works
	By region or country
3534.3	United States
3534.6.A-Z	Other regions or countries, A-Z
	e.g.
3534.6.A7	Argentina
3534.6.B6	Brazil
3534.6.B8	Bulgaria
3534.6.C2	Canada
3534.6.C45	China
3534.6.D65	Dominican Republic
3534.6.F8	France
3534.6.G3	Germany
3534.6.G7	Great Britain
3534.6.H8	Hungary
3534.6.I74	Ireland
3534.6.I8	Italy
3534.6.L29	Latin America
3534.6.M6	Mexico
3534.6.N4	Netherlands
3534.6.P4	Peru
3534.6.P7	Poland
3534.6.S7	Spain
3534.6.T9	Turkey
3534.6.U6	Ukraine
3534.6.U8	Uruguay
3535	Rockabilly music
3535.5	Salsa
3536	Skiffle
3537	Soul music
3539	Swamp pop
3540	Techno music
3540.5	Underground dance music
3540.7	Video game music
3541	Western swing music

History and criticism
  Popular music
    Types and styles -- Continued

(3543)   Pageants, folk festivals, community music, etc.
         For individual festivals see ML35+
         For social and political aspects see ML3916+
         For community music see MT87
         For administration see MT88
         For production see MT955
    Folk, national, and ethnic music
      Class here works about folk, national, ethnic, patriotic, political
        music, etc.
      For collections of national music with critical or historical
        commentary see M1627+
      For popular music see ML3469+

3544   Periodicals. Societies. Serials
3544.5   Festivals. Congresses
      Prior to 1993, works about folk festivals were classified in
        ML3500
      For individual festivals see ML35+
      For social and political aspects see ML3916+
      For community music see MT87
      For administration see MT88
      For production see MT955

3545   General works
(3547)   Primitive (General), including ethnomusicology
      For specific places see the place
      For ethnomusicology see ML3797.6+
    By region or country
      America
3549-3549.6   General works (Table M3)
        Including Latin America
      North America
3550-3550.6   General works (Table M3)
        United States
3551-3551.9   General works (Table M4)
(3552)   Archive of American Folksong, Library of Congress
        By ethnic group
3553   British American
3554   Irish American
3555   German American. Scandinavian American.
           Dutch American

History and criticism
  Folk, national, and ethnic music
    By region or country
      America
        North America
          United States
            By ethnic group -- Continued

3556	African American
	Including spirituals
	For African American gospel music see ML3186.8+
	For general works on African American popular music see ML3478+
	For types and styles of African American popular music, e.g., jazz, soul music see ML3505.8+
	For blues, traditional or popular see ML3520.8+
3557	Indian nations and tribes
3558	Latin American
	Including Creole
(3559)	Other racial
	see the ethnic group
3560.A-Z	Other ethnic groups, A-Z
3560.C25	Cajun
3560.C5	Chinese American
3560.E8	Eskimo
	Filipino American see ML3560.P4
3560.H25	Haitian American
3560.H3	Hawaiian
3560.H5	Hmong American
3560.H8	Hungarian American
3560.P4	Philippine American. Filipino American
3560.P64	Polish American
3560.S9	Swedish American
3560.V5	Vietnamese American
3560.Y84	Yugoslav American
3561.A-Z	Songs. By topic or title, A-Z
	e.g.
3561.S8	Star-spangled banner
3561.W3	War songs
3562	Other topics (not A-Z)
3563-3563.9	Canada (Table M4)
3565	West Indies. Caribbean Area
	Including individual West Indian island, countries, etc. (not A-Z)
3570-3570.9	Mexico (Table M4)

History and criticism
Folk, national, and ethnic music
By region or country
America -- Continued
Central America

3571-3571.6	General (Table M3)
3572.A-Z	By region or country, A-Z
	Subdivide each region or country by Table M7 or M8
3572.C6-.C69	Costa Rica (Table M8)
3572.G9-.G99	Guatemala (Table M8)
3572.N5-.N59	Nicaragua (Table M8)
3572.P35-.P359	Panama (Table M8)

South America

3575.A1-.A3	General works (Table M7)
3575.A4-Z	By region or country, A-Z
	For obsolete numbers formerly used under this span see Table MZ18
	Subdivide each region or country by Table M7 or M8
3575.A475-.A4756	Andes Region (Table M7)
3575.A7-.A79	Argentina (Table M8)
3575.B6-.B69	Bolivia (Table M8)
3575.B7-.B79	Brazil (Table M8)
3575.C5-.C59	Chile (Table M8)
3575.C7-.C79	Colombia (Table M8)
	Dutch Guiana see ML3575.S97+
3575.E2-.E29	Ecuador (Table M8)
3575.F9-.F99	French Guiana (Table M8)
3575.P3-.P39	Paraguay (Table M8)
3575.P4-.P49	Peru (Table M8)
3575.S97-.S979	Suriname. Dutch Guiana (Table M8)
3575.U78-.U789	Uruguay (Table M8)
3575.V3-.V39	Venezuela (Table M8)

Europe

	For obsolete numbers formerly used under this span see Table MZ18
3580-3580.6	General works (Table M3)
3586-3586.9	Austria (Table M4)
3590-3590.9	Czechoslovakia. Czech Republic (Table M4)
3591-3591.9	Slovakia (Table M4)
3593-3593.9	Hungary (Table M4)
	Including Romanies in Hungary

Balkan Peninsula

3600-3600.6	General works (Table M3)
3601-3601.9	Albania (Table M4)
3602-3602.9	Bulgaria (Table M4)
3604-3604.9	Greece (Table M4)
3606-3606.9	Montenegro (Table M4)

	History and criticism
	Folk, national, and ethnic music
	By region or country
	Europe
	Balkan Peninsula -- Continued
	For Serbia and Montenegro see ML3611.S47+
3608-3608.9	Romania (Table M4)
3610-3610.9	Yugoslavia (Table M4)
3611.A-Z	Other Balkan regions or countries, A-Z
	Subdivide each region or country by Table M7 or M8
3611.B54-.B549	Bosnia and Hercegovina (Table M8)
3611.C76-.C769	Croatia (Table M8)
3611.I745-.I7459	Istria (Table M8)
3611.M3-.M39	Macedonia (Republic) (Table M8)
3611.S47-.S479	Serbia and Montenegro (Table M8)
	For Montenegro see ML3606+
3611.S62-.S629	Slovenia (Table M8)
	Belgium
	Including Netherlands to about 1600
3615-3615.9	General works (Table M4)
3616.A-Z	Songs. By topic or title, A-Z
3617	Other topics (not A-Z)
3619	Finland (Table M4)
	France
3620-3620.9	General works (Table M4)
3621.A-Z	Songs. By topic or title, A-Z
	e.g.
3621.C65	Commune, 1871
3621.M37	Marseillaise
3621.P76	Protest songs
3621.R48	Revolution, 1789-1793
3621.W37	War songs
3622	Other topics (not A-Z)
(3628)	Marseillaise
	see ML3621.M37
	Germany
	For obsolete numbers formerly used under this span see Table MZ18
3630-3630.9	General works (Table M4)
3645.A-Z	Songs. By topic or title, A-Z
3645.D4	Deutschland, Deutschland über alles
3645.E4	Eifersüchtige Knabe
3645.F73	Franco-Prussian War, 1870-1871
3645.H47	Herders
3645.L54	Lili Marleen
3645.N36	Napoleon I, Emperor of the French, 1769-1821
3645.O3	O Deutschland hoch in Ehren

History and criticism
  Folk, national, and ethnic music
    By region or country
      Europe
        Germany
          Songs. By topic or title, A-Z -- Continued

3645.S63	Soccer
3645.S78	Students' songs
3645.Y6	Yodels. Yodeling
3646	Other topics (not A-Z)
	Great Britain. Ireland
3650-3650.6	General works (Table M3)
3652-3652.9	England (Table M4)
3653-3653.9	Wales (Table M4)
3654-3654.9	Ireland. Northern Ireland (Table M4)
3655-3655.9	Scotland (Table M4)
3656.A-Z	Songs. By topic or title, A-Z
	e.g.
3656.G6	God save the King
	Other topics (not A-Z)
(3658)	God Save the King
	see ML3656.G6
	Italy
3660-3660.9	General works (Table M4)
3661.A-Z	Songs. By topic or title, A-Z
3662	Other topics (not A-Z)
	Netherlands
	For Netherlands to about 1600 see ML3615+
3670-3670.9	General works (Table M4)
3671.A-Z	Songs. By topic or title, A-Z
3672	Other topics (not A-Z)
3677-3688.9	Poland (Table M4)
3680-3680.9	Russia. Soviet Union. Russia (Federation) (Table M4)
	For former Soviet republics in Asia see ML3740+
3681.A-Z	Baltic States, A-Z
	For obsolete numbers formerly used under this span see Table MZ18
3681.A1-.A16	General works (Table M7)
3681.E8-.E89	Estonia (Table M8)
3681.L4-.L49	Latvia (Table M8)
3681.L6-.L69	Lithuania (Table M8)
3684-3684.9	Belarus (Table M4)
3689-3689.9	Moldova (Table M4)
3690-3690.9	Ukraine (Table M4)
(3693.A-Z)	Other regions and countries (Russia), A-Z
	For obsolete numbers formerly used under this span see Table MZ18

History and criticism
  Folk, national, and ethnic music
    By region or country
      Europe
        Other regions and countries (Russia), A-Z -- Continued

(3695.A-Z)	Songs. By topic or title, A-Z
	For obsolete numbers formerly used under this span
	see Table MZ19
	Scandinavia
3700-3700.6	General works (Table M3)
3702-3702.9	Denmark (Table M4)
3704-3704.9	Norway (Table M4)
3706-3706.9	Sweden (Table M4)
3708	Other
	Spain
3710-3710.9	General works (Table M4)
3712	Flamenco. Cante hondo
3713.A-Z	Songs. By topic or title, A-Z
3714	Other topics (not A-Z)
	Portugal
3717-3717.9	General works (Table M4)
3718.A-Z	Songs. By topic or title, A-Z
3719	Other topics (not A-Z)
	Switzerland
3720-3720.9	General works (Table M4)
3721	Yodels. Yodeling
3722.A-Z	Songs. By topic or title, A-Z
	e.g.
3722.N54	Nikolaus, von der Flüe, Saint, 1417-1487
3723	Other topics (not A-Z)
3730.A-Z	Other European regions or countries, A-Z
	For obsolete numbers formerly used under this span see
	Table MZ18
	Subdivide each region or country by Table M7 or M8
	Asia
3740-3740.6	General works (Table M3)
	By region or country
3742-3742.9	Saudi Arabia (Table M4)
3744-3744.9	Armenia (Table M4)
3746-3746.9	China (Table M4)
3747-3747.9	Taiwan (Table M4)
3748-3748.9	India (Table M4)
3750-3750.9	Japan (Table M4)
3752-3752.9	Korea (Table M4)
	Including South Korea
3753-3753.9	Korea (North) (Table M4)
3754-3754.9	Israel. Palestine (Table M4)

History and criticism
  Folk, national, and ethnic music
    By region or country
      Asia
        By region or country -- Continued

3756-3756.9	Iran (Table M4)
3757-3757.9	Turkey (Table M4)
3758.A-Z	Other Asian regions or countries, A-Z

           For obsolete numbers formerly used under this span
              see Table MZ18
           Subdivide each region or country by Table M7 or M8

3758.A3-.A39	Afghanistan (Table M8)
3758.A75-.A759	Armenia (Table M8)
3758.A783-.A7836	Asia, Central (Table M7)
3758.A98-.A989	Azerbaijan (Table M8)
3758.B3-.B39	Bangladesh (Table M8)
3758.B78-.B789	Brunei (Table M8)
3758.B87-.B879	Burma (Table M8)
3758.C16-.C169	Cambodia (Table M8)
3758.C9-.C99	Cyprus (Table M8)
3758.G28-.G289	Georgia (Table M8)
3758.I52-.I529	Indochina (Table M8)
3758.I53-.I539	Indonesia (Table M8)
3758.I7-.I79	Iraq (Table M8)
3758.K4-.K49	Kazakhstan (Table M8)
3758.K87-.K876	Kurdistan (Table M7)
3758.K92-.K929	Kuwait (Table M8)
3758.K98-.K989	Kyrgyzstan (Table M8)
3758.M42-.M429	Malaysia (Table M8)
3758.M45-.M459	Mauritius (Table M8)
3758.M6-.M69	Mongolia (Table M8)
3758.N35-.N359	Nepal (Table M8)
3758.O45-.O459	Oman (Table M8)
3758.P32-.P329	Pakistan (Table M8)
3758.P36-.P369	Papua New Guinea (Table M8)
3758.P5-.P59	Philippines (Table M8)
3758.Q2-.Q29	Qatar (Table M8)
3758.R4-.R49	Réunion (Table M8)
3758.S7-.S79	Sri Lanka (Table M8)
3758.T33-.T339	Tajikistan (Table M8)
3758.T5-.T59	Thailand (Table M8)
3758.T9-.T99	Turkmenistan (Table M8)
3758.U9-.U99	Uzbekistan (Table M8)
3758.V5-.V59	Vietnam (Table M8)
3758.Y4-.Y49	Yemen (Table M8)
3760-3760.6	Africa (Table M3)

	History and criticism
	Folk, national, and ethnic music
	By region or country -- Continued
3770	Australia (Table M4)
	Prior to 2007, also used for Oceania, etc.
	For Oceania and other regions or countries not elsewhere provided for see ML3774+
3771-3771.9	New Zealand (Table M4)
	Oceania. Other
3774-3774.6	General (Table M3)
3775.A-Z	By region, country, island group, or island, A-Z
	For obsolete numbers formerly used under this span see Table MZ18
	Subdivide each region, country, island group, or island by Table M7 or M8
3775.C66-.C669	Cook Islands (Table M8)
3775.S35-.S359	Samoa (Table M8)
3775.S65-.S659	Solomon Islands (Table M8)
3775.S65-.S659	Solomon Islands (Table M8)
3775.T65-.T659	Tonga (Table M8)
3775.T75-.T759	Tristan da Cunha (Table M8)
3776	Music of the Jews
	Class here works about secular music of the Jews in all countries
	For ancient music see ML166
	For sacred vocal music see ML3195
3780	Music on particular topics
	Class here works on labor songs, sea songs, etc.
3785	Musical journalism
	Music trade
	Including the sound recording industry
	For collective biographies of manufacturers of instruments see ML404
	For collective biographies of music publishers, printers, dealers see ML405
	For biographies of individual manufacturers of instruments see ML424.A+
	For biographies of individual music publishers, printers, dealers see ML427.A+
3790	General works
3792.A-Z	Individual record companies and labels, A-Z
3795	Music as a profession. Vocational guidance
	Including social and economic conditions of musicians
	For works about social aspects of music see ML3916+
	Musical research
	Including methods of research
	Musicology

ML

	Musical research
	Musicology -- Continued
3797	General works
3797.1	Addresses, essays, lectures
3797.2.A-Z	By region or country, A-Z
	Ethnomusicology
3797.6	Periodicals. Societies. Serials
3797.7	Congresses
3798	General works
3799	Addresses, essays, lectures
3799.5	Music archaeology
	Philosophical and societal aspects of music. Physics and acoustics of music. Physiological aspects of music
	Including metaphysics and origin of music
3800	General works
	Physics and acoustics
3805	General works
3807	Physical characteristics of musical sound
3809	Intervals, temperament, etc.
3811	Tonality, atonality, polytonality, etc.
3812	Scales
	Including church modes, etc.
3813	Rhythm
3815	Harmony
3817	Other (not A-Z)
	Physiological aspects of music
3820	General works
(3822)	Special
	Hand (Piano) see MT221
	Hand (Violin) see MT261
	Voice see MT821
	Psychology
	For moral influence of music see ML3919+
3830	General works
3832	Rhythm
3834	Melody
3836	Harmony
3838	Other (not A-Z)
3840	Music and color
	Aesthetics
3845	General works
3847	The beautiful in music
3849	Relations between music and other arts
	For radio, television, etc., and music see ML68
	For literary authors and music see ML79+
	For music and musical instruments in art see ML85
	For influence of music on literature see PN56.M87

Philosophical and societal aspects of music. Physics and
acoustics of music. Physiological aspects of music
Aesthetics -- Continued

3850	Rhythm
3851	Melody
3852	Harmony
3853	Interpretation
3854	Absolute music
3855	Program music
	Dramatic music
3857	General works
3858	Opera, ballet, opera-ballet, etc.
3860	Incidental music
3861	Melodrama
3862	Other
	Sacred music
3865	General works
3867	Oratorio
3869	Church music
3871	Other (not A-Z)
	Secular vocal music (non-dramatic)
3872	General works
3873	Choral music
3875	Song forms
	Including lied, ballad, etc.
3876	Electronic music. Computer music
3877	Other (not A-Z)
	Criticism
3880	General works
3890	The musical canon
	Class here works on that group of compositions generally accepted as superior and lasting
	For works on the canon as a musical form see ML446
3915	Methodology and practice of criticism
(3915.6.A-Z)	Newspaper clippings. By person or topic, etc., A-Z
	Social and political aspects of music
	For social and economic conditions of musicians see ML3795
3916	General works
3917.A-Z	By region or country, A-Z
	e.g.,
3917.B6	Brazil
3917.F5	Finland
3917.F8	France
3917.G3	Germany
3917.I4	India
3917.R6	Romania

Philosophical and societal aspects of music. Physics and
acoustics of music. Physiological aspects of music
Social and political aspects of music
By region or country, A-Z -- Continued

3917.R8	Russia. Soviet Union. Russia (Federation)
(3917.S65)	Soviet Union
	see ML3917.R8
3917.U6	United States
3918.A-Z	Forms and types, A-Z
3918.B57	Blues
3918.D37	Darkwave (Music)
3918.F65	Folk music
3918.F86	Funk
3918.G68	Gothic rock music
3918.J39	Jazz
3918.K36	Karaoke
3918.M85	Musical theater
3918.M87	Musicals. Revues
3918.O64	Opera
3918.P67	Popular music
3918.R37	Rap music
3918.R44	Reggae music
	Revues see ML3918.M87
3918.R63	Rock music
3918.S26	Salsa
3918.S74	Street music
3918.T43	Techno music
3918.U53	Underground dance music
	Moral influence of music. Therapeutic use of music
	Including influence on animals
	For music in special education see MT17
3919	Periodicals. Societies. Serials
3920	General works
	Religious aspects of music
	Class here works on music in general or on secular music
	For works on sacred vocal music see ML2900+
3921	General works
	Individual religions and denominations
	Christianity
3921.2	General works
3921.4.A-Z	By denomination, A-Z
3921.4.C38	Catholic Church
3921.4.S48	Seventh-Day Adventists
3921.6.A-Z	Other religions, A-Z
3921.6.H56	Hinduism
3921.6.I85	Islam
3921.6.J83	Judaism

	Philosophical and societal aspects of music. Physics and acoustics of music. Physiological aspects of music
	Religious aspects of music -- Continued
3921.8.A-Z	Forms and types, A-Z
3921.8.B68	Blues
3921.8.F65	Folk music
3921.8.J39	Jazz
3921.8.P67	Popular music
3921.8.R36	Rap music
3921.8.R63	Rock music
3922	Music in the workplace
(3923)	Music and physical education
	see GV364.3
(3925)	Fiction
	see subclasses PA-PZ
	Literature for children
	For music theory and instruction in musical performance for children see subclass MT
3928	History and criticism
	Class here general works
	Class works on particular topics with adult works on the topic, e. g., ML459+ Instruments and instrumental music
	Biography
3929	Collective
3930.A-Z	Individual, A-Z
	Including works on individual performance groups
	e. g.
3930.B39	Beatles
3930.C4	Chaĭkovskiĭ, Petr Il'ich, 1840-1893
	Tchaikovsky, Peter Ilich, 1840-1893 see ML3930.C4
3930.W2	Wagner, Richard, 1813-1883

ML

	Instruction and study
1	General works
	Including history and theory of music education
	Class here general music instruction for educational levels through high school
	For music instruction in colleges and universities see MT18
(2)	History
	For general works see MT1
	For individual regions or countries see MT3.A+
	For individual institutions see MT4+
2.5	Music study abroad
	Class here music study outside of the United States
	For collective biography of Americans who studied abroad see ML385+
	For individual biography of Americans who studied abroad see ML410+
	For vocational guidance see ML3795
	History
	Class here history by place or institutuion
	For general history of music education see MT1
3.A-Z	By region or country, A-Z
	Individual institutions
4.A-Z	United States. By city, A-Z
	Subarrange by institution
	Subarrange individual institutions by Table M20
5.A-Z	Other countries. By city, A-Z
	Subarrange by institution
	Subarrange individual institutions by Table M20
	Music theory
	Including instruction on how to analyze musical works
	For general music instruction for educational levels through high school see MT1
	For dictation and ear training see MT35
	For elements and techniques of music see MT40+
	For sight-singing and solfeggio see MT875
5.5	Through 1600
	Including manuscripts, published editions, and commentaries on such works from any period
	1601-
	Including manuscripts and commentaries
6	General works
(6.A1)	History
	see MT6
(6.A2)	Works published through 1800
	For early works through 1600 see MT5.5
	For 1601- see MT6

	Music theory
	1601- -- Continued
(6.5)	Collections of music for analysis and appreciation
	see MT91
7	Rudiments. Elementary works
	Including basic music theory for children
	Class rudiments combined with instruction for a specific
	instrument with the instrument
	For specific aspects of theory for children, e. g.,
	harmony see MT155
	Printed pedagogical aids
	For audio-visual aids see MT150
9	Examinations, exercises, etc.
10	Teachers' and supervisors' manuals, etc.
15	Charts, diagrams, etc.
(16)	Uncataloged pamphlets, charts, clippings, etc., and other
	miscellaneous matter
17	Music in special education
	For music therapy see ML3920
18	Music in colleges and universities
	Systems and methods
	Class here general instruction in music
	For individual instruments see the instrument, e. g., Violin, MT262
	For several instruments treated together see MT172
	For singing and vocal technique see MT825+
20	Galin-Paris-Chevé
22.A2-Z	Jaques-Dalcroze
	Literature
	Collections
22.A2-.A64	By Jaques-Dalcroze and others
22.A65-.A69	By Jaques-Dalcroze
22.A7-.A74	Separate works
	Musical compositions for use in the method
22.A75	By Jaques-Dalcroze
22.A8	By others
22.A85-Z	Works about the method
23	Kodály
24	Logier
26	Orff
30	Tonic sol-fa
32	Other (not A-Z)
33	Correspondence school, etc. methods
34	Club and study group courses
	Notation
35	General works
	Including dictation, ear-training, music copying, and manuscript
	preparation

MT

Composition. Elements and techniques of music
    Forms and genres
        Other, A-Z -- Continued

64.V63   Vocal music
                Class here general works
                For works on specific types of vocal music see the type, e.
                    g. MT64.S6 , Song

64.W3   Waltz
67   Popular music
                Class here works about composition, writing of song texts,
                  etc.
                Including commercials

68   Improvisation. Accompaniment. Transposition
                Class here general works on improvisation and improvisation on
                  instruments for which there is no more specific class
                For organ accompaniment of Gregorian chant and other
                  liturgical music see MT190
                For organ improvisation see MT191.I5
                For piano accompaniment see MT236
                For piano accompaniment and improvisation of popular
                  music see MT239
                For piano accompaniment of hymns see MT240.H9
                For vocal improvisation see MT866

        Instrumentation and orchestration
            Including vocal and choral arranging
            Orchestra

70   General works
70.5   Vocal and choral arranging
71   Separate orchestral choirs
                Class here works about string sections, wind sections, etc.

73   Band
73.5   Jazz band, dance band, etc.
74   Plucked instrument orchestras
75   Interpretation
                Class here works about phrasing, dynamics, articulation, and
                  other performance techniques

80   Embellishment
                 For ornamentation for piano see MT240.O7

82   Memorizing
85   Conducting. Score reading and playing
(86)   Jazz band, dance band, etc., instruction, including conducting,
            organization, and management
                For organization and management see ML3795
                For conducting see MT85
                For instruction in ensemble performance see MT733.7

87   Community music

88	Administration and instruction of vocal groups
	Including music in worship services
	Analysis and appreciation of music
	Class here works consisting primarily of analysis of musical compositions
	For works about the music of individual composers that are 20% or more biographical or historical in content see ML410+
90	General works
91	Collections of music for analysis and appreciation
92.A-Z	Individual composers. By composer, A-Z
	Class here analytical works more general than MT100, MT115, etc.
	Dramatic music
	Including synopses
95	Two or more composers
100.A-Z	One composer. By composer, A-Z
	Including pasticcios
	e.g.
	Wagner, Richard, 1813-1883
100.W2	General works
100.W21	Early operas
	Including Der fliegende Holländer
100.W22	Tannhäuser
100.W23	Lohengrin
100.W24	Tristan und Isolde
	Ring des Nibelungen
100.W25	Complete
100.W26	Rheingold
100.W27	Walküre
100.W28	Siegfried
100.W29	Götterdämmerung
100.W3	Meistersinger
100.W31	Parsifal
	Choral music
	Including oratorios, cantatas, etc.
110	Two or more composers
115.A-Z	One composer. By composer, A-Z
	Solo voice(s)
	Including songs, part songs, etc.
120	Two or more composers
121.A-M121.Z	One composer. By composer, A-Z
	Orchestral music
125	Two or more composers
130.A-Z	One composer. By composer, A-Z
	Band music
135	Two or more composers

	Analysis and appreciation of music
	Band music -- Continued
136.A-Z	One composer. By composer, A-Z
	Chamber and solo instrumental music
140	Two or more composers
145.A-Z	One composer. By composer, A-Z
	e.g.
	Beethoven, Ludwig van, 1770-1827
145.B4	Chamber music (General)
145.B42	Piano sonatas
145.B422	Sonatas for violin and piano
145.B425	String quartets
145.B426	Other string ensembles
145.B428	Vocal music
146	Popular music
	Class here general works and works about individual types
150	Audio-visual aids
155	Music theory for children
	Class here specific aspects of theory, e. g., harmony, composition
	For rudiments of music see MT7
165	Tuning
	Class here general works and works on particular instruments or groups of instruments
	Instrumental techniques
	For instrumental techniques for children see MT740+
170	General works
172	Methods for several instruments in one work
	Keyboard instruments
179	General works
	Organ
180	General works
182	Systems and methods
	Studies and exercises
	Class here pedagogical works
	For concert works titled Studies see M11+
185	General works
	Specific techniques
187	Pedal
189	Registration
190	Accompaniment of Gregorian chant and other liturgical music
191.A-Z	Other, A-Z
191.A3	Accompaniment
(191.A8)	Arranging
	see MT180
191.C5	Chorale preludes
	Class here playing and improvisation

	Instrumental techniques
	Keyboard instruments
	Organ
	Studies and exercises
	Specific techniques
	Other, A-Z -- Continued
191.H4	Harmony
191.I5	Improvisation
	For improvisation of chorale preludes see MT191.C5
191.M6	Modulation
(191.P7)	Preluding
	For playing and improvisation of chorale preludes see MT191.C5
	For general improvisation see MT191.I5
191.T7	Trio playing
192-192.8	Electronic keyboard instruments (Table M5)
	Including synthesizers with keyboards
193	Teaching pieces
	Class here works composed principally for pedagogical purposes
	Instructive editions
	Class here works heavily annotated with textual instructions for practice and interpretation
195	Two or more composers
197	One composer
198	Self-instructors
	Reed organ
200	General works
202	Systems and methods
205	Studies and exercises
208	Self-instructors
(210-219)	Other kinds of organ
	For electronic keyboard instruments see MT192+
	Piano
	Including predecessors of the piano, variant keyboards, and practice instruments
220	General works
221	Physiology of the hand
	Including hand exercises
222	Systems and methods
224	Rudiments of music
	Class here rudiments of music combined with piano instruction
	Studies and exercises
	Class here pedagogical works
	For concert works titled Studies see M21+

MT

Instrumental techniques
Keyboard instruments
Piano -- Continued
Instructive editions
Class here works heavily annotated with textual instructions
for practice and interpretation
245 Two or more composers
247 One composer
248 Self-instructors
(249.A-Z) Instructive courses, anthologies, etc., in several volumes.
By editor or title, A-Z
see MT222
Specific types of instrument
Including early instruments
250 General works
252 Predecessors of the piano
Including harpsichord, clavichord, etc.
255 Variant keyboards
Class here Janko, double keyboard, etc.
257.A-Z Other, A-Z
257.A3 Aeolian
257.D6 Dolceola
257.P3 Pianoette
257.T7 Toy piano
258 Practice instruments
Including Virgil clavier, technicon, etc.
Stringed instruments. Bowed stringed instruments
Class here general works on instruments with strings that are
bowed, hammered, or plucked, as well as works limited to
bowed stringed instruments
For stringed instruments with keyboard see MT179+
For plucked instruments see MT539+
259 General works
Violin
260 General works
261 Physiology of the hand
For hand exercises see MT221
262 Systems and methods
Studies and exercises
Including accompanied works
265 General works
266 Orchestral excerpts
Specific techniques
267 Bowing
268 Positions
269 Chords
270 Harmonics

MT

Instrumental techniques
  Stringed instruments. Bowed stringed instruments
    Viola -- Continued
      Instructive editions
        Class here works heavily annotated with textual instructions
          for practice and interpretation

295	Two or more composers
297	One composer
298	Self-instructors
	Violoncello
300	General works
302	Systems and methods
	Studies and exercises
	Including accompanied works
305	General works
306	Orchestral excerpts
	Specific techniques
307	Bowing
308	Positions
309	Chords
310	Other (not A-Z)
312	Two violoncellos
314	Teaching pieces

        Class here works composed principally for pedagogical
          purposes
      Instructive editions
        Class here works heavily annotated with textual instructions
          for practice and interpretation

315	Two or more composers
317	One composer
318	Self-instructors
	Double bass
320	General works
322	Systems and methods
330	Studies and exercises
	Including accompanied works
331	Orchestral excerpts
333	Teaching pieces

        Class here works composed principally for pedagogical
          purposes

333.4	Instructive editions

        Class here works heavily annotated with textual instructions
          for practice and interpretation

333.6	Two double basses
334	Self-instructors
335.A-Z	Other. By instrument, A-Z

      For early Western stringed instruments see MT336+

	Instrumental techniques
	Stringed instruments. Bowed stringed instruments
	Other. By instrument, A-Z -- Continued
	Ban hu see MT335.P3
335.C36	Campanula
335.C5	Ching hu. Jing hu
335.C56	Chui ch'in. Zhui qin
335.C58	Chung hu. Zhong hu
	Da tong see MT335.T3
335.E7	Er hu
	Gao hu see MT335.K32
335.G45	Ghichak
335.G8	Gŭdulka
335.H36	Haegŭm
335.H4	Hardanger fiddle
(335.H8)	Hu qin. Jing hu
	see MT335.E7
335.H83	Hu hu
	Jing hu see MT335.C5
335.J68	Jouhikko
335.K32	Kao hu. Gao hu
335.M67	Morin khuur
335.P3	Pan hu. Ban hu
335.S7	Sǫ ū
335.T3	Ta t'ung. Da tong
	Zhong hu see MT335.C58
	Zhui qin see MT335.C56
	Early stringed instruments
336	Viola d'amore
337	Viola da gamba
338	Other (not A-Z)
	Wind instruments
339	General works
339.5	Woodwind instruments (General)
	Flute
340	General works
342	Systems and methods
343	Teaching pieces
	Class here works composed principally for pedagogical purposes
344	Instructive editions
	Class here works heavily annotated with textual instructions for practice and interpretation
345	Studies and exercises
	Including accompanied works
346	Orchestral excerpts
347	Two flutes

	Instrumental techniques
	Wind instruments
	Flute -- Continued
348	Self-instructors
	Other instruments of the flute family
	Recorder
350	General works
351	Systems and methods
352	Studies and exercises
352.5	Teaching pieces
352.6	Instructive editions
352.7	Two recorders
353	Self-instructors
356	Fife
	For fife and drum see MT735
357-357.8	Piccolo (Table M5)
358.A-Z	Other. By instrument, A-Z
358.A8	Atenteben
358.B36	Bānsurī
(358.C68)	Courting flute
	see MT358.N38
358.C9	Csakan
	Di zi see MT358.T5
358.F58	Flaviol
358.G3	Galoubet
(358.H7)	Hsiao
	see MT358.X53
358.M4	Melody flute
358.N38	Native American flute
358.N4	Nāy
	Ocarina see MT526
358.O7	Orkon
358.P45	Penny whistle
358.P5	Piccolet
358.P6	Pipe
358.Q4	Quena
358.S36	Sáo
358.S4	Saxoflute
358.S52	Shakuhachi
358.S55	Shinobue
358.S6	Siku
358.S9	Suifūkin
358.T3	Tanso
358.T5	Ti tzu. Di zi
358.T6	Tonette
358.X53	Xiao
359	Flageolet

MT

Instrumental techniques
Wind instruments
Bassoon -- Continued
403 Teaching pieces
Class here works composed principally for pedagogical
purposes
404 Instructive editions
Class here works heavily annotated with textual instructions
for practice and interpretation
405 Studies and exercises
Including accompanied works
406 Orchestral excerpts
407 Two bassoons
408 Self-instructors
Other instruments of the bassoon family
412 Contrabassoon
415 Sarrusophone
418 Brass instruments (General)
Horn
420 General works
422 Systems and methods
423 Teaching pieces
Class here works composed principally for pedagogical
purposes
424 Instructive editions
Class here works heavily annotated with textual instructions
for practice and interpretation
425 Studies and exercises
Including accompanied works
426 Orchestral excerpts
427 Two horns
428 Self-instructors
Other instruments of the horn family
432 Alphorn
Trumpet. Keyed trumpet. Cornet
440 General works
442 Systems and methods
443 Teaching pieces
Class here works composed principally for pedagogical
purposes
444 Instructive editions
Class here works heavily annotated with textual instructions
for practice and interpretation
445 Studies and exercises
Including accompanied works
446 Orchestral excerpts
447 Two instruments

MT

	Instrumental techniques
	Wind instruments
	Saxophone -- Continued
503	Teaching pieces
	Class here works composed principally for pedagogical purposes
504	Instructive editions
	Class here works heavily annotated with textual instructions for practice and interpretation
505	Studies and exercises
	Including accompanied works
506	Orchestral excerpts
507	Two saxophones
508	Self-instructors
510	Other instruments of the saxophone family
520	Early wind instruments (not A-Z)
526	Ocarina
530	Bagpipe and similar instruments
533.A-Z	Other. By instrument, A-Z
	Cf. MT520 Early Western instruments
533.D53	Didjeridu
533.K36	Kazoo
(533.M4)	Melodica
	see MT686.M4
533.P3	Panpipes. Syrinx
(533.S95)	Syrinx
	see MT533.P3
(537)	Ensemble studies for wind and other instruments
	see MT728+
(538)	Tablatures for wind instruments (General)
	see instructional works for specific instruments
	Plucked instruments
539	General works
	Harp
540	General works
542	Systems and methods
543	Teaching pieces
	Class here works composed principally for pedagogical purposes
544	Instructive editions
	Class here works heavily annotated with textual instructions for practice and interpretation
545	Studies and exercises
	Including accompanied works
546	Orchestral excerpts
547	Two harps
548	Self-instructors

	Instrumental techniques
	Plucked instruments
	Harp -- Continued
	Other instruments of the harp family
552	Celtic harp
555	Kong hou
557	Piano-harp and similar instruments
	Banjo
560	General works
562	Systems and methods
563	Teaching pieces
	Class here works composed principally for pedagogical purposes
564	Rudiments of music
	Class here rudiments of music combined with banjo instruction
565	Studies and exercises
	Including accompanied works
567	Two banjos
568	Self-instructors
569	Instructive editions
	Class here works heavily annotated with textual instructions for practice and interpretation
570	Other instruments of the banjo family (not A-Z)
	For banjo ukulele see MT646
(579)	Cello banjo
	see MT570
	Guitar
580	General works
582	Systems and methods
583	Teaching pieces
	Class here works composed principally for pedagogical purposes
584	Rudiments of music
	Class here rudiments of music combined with guitar instruction
585	Studies and exercises
	Including accompanied works
586	Orchestral excerpts
587	Two guitars
588	Self-instructors
589	Instructive editions
	Class here works heavily annotated with textual instructions for practice and interpretation
	Other instruments of the guitar family
590-590.8	Hawaiian guitar (Table M5)
592-592.8	Bandurria (Table M5)

MT

	Instrumental techniques
	Plucked instruments
	Guitar
	Other instruments of the guitar family -- Continued
594	Bandolon
599.A-Z	Other. By instrument, A-Z
599.B35	Bajo sexto
599.B4	Bass guitar
599.C45	Charango
(599.C52)	Cittern
	see MT654.C58
599.D6	Dobro
	Electric bass guitar see MT599.B4
599.E4	Electric guitar
599.G85	Guitarrón
599.T74	Tres
	Mandolin
600	General works
602	Systems and methods
603	Teaching pieces
	Class here works composed principally for pedagogical
	purposes
604	Rudiments of music
	Class here rudiments of music combined with mandolin
	instruction
605	Studies and exercises
	Including accompanied works
606	Orchestral excerpts
607	Two mandolins
608	Self-instructors
608.5	Instructive editions
	Class here works heavily annotated with textual instructions
	for practice and interpretation
	Other instruments of the mandolin family
610	General works
611	Mandola
612	Mandoloncello
	Zither
620	General works
622	Systems and methods
623	Teaching pieces
	Class here works composed principally for pedagogical
	purposes
624	Rudiments of music
	Class here rudiments of music combined with zither
	instruction

Instrumental techniques
Plucked instruments
Zither -- Continued

625	Studies and exercises
	Including accompanied works
627	Two zithers
628	Self-instructors
628.5	Instructive editions
	Class here works heavily annotated with textual instructions for practice and interpretation
	Other instruments of the zither family
632-632.8	Autoharp (Table M5)
(633)	Metaharp
	see MT634.M48
634.A-Z	Other. By instrument, A-Z
634.A85	Audeharp
634.A9	Autoharp
634.B84	Bulbultarang
634.C4	Citaharp
(634.C4)	Cither harp
	see MT634.H37
(634.D9)	Dulcimer
	For Appalacian dulcimer, see MT654.A7
	For hammered dulcimer, see MT717+
(634.G5)	Guitar zither
	see MT634.H37
634.H36	Harp-lute guitar
634.H37	Harp zither. Guitar zither
634.H38	Harpola
634.I3	Ideal harp
634.K3	Kannel
634.K35	Kantele
634.K65	Kokle
(634.M2)	Mandolin zither
	see MT634.M35
634.M35	Mandolin guitar. Mandolin zither
634.M44	Meloharp
634.M48	Meta-harp
634.N48	New century harp
634.N49	New century zither
634.O58	Ongnyugŭm
634.P5	Piano-zither
634.V35	Valiha
634.Y36	Yanggŭm
634.Z58	Zitho-harp
640-640.8	Lute (Table M5)

	Instrumental techniques
	Plucked instruments -- Continued
(642)	Other plucked instruments (General)
	see MT539
643-643.8	Balalaika, dömbra, etc. (Table M5)
644	Lyre
645-645.8	Ukulele (Table M5)
646	Banjo ukulele
647	Tambi
648	Cuatro
649-649.8	Sitar (Table M5)
650	Tambura (Fretted lute)
654.A-Z	Other. By instrument, A-Z
654.A7	Appalachian dulcimer
654.B3	Bağlama
654.B35	Bandura
654.B69	Bouzouki
654.C47	Cheng
654.C5	Ch'in. Qin
654.C58	Cittern
654.E6	Epinette des Vosges
654.K4	Kayagŭm
654.K7	Koto
654.L58	Liu qin
654.M38	Mbira
654.O9	Oud
654.P5	Pi pa
	Qin see MT654.C5
654.R33	Rabāb
654.S26	San xian
654.S5	Shamisen
654.S58	Shudraga
654.T36	Ṭanbūr
654.T54	Theorbo
654.V56	Vina
654.Y83	Yue qin
	Percussion and other instruments
655	Percussion instruments (General)
	For percussion ensemble see MT736
660-660.8	Timpani (Table M5)
662-662.8	Drums (Table M5)
	Class here drums commonly used in the Western symphony orchestra, such as bass drum, snare drum, etc., instruction for the entire batterie, and drum set
	For timpani see MT660+
	For percussion ensemble see MT736
	Cf. MT663+ Bongos. Congas

Instrumental techniques

Percussion and other instruments -- Continued

663-663.8	Bongos. Congas (Table M5)
	Including individual sizes of congas, e.g. quinto
664-664.8	Tabla (Table M5)
670	Glass harmonica
680-680.8	Accordion (Piano accordion) (Table M5)
681-681.8	Concertina. Button-key accordion (Table M5)
	Mouth organs
682-682.8	Harmonica (Table M5)
683	Kaen
684	Sheng
685	Shō
686.A-Z	Other instruments of the mouth organ family. By instrument, A-Z
686.M4	Melodica
700	Player piano and similar instruments
703	Phonograph and similar instruments
	Including turntablism
(705)	Whistling
	see MT949.5
710	Carillon, bell ringing, etc.
	Including change ringing, peals, etc.
711	Handbell ringing
	Including change ringing for handbells
717-717.8	Dulcimer (Table M5)
719-719.8	Xylophone and similar instruments (Table M5)
	Including marimba, vibraphone, etc.
720	Tubular bells. Chimes
	Including glockenspiel
	Prior to 1980, used for various percussion and other instruments
722	Implements put to musical use
	Class here musical saw, kitchen utensils, etc.
	For bones see MT725.B6
	Electronic instruments
	Including instruction in operation of analog electronic instruments and devices, such as ondes Martenot, Theremin, and trautonium
	For composition of electronic or computer music see MT56
	For performance on electronic keyboard instruments, including synthesizers with keyboards see MT192+
723	Computer sound processing
	Class here instruction in computer-based instruments and devices

MT

	Instrumental techniques
	Percussion and other instruments
	Electronic instruments -- Continued
724	General works
	Including works on individual electronic instruments
724.5	Drum machine
725.A-Z	Other. By instrument, A-Z
725.B3	Balo
725.B55	Bodhrán
725.B6	Bones
725.C4	Castanets
725.C45	Changgo
725.C5	Chin ch'ien pan. Jin qian ban
725.C55	Cimbalom
725.C6	Claves
725.C9	Cymbals
725.D37	Darabukka
725.D54	Djembe
725.F46	Fêli
725.G4	Gender
725.G53	Ghatam
725.G8	Gumlā
725.H37	Hardwood drum
725.H87	Hurdy-gurdy
725.J5	Jew's harp
	Jin qian ban see MT725.C5
725.L58	Lithophone
(725.L6)	Lo ku
	see MT736
725.M4	Maracas
725.M7	Mridanga
725.P5	Phonofiddle
725.P8	Pung
725.S26	Santūr
725.S7	Steel drum
725.T3	Tambourine
725.T38	Tavil
725.T5	Tinglik
(725.T7)	Toy piano
	see MT257.T7
725.T8	Tubaphone. Tubuphone
725.Y3	Yang qin
725.Y34	Yanggŭm
725.Y66	Yoochin (Dulcimer)
725.Z37	Zarb
	Ensembles
	Chamber music

Instrumental techniques
Ensembles
Chamber music -- Continued
728   General works
Instructive editions
Class here works heavily annotated with textual instructions for practice and interpretation
728.2   Two or more composers
728.3   One composer
730   Orchestra
Band
733   General works
733.4   Marching bands and maneuvers
733.5   Drum majoring
733.6   Baton twirling
733.7   Big band. Dance band. Jazz band
734   Plucked instruments
735   Field music
Class here works about signals and fife and drum music
736   Percussion
737   Motion picture accompanying
Instrumental techniques for children
For group instruction see MT937+
740   General works
742   Systems and methods (General)
Keyboard instruments
745   General works
746   Systems and methods
750   Specific techniques
755   Studies and exercises
Including accompanied works
756   Four hands. Two keyboard instruments
758   Teaching pieces
Class here works composed principally for pedagogical purposes
Stringed instruments
General see MT801.S8
Violin. Viola
760   General works
761   Systems and methods
765   Specific techniques
775   Studies and exercises
Including accompanied works
776   Two instruments
778   Teaching pieces
Class here works composed principally for pedagogical purposes

MT

Instrumental techniques
Instrumental techniques for children
Stringed instruments -- Continued
Violoncello
785	General works
786	Systems and methods
790	Specific techniques
795	Studies and exercises
	Including accompanied works
796	Two violoncellos
798	Teaching pieces
	Class here works composed principally for pedagogical purposes
	Other instruments
800	General works
801.A-Z	By instrument, A-Z
801.A3	Accordion
801.A66	Appalachian dulcimer
801.A85	Autoharp
801.B3	Banjo
801.B5	Bells
801.B72	Brass instruments (General)
801.C6	Clarinet
801.C66	Cornet
	For trumpet see MT801.T7
801.C8	Cuatro
801.D65	Double bass
801.D7	Drum
801.F4	Flageolet
801.F5	Flute
	Flutophone see MT801.T6
801.G8	Guitar
801.H35	Handbells
801.H4	Harmonica
801.H43	Harp
801.H7	Horn
801.M3	Mandolin
	Melody flute see MT801.T6
(801.M68)	Mouth organ
	see MT801.H4
801.O7	Organ
801.P46	Penny whistle
801.P55	Pipe
801.R4	Recorder
801.S4	Saxophone
801.S5	Sheng
801.S8	Stringed instruments (General)

Instrumental techniques
  Instrumental techniques for children
    Other instruments
      By instrument, A-Z -- Continued

801.T6	Tonette, flutophone, melody flute, and similar melody instruments
801.T67	Trombone
801.T7	Trumpet
	For cornet see MT801.C66
801.T8	Tuba
801.U4	Ukulele
801.W5	Wind instruments (General)
801.X9	Xylophone and other mallet instruments
(805)	Special techniques and exercises
	see the instrument, family of instruments, or ensemble
810	Ensembles
	Class here orchestral music, chamber music, rhythm band, etc.

Singing and vocal technique

820	General works
821	Physiology and care of the voice
	For voice disorders of singers see RF511.S55
(823)	History of vocal instruction and study
	see ML1460

  Systems and methods

825	American
830	English
835	French
840	German
845	Italian
850	Other (not A-Z)
853	Systems using audio-visual aids and computer instruction
	For audio-visual aids in general musical instruction and study see MT150

  Specific techniques

855	General works
860	Chanting
	Including Gregorian chant intonations, etc.
(865)	Protestant chorale
	see MT875
(866)	Improvisation
	Including scat singing
868	Jazz vocals
870	Sight-singing
	Including solfeggio
(872)	Declamation
875	Chorus and part-singing

	Singing and vocal technique
	Specific techniques -- Continued
878	Breath control
882	Tone production
883	Pronunciation. Diction
884	Yodeling
885	Studies and exercises
	Including accompanied works
890	Instructive editions. Teaching pieces
	Class here works heavily annotated with textual instructions for practice and interpretation, and works composed principally for pedagogical purposes
892	Interpretation, phrasing, expression, etc.
893	Self-instructors
	Vocal techniques for children
898	General works
900	Systems and methods
905	Specific techniques
915	Choir training
	School music
918	General works
	Kindergarten
920	General works
925	Methods. Studies and exercises
	Including studies and exercises with accompaniment
	Elementary schools. Junior high schools. High schools
930	General works
935	Vocal methods
(936)	Outlines of courses, etc.
	see MT10
	Instrumental methods
	Class here group instruction
937	Methods
	Cf. MT740+ Instrumental techniques for children
945	Studies and exercises
	Including accompanied works
948	Action songs. Drill songs. Musical games
	Cf. M1993 Action songs. Drill songs. Musical games
(949)	Other
949.5	Whistling
950	Music to accompany instruction in ballet, folk dancing, gymnastics, etc.
	Class here music composed or compiled for such accompaniment
	Cf. GV1755+ Folk dance instruction
	Musical theater
	Class here works about opera, musicals, etc.

Musical theater -- Continued
955	Production
	Class here works about direction, costume, scenery, etc.
956	Performing
	Class here works on singing, acting, etc.
960	Music in the theater

Assign Cutters for regions as needed in individual classes

.A3	Alabama
.A4	Alaska
.A5	Arizona
.A7	Arkansas
.C15	California
.C3	Carolina (General)
.C5	Colorado
.C7	Connecticut
.D3	Dakota (General)
.D33	Delaware
.D5	District of Columbia
.F6	Florida
.G4	Georgia
.H4	Hawaii
.I2	Idaho
.I3	Illinois
.I39	Indiana
.I6	Iowa
.K2	Kansas
.K4	Kentucky
.L8	Louisiana
.M2	Maine
.M3	Maryland
.M4	Massachusetts
.M5	Michigan
.M55	Minnesota
.M6	Mississippi
.M68	Missouri
.M7	Montana
.N36	Nebraska
.N5	Nevada
.N53	New Hampshire
.N55	New Jersey
.N57	New Mexico
.N6	New York
.N85	North Carolina
.N88	North Dakota
.O37	Ohio
.O5	Oklahoma
.O66	Oregon
.P4	Pennsylvania
.R47	Rhode Island
.S6	South Carolina
.S8	South Dakota
.T3	Tennessee

TABLES

.T35	Texas
.U89	Utah
.V5	Vermont
.V8	Virginia
.W3	Washington
	Washington (D.C.) see M1 .D5
.W5	West Virginia
.W6	Wisconsin
.W9	Wyoming

TABLES

1	Miscellaneous collections
	Class here collections containing original works and arrangements
	Original compositions
2	Collections
3	Separate works
	Arrangements
4	Collections
5	Separate works

0	General works
0.1	Addresses, essays, lectures
	By period
0.2	Through 1700
0.3	1701-1800
0.4	1801-1900
0.5	1901-2000
0.6	2001-

TABLES

0	General works
0.1	Addresses, essays, lectures
	By period
0.2	Through 1700
0.3	1701-1800
0.4	1801-1900
0.5	1901-2000
0.6	2001-
0.7A-.7Z	By state, province, etc., A-Z
	For regions and states of the United States, see Table M1
0.8A-.8Z	By city, A-Z
	For works on a city in relation to a topic, see the topic, e.g., ML1711.8.P5 Opera in Philadelphia; for works on a specific society, including performing ensembles, see ML26+ ; for works on a specific festival, including performance festivals, see ML36+
0.9	Other

0	General works
0.2	Systems and methods
0.3	Studies and exercises
	Including accompanied works
0.4	Orchestral excerpts
0.5	Teaching pieces
	Class here works composed principally for pedagogical purposes
0.6	Instructive editions
	Class here works heavily annotated with textual instructions for practice and interpretation
0.7	Two instruments
0.8	Self-instructors

TABLES

	Use an initial letter for the language according to English terminology, e.g., .E1-.E99 English, .G1-.G99 German, etc. If more than one language is present, one of which is Latin, assign .L
	For special texts not listed below see the medium of performance, e.g., M2072 for Domine probasti me (Psalm 139) for mixed chorus with keyboard accompaniment
.x1	Two or more of the texts listed below
	For combinations like Magnificat and Nunc dimittis, etc., see under particular headings
.x11	Adeste fidelis
.x114	Adoro te
.x12	Agnus Dei (O Lamb of God)
.x13	Alma Redemptoris Mater
.x14	Amens
.x144	Antiphons
	Class here sets only
	For individual antiphons, see M6 .x13, etc.
.x15	Asperges me
.x16	Ave Maria
.x161	Ave Maris Stella
.x163	Ave Regina laetare
.x165	Ave verum corpus
.x168	Beatitudes
.x169	Beatus vir, qui non abiit; Psalm 1
.x17	Benedic anima mea et omnia (Bless the Lord, O my soul); Psalm 103
.x18	Benedicite omnia opera (O all ye works of the Lord)
.x2	Benedictus Dominus (Blessed be the Lord); Psalm 144
.x21	Benedictus qui venit (Blessed is He that cometh)
	Bless the Lord, O my soul see M6 .x17
	Blessed be the Lord see M6 .x2
	Blessed is He that cometh see M6 .x21
.x22	Bone pastor
.x23	Bonum est confiteri (It is a good thing); Psalm 92
.x25	Cantate Domino canticum novum, cantate Domino (O sing unto the Lord); Psalm 96
.x27	Collects
	Class here sets only
.x28	Cor Jesu
	Creeds
.x3	Nicene: Credo in unum Deum (I believe in one God, the Father almighty)
.x31	Athanasian
.x32	Apostles
.x34	De profundis; Psalm 130
.x35	Deus misereatur (God be merciful); Psalm 67

.x37	Dies irae
.x373	Dixit Dominus; Psalm 110
.x38	Ecce panis
.x382	Ecce sacerdos
.x39	Gaude Virgo
.x4	Gloria in excelsis Deo (Glory be to the Lord on high)
.x41	Gloria Patri (Glory be to the Father)
.x413	Gloria tibi (Glory be to thee)
	Glory be to the Father see M6 .x41
	Glory be to the Lord on high see M6 .x4
	Glory be to thee see M6 .x413
	God be merciful see M6 .x35
.x416	Graduals

           Class here sets only
           Including works with offertories added
           For separate sets of offertories see M6 .x73

.x42	Haec dies
	Have mercy upon me, O God see M6 .x62
	Holy, Holy, Holy, Lord God of hosts see M6 .x8
.x43	Hymns

           Class here sets only
           I believe in one God, the Father almighty see M6 .x3

.x435	In te, Domine, speravi (In thee, O Lord, do I put my trust); Psalm 31
	In thee, O Lord, do I put my trust see M6 .x435
.x438	Introits

           Class here sets only
           It is a good thing see M6 .x23

.x44	Jesu dulcis memoria
.x445	Jesu Redemptor omnium
.x45	Jubilate Deo omnis terra, servite Domino; Psalm 100
.x47	Justus ut palma
.x5	Kyrie eleison (Lord have mercy upon us)

           For the Greek text, Kyrie eleison, assign the Cutter .L

.x52	Lauda Sion
.x53	Laudate Dominum in sanctis eius; Psalm 150
.x535	Laudate, pueri, Dominum; Psalm 113
.x54	Libera me
	Lift up your hearts see M6 .x85
.x55	Litanies

           Class here sets only
           Lord have mercy upon us see M6 .x5
           Lord now lettest Thou see M6 .x7
           Lord's prayer see M6 .x74

.x59	Lucis creator
.x6	Magnificat (My soul doth magnify)

           Class here Magnificats with or without Nunc dimittis following

TABLES

.x61	Media vita
.x62	Miserere mei, Deus, secundum magnum misericordiam (Have mercy upon me, O God); Psalm 51
	My soul doth magnify see M6 .x6
.x67	Nato nobis Salvatore
.x7	Nunc dimittis (Lord now lettest Thou)
	Class here separate works only
	Cf. M6 .x6 Magnificat
	O all ye works of the Lord see M6 .x18
	O come let us sing see M6 .x95
.x713	O cor amoris victima
	O Lamb of God see M6 .x12
.x718	O sacrum convivium
.x72	O salutaris (hostia)
	O sing unto the Lord see M6 .x25
.x73	Offertories
	Class here sets only
.x735	Pange lingua
.x737	Panis angelicus
.x74	Pater noster (Lord's prayer)
.x745	Pie Jesu
.x75	Processionals
	Class here sets only
	Psalm 1 see M6 .x169
	Psalm 31 see M6 .x435
	Psalm 51 see M6 .x62
	Psalm 67 see M6 .x35
	Psalm 92 see M6 .x23
	Psalm 95 see M6 .x95
	Psalm 96 see M6 .x25
	Psalm 100 see M6 .x45
	Psalm 103 see M6 .x17
	Psalm 110 see M6 .x373
	Psalm 113 see M6 .x535
	Psalm 130 see M6 .x34
	Psalm 144 see M6 .x2
	Psalm 150 see M6 .x53
.x756	Quid retribuam
.x76	Recessionals
	Class here sets only
.x77	Regina Caeli
.x78	Responses
	Class here sets only
	Sadly stood the Mother weeping see M6 .x82
.x79	Salve Regina
.x8	Sanctus (Holy, Holy, Holy, Lord God of hosts)
.x82	Stabat Mater dolorosa (Sadly stood the Mother weeping)

.x85	Sursum corda (Lift up your hearts)
.x87	Tantum ergo
.x9	Te Deum laudamus (We praise Thee O God)
.x91	Terra tremuit
.x914	Tollite hostias
.x916	Tota pulchra
.x918	Tu es Petrus
.x92	Veni Creator Spiritus
.x94	Veni Sancte Spiritus
.x95	Venite, exultemus Domino (O come let us sing); Psalm 95
.x96	Vesper prayers, hymns, etc.

Class here sets only

For vesper services see M2014.6, Catholic, and M2016.4, Anglican

.x97	Vidi aquam
.x975	Virgin Mary

Class here sets not elsewhere provided for, as e.g., under Litanies

We praise Thee O God see M6 .x9

TABLES

.x	General works
.x1	Addresses, essays, lectures
	By period
.x2	Through 1700
.x3	1701-1800
.x4	1801-1900
.x5	1901-2000
.x6	2001-

.x	General works
.x1	Addresses, essays, lectures
	By period
.x2	Through 1700
.x3	1701-1800
.x4	1801-1900
.x5	1901-2000
.x6	2001-
.x7A-.x7Z	By state, province, etc., A-Z
	For regions and states of the United States, see Table M1
.x8A-.x8Z	By city, A-Z
	For works on a specific city in relation to a topic, see the topic, e.g., ML1711.8.P5 Opera in Philadelphia; for works on a specific society, including performing ensembles, see ML26+ ; for works on a specific festival, including performance festivals, see ML36+
.x9	Other

TABLES

0	General works
0.1	Addresses, essays, lectures
0.7A-.7Z	By state, province, etc., A-Z
	Use Cutter numbers in Table M1 for regions and states of the United States
0.8A-.8Z	By city, A-Z

.x	General works
.x1	Addresses, essays, lectures
.x7A-.x7Z	By state, province, etc., A-Z
	For regions and states of the United States, see Table M1
.x8A-.x8Z	By city, A-Z

TABLES

.x0	General works
.x4	History
.x5	Annual reports. By date
.x6	Other reports
.x7	Programs. By date
	For opera, concert, etc., programs see ML40+
.x9	Other

| .xA-.xA39 | Thematic catalogs |
| .xA4-Z | General. By compiler |

a	Legal documents, correspondence, etc., relating to the establishment of the Foundation
	Music
	Manuscripts
c	Holographs
d	Other
e	Printed music
	Including photocopies
f	Radio broadcasts
g	Books and miscellaneous
	Correspondence
i	From the founder
j	To the founder
k	Other business correspondence
	Concert programs of the Foundation and related printed matter
	Public concerts
l	Autographed items
m	Items without autographs
	Private concerts
n	Autographed items
o	Items without autographs
	Newspaper clippings
p	Relating to the Foundation
q	Relating to the Founder
r	Pictures

0.2	Louis C. Elson Foundation
0.23	Fromm Music Foundation Collection
	George Gershwin Collection
	Music
0.25a	Holographs
0.25e	Printed music
	Including photocopies
0.25g	Books
	Ira and Leonore Gershwin Fund Collection
	Music
	Manuscripts
0.27a	Holographs not commissioned by the Ira and Leonore Gershwin Fund
0.27b	Holographs commissioned by the Ira and Leonore Gershwin Fund
0.27e	Correspondence
0.27f	Legal and financial documents
0.27g	Photographs
	Serge Koussevitzky Music Foundation
0.3a	Legal documents, correspondence, etc., relating to the establishment of the Foundation
	Music
	Manuscripts
0.3c	Holograph manuscripts of works commissioned by the Serge Koussevitzky Music Foundation
0.3c2	Holograph manuscripts of works commissioned by the Koussevitzky Music Foundation, Inc.
0.3c3	Holograph manuscripts of works not commissioned by either foundation
0.3d	Other
	Printed music
0.3e	With Koussevitzky's conducting markings
0.3e2	Other
	Including photocopies
0.3g	Books
	Including manuscripts
	Correspondence
0.3i	From the founder
0.3j	To the founder
0.3k	Business correspondence
	Including related business documents
	Programs and related printed matter
	For newspaper clippings see M14 0.3o+
	Relating to the Foundation
0.3l	Autographed
0.3m	Without autographs

TABLES

	Serge Koussevitzky Music Foundation
	Programs and related printed matter -- Continued
0.3n	Relating to the Founder's career
	Newspaper clippings
0.3o	Relating to the Serge Koussevitzky Music Foundation
0.3p	Relating to the Koussevitzky Music Foundation, Inc.
0.3r	Relating to the founder
0.3s	Pictures, photographs, etc.
0.3u	Sound recordings
	Dayton C. Miller Foundation
0.4a	Instruments
0.4b	Literature
0.4c	Music
0.4d	Art
0.4e	Portraits. Photographs. Autograph letters
0.4g	Slides. Photographs
0.4k	Sound recordings
0.4p	Correspondence. Memorabilia
0.4r	Legal and business correspondence
0.4z	Other
	Sergei Rachmaninoff Archives
	Music
	Holographs
0.55a	Original manuscripts
0.55a2	Photocopies
0.55a3	Publications
0.55b	Correspondence from and to Rachmaninoff
0.55c	Lists of compositions, transcriptions, and revisions. List of works recorded, including Ampico rolls
	Concerts
0.55d	Performances: Russia, Europe, United States, Canada, 1891-1943
	Including charts concerning concerts in the U.S.
0.55e	Programs: Russia and Europe, 1891-1917; Europe, 1918-1939, United States and Canada, 1901-1910 and 1918-1943
0.55f	Works performed as pianist, with conductors of orchestral performances. Works conducted. Authors of texts set, epigraphs used, etc.
	First performances
	Including programs, reviews, letters, etc.
0.55g1	Concertos and Rapsodie sur un thème de Paganini
0.55g2	Symphonies
0.55g3	Other orchestral works
	Literature about Rachmaninoff
	Including Natalie A. Rachmaninoff

	Sergei Rachmaninoff Archives
	Literature about Rachmaninoff -- Continued
	Career
0.55h	1891-1917, published in Russia before the Revolution
0.55i	1918-1943, in Russian
0.55j	1899, 1907, 1918-1943, in other languages, published in Europe
0.55k	1909, 1918-1943, published in the United States
0.55l	Homages, testimonials, prizes, awards
0.55m	Interviews. Letters to Russian and American newspapers and journals. Unpublished reminiscences about Russia. Material relating to future musical compositions
0.55n	Unpublished biographical works
0.55o	Obituaries, in English, German, and Russian
0.55p	Published after his death, in English, German, and Russian
0.55q	Natalie A. Rachmaninoff (Mrs. Sergei): correspondence, photographs, obituaries, etc.
0.55r	Biographies in Russian and English. Book reviews
0.55x	Bibliography (unfinished)
0.55y	Memorial concerts in the United States, Russia, Switzerland
0.55z	Other
	Richard Rodgers Collection
0.58a	Holograph music manuscripts
0.58b	Other manuscript music
	Leopold Stokowski Collection
0.6a	Holograph music manuscripts
0.7	Prentiss Taylor Archives
	Gertrude Clark Whittall Foundation
0.8a	Instruments
	Music and correspondence of musicians
	Holograph music manuscripts
0.8b	Original
0.8c	Photocopies
	Correspondence
0.8d	Holographs
0.8e	Photocopies
	Unit collections
0.8j	Mendelssohn
0.8k	Paganini
0.8p	Other manuscripts
0.8q	Sound recordings
0.8s	Programs
0.8t	Portraits. Other pictures
0.8u	Art
0.8v	Books. Pamphlets
	Business documents

TABLES

Gertrude Clark Whittall Foundation
Business documents -- Continued
0.8w   Legal documents
0.8x   Business correspondence and other documents
0.8z   Other

.A4	Amateur Hour Collection
.A58	George Antheil Collection
.A9	Lauro Ayestarán Collection
.B23	Ernst Bacon Collection
.B4	John Davis Batchelder Collection
.B43	Harold Bauer Collection
.B45	Edward Beach Collection
.B49	Leonard Bernstein Collection
.B56	Ernest Bloch Collection
.B63	Franziska Boas Collection
.B7	William B. Bradbury Collection
.D3	Da Capo Fund Collection
.D53	Serge Diaghilev / Serge Lifar Collection
.D55	Robert Di Domenica Collection
.F43	Federal Music Project (U.S.) Collection
.G55	Julius Gold Collection
.G6	Gold and Fizdale Collection
.G75	Serge Grigoriev/Ballets Russes Archive
.G8	Glenn Dillard Gunn Collection
.H36	Charles Hambitzer Music Manuscripts
.H397	Joe Haymes Big Band Arrangements
	Jascha Heifetz Collection
	Music
.H4a	Manuscripts
.H4b	Printed music
	Including photocopies
.H4g	Books
	Including manuscripts
.H4i	Correspondence
.H43	Heinemann Foundation Collection
.I57	Inter-American Music Festival Foundation Papers
.J3	Carrie Jacobs-Bond Collection
.J64	Eric Johnson Collection of Ernest Bloch Photographs
.K4	Jerome Kern Collection
.K63	Rudolf Kolisch Collection
.K7	Fritz Kreisler Collection
.L39	Dorothea Dix Lawrence Collection
.L43	Minna Lederman Daniel Collection
.M24	McKim Fund Collection
.M43	Nikola Karlovich Medtner Collection
.M55	Gilbert Miller Collection
.P67	Cole Porter Collection
.R64	Artur Rodzinski Collection
.S28	Ira Gershwin Files from the Law Office of Leonard Saxe
.S3	Francis Maria Scala Collection

TABLES

	Gisella Selden-Goth Collection
	Music
.S4a	Holographs
.S4e	Printed music
	Including photocopies
.S4g	Books
	Sigma Alpha Iota Collection
.S5a	Music manuscripts
.S7	Edward and Clara Steuermann Collection
.S77	William Remsen Strickland Collection
.U5	Joint Army and Navy Committee on Welfare and Recreation, Sub-Committee on Music, Papers

	Under each language, compiler, publisher, title, ceremony, or occasion:
.x	Complete work. By date
.x2	Selections. By date

TABLES

.xA3	General
.xB3	Band music
.xB4	Bibliography
.xC5	Choral music
.xI5	Instruction and study
.xI6	Instrumental music
.xO7	Orchestral music
.xP5	Piano music
.xT5	Theater music
.xV6	Vocal music

	To construct classification numbers for biography of Richard Wagner, substitute ML410.W1 for .x in this table
	Writings
	Collections
	Class here complete collections and selections not assigned to more specific classes. By date of edition
.xA1	German
.xA105	Translations
	Selections. Special editions
	Subarrange by editor, translator, or compiler
.xA11-.xA119	Posthumous, unpublished, etc., works
	Including fragments, sketches, etc.
	Prose works
.xA12-.xA125	German
.xA126-.xA139	Translations
	Poems
	see PT2551.W35
	For opera librettos see ML50
.xA142-.xA169	Selections. Anthologies. Quotations
	Collected quotations from Wagner's writings
.xA17-.xA19	Individual operas
.xA191-.xA196	By topic
.xA197	Indexes to Wagner's works
	Class here separately published indexes
	Separate works. By date of edition
	Class here important early editions, including translations
	Class later editions with the topic, e.g., Über das Dirigieren in MT85
	The arrangement below is based on N. Oesterlein, Katalog einer Richard Wagner-Bibliothek
	For opera librettos, see ML50
	Philosophical, critical, etc., works
.xA204	Beethoven, 1870
.xA206	Bericht an den Deutschen Wagner-Verein, 1872
.xA208	Bericht an ... Ludwig II. von Bayern über ein in München zu errichtende deutsche Musikschule, 1865
.xA21	Ein Brief von Richard Wagner über Franz Liszt's Symphonische Dichtungen, 1857
.xA212	Das Bühnenfestspielhaus zu Bayreuth, 1873
.xA214	Deutsche Kunst und Deutsche Politik, 1868
.xA215	Ein deutscher Musiker in Paris, 1840-1841
.xA216	Herr Eduard Devrient und sein Styl, 1869
.xA218	Drei Operndichtungen nebst einer Mittheilung an seine Freunde, 1852
.xA22	Das Judenthum in der Musik, 1869
.xA222	Die Kunst und die Revolution, 1849
.xA224	Das Kunstwerk der Zukunft, 1850

TABLES

	Writings
	Separate works. By date of edition
	Philosophical, critical, etc., works -- Continued
.xA226	Lebens-Bericiht, 1884
	For the 1912 edition see ML410.W1W122
	Mein Leben, 1911
	see ML410.W1W14
.xA232	Offener Brief an Ernst von Weber, 1880
.xA234	Oper und Drama, 1852
.xA236	Ein Pilgerfahrt zu Beethoven, 1840
.xA238	Religion und Kunst, 1881
.xA24	Richard Wagner's Lehr- und Wanderjahre, 1871
.xA242	Richard Wagner's Programm zur Neunten Symphonie von Beethoven
.xA244	Ein Theater in Zürich, 1851
.xA246	Über das Dirigieren, 1869
.xA248	Über die Afführung des Bühnenfestspiels der Ring des Nibelungen, 1871
.xA25	Über die Afführung des Tannhäuser, 1852
.xA252	Über die Bestimmung der Oper, 1871
.xA254	Über die Schauspieler und Sänger, 1872
.xA256	Was is deutsch?, 1881
.xA258	Die Wibelungen, 1850
.xA26	Das Wiener Hof-Operntheater, 1863
.xA262	Zukunftsmusik, 1861
.xA264	Zwei Briefe von Richard Wagner, 1852
.xA266	Other
.xA267	Speeches, etc.
.xA269	Separates of magazine articles not published separately. By date
.xA271	Programs. By date
.xA273	Other
	Dramatic works
.xA28	Die Feen
.xA281	Die fliegende Holländer, 1843
.xA282	Iphigenia in Aulis, 1847
.xA283	Das Liebesmahl der Apostel, 1843
.xA284	Das Liebesverbot oder Die Novize von Palermo, 1911
.xA285	Lohengrin, 1850
.xA286	Die Meistersinger von Nürnberg, 1863
.xA287	Parsifal, 1877
.xA288	Rienzi, 1842
	Der Ring des Nibelungen
.xA289	Der Ring des Nibelungen, 1864
.xA29	Das Rheingold, 1869
.xA291	Die Walküre, 1870
.xA292	Siegfried, 1871

	Writings
	Separate works. By date of edition
	Dramatic works
	Der Ring des Nibelungen -- Continued
.xA293	Götterdämmerung, 1874
.xA294	Tannhäuser und der Sängerkrieg auf Wartburg, 1845
.xA295	Tristan und Isolde, 1859
.xA296	Other
.xA298A-.xA298Z	Parodies, etc. By title, A-Z
	Correspondence
.xA3-.xA309	Complete collections. By date
.xA31-.xA319	Selections (General). By date
.xA32-.xA449	Selections by topic, correspondent(s), etc. By date
.xA45-.xA459	Calendars, etc.
.xA47-.xA489	Letters written to Wagner
	Biography and criticism
	Including autobiography
.xA5	Periodicals. Societies. Serials
.xA55-.x2	Biography and autobiography
.xA6-.xZ	General works
.xW122-.xW14	Autobiography
.xW122	Lebens-Bericht, 1912
.xW14	Mein Leben, 1911
.x11	Particular periods in the life of Wagner. By author
.x2A-.x2Z	By region or country, A-Z
	Class here works about Wagner's influence, Wagner in France, in Italy, etc.
	Criticism and interpretation
	For analysis and appreciation of Wagner's works see MT90+
	Of several works by Wagner
.x3	General works
.x31	Addresses, essays, lectures
	Of individual works by Wagner
.x32	Early operas
	Including Der fliegende Holländer
.x35	Tannhäuser
.x37	Lohengrin
.x4	Tristan und Isolde
.x5	Ring des Nibelungen
.x6	Meistersinger
.x7	Parsifal
.x75	Other musical works
(.x8)	Literary works
	For works on Wagner's literary writings or influences see PT2551.W36
.x9	Other topics
	Pictorial works

TABLES

Biography and criticism
Criticism and interpretation
Pictorial works -- Continued
.x95   General
Including scenes from his operas, etc.
.x96   Portraits, caricatures, etc.

.x	General works
.x3	Constitution, by-laws, lists of members, etc. By date
.x4	History
.x5	Annual reports. By date
.x6	Other reports
.x7	Programs. By date
	For opera, concert, etc., programs see ML40+
.x9	Other

.x1	General works
.x3	Catalogs, calendars, etc. By date
.x4	History
.x5	Annual reports. By date
.x6	Other reports
.x7	Programs
.x9	Other

(M2.4)	Kinds and forms
	see M2+
(M2.6)	Instruments
	see M2+
(M2.7)	Einblattdrucke
	see M2+
(M2.8)	Manuscript facsimiles
	see M2+
(M2.9)	Other
	see M2+

TABLES

TABLE OF OBSOLETE NUMBERS FOR
INSTRUMENTS FORMERLY USED UNDER
M1138.4.A-Z

(M1138.4.A3)	Accordion
	see M1139.4.A3
(M1138.4.B3)	Bandoneon
	see M1139.4.B3
(M1138.4.C6)	Concertina
	see M1139.4.C6
(M1138.4.M6)	Mouth organ
	see M1139.4.H3
(M1138.4.O6)	Ondes Martenot
	see M1139.4.O5

(0.2)	Two solo voices or chorus parts
(0.3)	Three solo voices or chorus parts
(0.4)	Four solo voices or chorus parts
(0.5)	Five solo voices or chorus parts
(0.6)	Six or more solo voices or chorus parts
(0.7)	Solo voices with chorus
(0.8)	Cycles for solo voices in various combinations

TABLES

(2)	Two solo voices or chorus parts
(3)	Three solo voices or chorus parts
(4)	Four solo voices or chorus parts
(5)	Five solo voices or chorus parts
(6)	Six or more solo voices or chorus parts
(7)	Solo voices with chorus
(8)	Cycles for solo voices in various combinations

(2)	Two solo voices or chorus parts
(3)	Three solo voices or chorus parts
(4)	Four solo voices or chorus parts
(5)	Five solo voices or chorus parts
(6)	Six or more solo voices or chorus parts
(7)	Choruses and solo voices and part song cycles

TABLES

	Collections
(M1672.A5)	Alaska
	see M1629.7.A4 , M1658.A4
	American Samoa
	see M1844.S2, M1844.S218
(M1672.C2)	Canal Zone
	see M1684.P2
(M1672.C8)	Cuban revolution, 1895-1898
	see M1675.C8
(M1672.D2)	Danish West Indies
	see M1672.V5
	For West Indies see M1681.A1+
(M1672.H3)	Hawaii
	see M1629.7.H4 , M1658.A4
(M1672.P4)	Philippines
	see M1822 , M1823.18
(M1672.P8)	Puerto Rico
	see M1680.P6 , M1681.P618
(M1672.S2)	Samoa, American
	see M1844.S2 , M1844.S218
	Separate works
(M1673.A5)	Alaska
	see M1658.A4
	American Samoa
	see M1844.S2 , M1844.S22
(M1673.C2)	Canal Zone
	see M1685.P2
(M1673.C8)	Cuban revolution, 1895-1898
	see M1675.C8
(M1673.D2)	Danish West Indies
	see M1672.V5
	For West Indies see M1681.A1+
(M1673.H3)	Hawaii
	see M1658.A4
(M1673.P4)	Philippines
	see M1822 , M1823.2
(M1673.P8)	Puerto Rico
	see M1681.P6 , M1681.P62
(M1673.S2)	Samoa, American
	see M1844.S2 , M1844.S22

(M1722-1723)   Turkey
             see M1824.T8 , M1825.T8+

(M1737.3-.6)   East Germany
             see M1734+

(M1760-1761)   Finland
             see M1729.3+

(M1762-1763)   Poland
             see M1755.3+

(M1766.A7)   Armenia
             see M1800+

(M1766.A9)   Azerbaijan
             see M1824.A9 , M1825.A98+

(M1766.B35)   Bashkiria. Bashkir language
             see M1756+

(M1766.C3)   Carpathia
             see M1756+

(M1766.C35)   Caucasus
             see M1756+

(M1766.C55)   Chivashia
             see M1756+

(M1766.C7)   Crimea
             see M1756+

(M1766.K26)   Kabardia
             see M1756+

(M1766.K3)   Kaluzhskija Oblast'
             see M1756+

(M1766.K58)   Kyrgyzstan
             see M1824.K96

(M1766.M6)   Mordvinia
             see M1756+

(M1766.P4)   Perm'
             see M1756+

(M1766.S4)   Siberia
             see M1756+

(M1766.T8)   Turkmenistan
             see M1824.T9

(M1766.V5)   Volga
             see M1756+

(M1766.V6)   Vornezh
             see M1756+

(M1766.W5)   White Russia
             see M1756+

(M1767.A7-.A72)   Armenia
             see M1801 , M1801.2

TABLES

(M1767.A9-.A92)	Azerbaijan see M1825.A9 , M1825.A92
(M1767.B35-.B352)	Bashkiria (Bashkir language) see M1756+
(M1767.C3-.C32)	Carpathia see M1757 , M1757.2
(M1767.C35-.C352)	Caucasus see M1757 , M1757.2
(M1767.C55-.C552)	Chuvashia see M1757 , M1757.2
(M1767.C7-.C72)	Crimea see M1755 , M1755.2 , M1756+
(M1767.K26-.K262)	Kabardia see M1757 , M1757.2
(M1767.K3-.K32)	Kaluzhskaya Oblast' see M1757 , M1757.2
(M1767.K58-.K582)	Kyrgyzstan see M1825.K9+
(M1767.M6-.M62)	Mordvinia see M1757 , M1757.2
(M1767.P4-.P42)	Perm' see M1757 , M1757.2
(M1767.S4-.S42)	Siberia see M1757 , M1757.2
(M1767.T8-.T82)	Turkmenistan see M1825.T9+
(M1767.V5-.V52)	Volga River Region see M1757 , M1757.2
(M1767.V6-.V62)	Vornezh see M1757 , M1757.2
(M1767.W6-.W62)	White Russia see M1757.B4 , M1757.B42

(M1778)	Spain and Portugal
	    For Spain see M1779+
	    For Portugal see M1781+

(M1824.A7)	Armenia see M1800 , M1801.18
(M1824.B29)	Bali see M1824.I5
(M1824.C5)	Ceylon see M1824.S8
(M1824.D47)	Dervishes see M2188.S8
(M1824.I7)	Iran see M1820 , M1821.I8
(M1824.J4)	Java see M1824.I5
(M1824.P33)	Palestine see M1810 , M1811.18
(M1824.S5)	Siam see M1824.T48
(M1824.S6)	Sikkim see M1808 , M1809.18
(M1824.T5)	Tibet see M1804 , M1805.18
(M1825.A7-.A72)	Armenia see M1801 , M1801.18
(M1825.B29-.B292)	Bali see M1825.I5
(M1825.C5-.C52)	Ceylon see M1825.S8
(M1825.I7-.I72)	Iran see M1820 , M1821.18
(M1825.J4-.J42)	Java see M1825.I5
(M1825.P3-.P33)	Palestine see M1810 , M1811.18
(M1825.S5-.S52)	Siam see M1825.T48
(M1825.S6-.S62)	Sikkim see M1809 , M1809.2
(M1825.T5-.T52)	Tibet see M1805 , M1805.2
(M1831-1832)	African regions, ethnic groups, and languages For ethnic groups see M1831.A+ For regions see M1834+
(M1838.C65-.C652)	Congo (Brazzaville) see M1838.C67+

TABLES

(M1838.R45-.R452)   Réunion
                           see M1846.M4+

(M1838.R52-.R522)   Rhodesia
                           see M1838.Z34+

(M1838.U34-.U342)   Upper Volta
                           see M1838.B85+

(M1838.Z25-.Z252)   Zaire
                           see M1838.C67+

(M1844.F5-.F52)   Flores Island
                           see M1824.I5 , M1825.I5+

(M1844.H3-.H32)   Hawaii
                           see M1629.7.H4 , M1658.H4

(M1844.I5-.I52)   Indonesia
                           see M1824.I5 , M1825.I5+

(M1844.O4-.O42)   Okinawa
                           see M1812+

(M1844.P35-.P352)   Papua
                           see M1824.P36 , M1825.P36+

(M1844.P6-.P62)   Polynesia
                           For general works see M1844.A1
                           For Samoa see M1844.S2+
                           For Tahiti (French Polynesia) see M1844.T3+

(M1844.R95-.R952)   Ryukyu Islands
                           see M1812+

(M1845)   Primitive music not elsewhere classified
                           See the region or country

           Collections

(M1905.G4)   Gideon's International. Christian Commercial Travelers'
               Association of America
               see M1920.G5

(M1905.K4)   Kiwanis clubs. Kiwanis International
               see M1920.K5

(M1905.L4)   Lions clubs. Lions International
               see M1920.L6

(M1905.R5)   Rotary clubs. Rotary International
               see M1920.R6

           Separate works

(M1906.G4)   Gideon's International. Christian Commercial Travelers'
               Association of America
               see M1921.G5

(M1906.K4)   Kiwanis clubs. Kiwanis International
               see M1921.K5

(M1906.L4)   Lions clubs. Lions International
               see M1921.L6

(M1906.R5)   Rotary clubs. Rotary International
               see M1921.R6

           Collections

(M1920.G7)   Grange, National
               see M1905.P3

(M1920.I5)   Industrial Workers of the World
               see M1664.L3

(M1920.W6)   Woodmen of the World, Modern Woodmen of the World, and
               other foresters' organizations
               see M1905.W7

           Separate works

(M1921.G7)   Grange, National
               see M1905.P3

(M1921.I5)   Industrial Workers of the World
               see M1664.L3

(M1921.W6)   Woodmen of the World, Modern Woodmen of the World, and
               other foresters' organizations
               see M1905.W7

TABLES

(M2038-2041)	Collections
(M2038)	Miscellaneous
(M2039)	Full scores
(M2040)	Vocal scores with organ or piano accompaniment
(M2041)	Excerpts
(M2042-2057)	Separate works
(M2042-2048)	Full scores
(M2042)	Mixed voices
(M2043)	Men's voices
(M2044)	Women's voices
(M2045-2048)	Special seasons and occasions
(M2045)	Christmas
(M2046)	Easter
(M2047)	Harvest and Thanksgiving
(M2048)	Other
(M2052-2057)	Vocal scores with organ or piano accompaniment
(M2052)	Mixed voices
(M2053)	Men's voices
(M2054)	Women's voices
(M2055-2057)	Special seasons and occasions
(M2055)	Christmas
(M2056)	Easter
(M2057)	Harvest and Thanksgiving
(M2058)	Other

(M2100.2)	Greek
	see M2100+
(M2100.3-.4)	Original language
	see M2100+
(M2100.3)	Russian
	see M2100+
(M2100.4)	Other
	see M2100+
(M2100.6-.8)	Translations
	see M2100+
(M2100.6)	English
	see M2100+
(M2100.8)	Other languages
	see M2100+

TABLES

(M2113.5)	Soprano
(M2113.6)	Alto
(M2113.7)	Tenor
(M2113.8)	Baritone
(M2113.9)	Bass

(M2132.B6)	Bohemian
	see M2132.C9
(M2132.I5)	Indian languages of North America regardless of place of publication
	see the language
(M2132.Y5)	Yiddish
	see M2144
(M2141)	Swiss
	see the language
(M2142.B7)	Bohemian
	see M2142.C9
(M2142.C6)	Croatian
	see M2140.S35
(M2142.L3)	Lettish
	see M2142.L23
(M2142.S3)	Scottish
(M2142.S93)	Swedish
	see M2140.S8

TABLES

(ML207.S9)   Suriname
                              see ML239.S99
(ML245)   Austria-Hungary
                                   For Austria see ML246
                                   For Hungary see ML248
(ML271)   France: Arrêts, edicts, ordinances, etc.
                                   see ML270
(ML276)   Baden-Württemberg
                                   see ML275
(ML277)   Bavaria
                                   see ML275
(ML278)   Hesse
                                   see ML275
(ML279)   Prussia
                                   see ML275
(ML280)   Lower Saxony
                                   see ML275
(ML283.A4)   Alsace
                                   see ML270
(ML283.A51)   Alsace
                                   see ML270
(ML283.B485)   Beuthen
                                   see ML297
(ML283.B5)   Bielefeld
                                   see ML275
(ML283.B62)   Bochum
                                   see ML297
(ML283.B65)   Bonn
                                   see ML275
(ML283.B66)   Brandenburg
                                   see ML275
(ML283.B68)   Bremen
                                   see ML275
(ML283.B7)   Breslau
                                   see ML275
(ML283.B7)   Brunschweig-Wolfenbüttel
                                   see ML275
(ML283.B88)   Burgsteinfurt
                                   see ML275
(ML283.E6)   Erzgebirges
                                   see ML275
(ML283.F7)   Frankfurt an der Eder
                                   see ML275
(ML283.G2)   Gaggenau
                                   see ML275

(ML283.G3)	Gebweiler
	see ML275
(ML283.G7)	Gotha
	see ML275
(ML283.H19)	Hamburg
	see ML275
(ML283.K53)	Kiel
	see ML275
(ML283.K57)	Kleve, North Rhein-Westphalia
	see ML275
(ML283.K6)	Kłodzko, Lower Silesia
	see ML297
(ML283.K65)	Koblenz
	see ML275
(ML283.L8)	Ludwigshafen
	see ML275
(ML283.M4)	Mecklenburg-Schwerin
	see ML275
(ML283.N7)	Niederberg
	see ML275
(ML283.O4)	Oldenburg
	see ML275
(ML283.R6)	Rostocker
	see ML275
(ML283.S22)	Saarland
	see ML275
(ML283.S32)	Schleswig-Holstein
	see ML275
(ML283.S33)	Schwerin
	see ML275
(ML283.S5)	Silesia, Germany
	see ML275
(ML283.S6)	Sonderhausen
	see ML275
(ML283.S8)	Stettin
	see ML275
(ML283.S93)	Swabia
	see ML275
(ML283.T4)	Thuringia
	see ML275
(ML283.T7)	Trier
	see ML275
(ML283.W34)	Weimar
	see ML275

TABLES

(ML283.W4)	Westphalia see ML275
(ML283.W5)	Wiederbrück see ML275
(ML284)	East Germany see ML275
(ML306)	Poland see ML297
(ML309.A7)	Armenia see ML334
(ML309.A9)	Azerbaijan see ML345.A98+
(ML309.B93)	Byelorussia see ML309.B4+
(ML309.D3)	Daghestan see ML300
(ML309.G4)	Georgia see ML345.G28+
(ML309.K25)	Karelia see ML300
(ML309.K3)	Kazakhstan see ML345.K
(ML309.K5)	Kyrgyzstan see ML345.K
(ML309.L3)	Latvia see ML304
(ML309.L6)	Ladeynoye Pole see ML300
(ML309.T3)	Tajikstan see ML345.T3+
(ML309.U4)	Ukraine see ML308
(ML309.U9)	Uzbekistan see ML345.U95
(ML309.V6)	Volga Valley see ML300
(ML345.A7)	Armenia see ML334
(ML345.B3)	Bali see ML345.I5+
(ML345.C5)	Ceylon see ML345.S7+
(ML345.J3)	Java see ML345.I5+

MZ14   TABLE OF OBSOLETE NUMBERS FOR REGIONS
AND COUNTRIES FORMERLY USED FOR GENERAL
HISTORY OF MUSIC   MZ14

(ML370)   Other regions and countries
see the region or country

TABLES

(ML500)	East Germany
	see ML499
(ML508.3)	Estonia
	see ML508.E8+
(ML508.5)	Latvia
	see ML508.L4+
(ML508.7)	Lithuania
	see ML508.L6+
(ML511.A75)	Armenia
	see ML334
(ML511.A9)	Azerbaijan
	see ML541.A98+
(ML511.G4)	Georgia
	see ML541.G28+
(ML511.U38)	Ukraine
	see ML507
(ML522.T9)	Turkey
	see ML541.T78+
(ML522.Y8)	Yugoslavia
	see ML522.S5+
(ML541.A785)	Asia, Southeastern
	see ML541.S68+
(ML541.I4)	India
	see ML533
(ML541.M35)	Manchuria
	see ML531
(ML541.N4)	Near East
	see ML541.N42+
(ML541.T55)	Tibet
	see ML531
(ML592.T7)	Trieste
	see ML580
(ML592.Y8)	Yugoslavia
	see ML592.S4+
(ML842.C9)	Czechoslovakia
	see ML842.C89+

(ML990.A4)	Accordion
	see ML1083
(ML990.B3)	Bandoneon
	see ML1083
(ML990.C6)	Concertina
	see ML1083
(ML990.C68)	Courting flute
	see ML990.N37
(ML990.H75)	Hsiao
	see ML990.X53
(ML990.M7)	Mouth organ
	see ML1088
(ML990.P6)	Pommer
	see ML990.S515
(ML990.S52)	Sheng
	see ML1089.S5
(ML1015.D8)	Dulcimer
	see ML1015.A6
(ML1015.S34)	Santūr
	see ML1038.S26
(ML1015.S35)	Sanza
	see ML1015.M35
(ML1016.B3)	Banjo
	see ML1015.B3
(ML1016.D8)	Dulcimer
	see ML1015.A6
(ML1016.G8)	Guitar
	see ML1015.G9
(ML1016.H4)	Electric guitar
	see ML1015.G9
(ML1018)	Other instruments. Music and playing. By instrument, A-Z
	see ML1015.A+
(ML1040)	Other percussion instruments (not A-Z)
	see ML1049
(ML1051)	Mechanical instruments, devices, etc. Construction
	For individual instruments see the instrument
	For general works see ML1050
(ML1053)	Mechanical instruments, devices, etc. Music and playing
	see individual instruments

TABLES

(ML1551.B45)	Belgian Congo
	see ML1551.C74+
(ML1551.S5)	Silesia (General)
	see ML1551.S52+
(ML1551.Y8)	Yugoslavia
	see ML1551.S4+
(ML1738.3)	Estonia
	see ML1738.E8+
(ML1738.5)	Latvia
	see ML1738.L4+
(ML1738.7)	Lithuania
	see ML1738.L5+
(ML1741.A75)	Armenia
	see ML1751.A7+
(ML1741.A9)	Azerbaijan
	see ML1751.A98+
(ML1741.G4)	Georgia
	see ML1751.G28+
(ML1751.A9)	Australia
	see ML1751.A92+
(ML1751.I73)	Ireland
	see ML1731
(ML1751.L58)	Lithuania
	see ML1738.L5+
(ML1751.S7)	South Africa
	see ML1751.S71+
(ML1751.T5)	Tibet
	see ML1751.C5+
(ML1751.Y8)	Yugoslavia
	see ML1751.S4+
(ML2551.T55)	Tibet
	see ML2551.C5+
(ML2851.Y8)	Yugoslavia
	see ML2851.S47+
(ML2881.Y8)	Yugoslavia
	see ML2881.S4+
(ML3051.B6)	Bohemia
	see ML3051.C9+
(ML3051.Z25)	Zaire
	see ML3051.C74+

(ML3486.C8)	Cuba see ML3486.C82+
(ML3491)	East Germany see ML3490
(ML3499.S9)	Sweden see ML3499.S91+
(ML3499.Y8)	Yugoslavia see ML3499.S42+
(ML3502.H55)	Hong Kong see ML3502.C5+
(ML3503.A358)	Africa, General see ML3502.5
(ML3503.Z25)	Zaire see ML3505.C68+
(ML3503.Z58)	Zanzibar see ML3503.T34+
(ML3509.B4)	Belgium see ML3509.B42+
(ML3509.G35)	East Germany see ML3509.G3+
(ML3509.I8)	Israel see ML3509.I82+
(ML3509.S7)	Soviet Union see ML3509.R8+
(ML3575.I5)	Indians of South America see ML3575.A2
(ML3585)	Austria see ML3586
(ML3610)	Yugoslavia see ML3611.S47+
(ML3612)	Turkey see ML3757
(ML3613)	Other regions and countries see the region or country
(ML3632)	Baden-Württemberg see ML3630+
(ML3634)	Bavaria see ML3630+
(ML3636)	Hesse see ML3630+
(ML3638)	Prussia see ML3630+
(ML3640)	Lower Saxony see ML3630+

TABLES

(ML3642)   Württemberg
                           see ML3630+
(ML3643.A4)   Altmark
                           see ML3630+
(ML3643.F7)   Franconia
                           see ML3630+
(ML3643.H3)   Harz Mountains Region
                           see ML3630+
(ML3643.H55)   Hinsbeck
                           see ML3630+
(ML3643.P28)   Palatinate
                           see ML3630+
(ML3643.R5)   Rhine Valley. Rhineland
                           see ML3630+
(ML3643.R55)   Rhineland-Palatinate
                           see ML3630+
(ML3643.W3)   Waldeck (Hesse)
                           see ML3630+
(ML3647)   East Germany
                           see ML3630+
(ML3681.3)   Eastonia
                           see ML3681.E8+
(ML3681.5)   Latvia
                           see ML3681.L4+
(ML3681.7)   Lithuania
                           see ML3681.L6+
(ML3682)   Armenia
                           see ML3758.A75+
(ML3683)   Azerbaijan
                           see ML3758.A98+
(ML3685)   Finland
                           see ML3619
(ML3688)   Georgia
                           see ML3758.G28+
(ML3693.A2)   Abkhazia
                           see ML3758.G28+
(ML3693.A75)   Armenia
                           see ML3758.A75+
(ML3693.A95)   Azerbaijan
                           see ML3758.A98+
(ML3693.B9)   Belarus
                           see ML3684
(ML3693.E8)   Estonia
                           see ML3681.E8+

TABLE OF OBSOLETE NUMBERS FOR REGIONS
AND COUNTRIES FORMERLY USED FOR HISTORY
OF POPULAR, FOLK, ETHNIC, AND NATIONAL
MUSIC

(ML3693.F55)	Finno-Ugrians (Russia)
	see ML3680
(ML3693.G46)	Georgia
	see ML3758.G28+
(ML3693.H4)	Hebrews
	see ML3776
(ML3693.I2)	Iakutsk
	see ML3680
(ML3693.K36)	Karelia
	see ML3680
(ML3693.K39)	Kazakhstan
	see ML3758.K4+
(ML3693.K57)	Kyrgyzstan
	see ML3758.K98+
(ML3693.L58)	Lithuania
	see ML3681.L6+
(ML3693.M64)	Moldova
	see ML3689
(ML3693.S55)	Siberia
	see ML3680
(ML3693.T4)	Tatarstan
	see ML3680
(ML3693.T7)	Tuva
	see ML3680
(ML3693.U9)	Uzbekistan
	see ML3758.U9+
(ML3693.W5)	White Russia
	see ML3684
(ML3693.Y3)	Yakut
	see ML3680
(ML3730.A4)	Albania
	see ML3601
(ML3730.C9)	Cyprus
	see ML3758.C9+
(ML3730.G28)	Georgia
	see ML3758.G28+
(ML3730.T8)	Turkey
	see ML3757
(ML3758.A75)	Armenia
	see ML3740
(ML3758.I5)	Indochina
	see ML3758.I52+
(ML3758.J3)	Java
	see ML3758.I53+

TABLES

(ML3758.K9)	Kuwait
	see ML3758.K92+
(ML3758.M4)	Malaysia
	see ML3758.M42+
(ML3758.P3)	Pakistan
	see ML3758.P32+
(ML3770)	Oceania, etc.
	see ML3774+
(ML3775.M45)	Mauritius
	see ML3758.M45+
(ML3775.N45)	New Zealand
	see ML3771
(ML3775.P6)	Philippines
	see ML3758.P5+
(ML3775.V3)	Venezuela
	see ML3575.V3+

(ML3695.A-Z)	By topic or title, A-Z
	see ML3580
(ML3695.R5)	Revolutions
	see ML3680
(ML3696)	Other topics (not A-Z)
	see ML3680

(M1831.B34)	Bambute
	see M1831.M4
(M1831.B42)	Batutsi
	see M1831.T87
(M1831.B88)	Bushmen
	see M1831.S26
(M1831.L85)	Lunda
	see M1831.R98
(M1831.M37)	Mashona
	see M1831.S5
(M1831.M72)	Mpangwe
	see M1831.F33
(M1831.S45)	Senga language
(M1831.S65)	Somali
	see M1838.S65+
(M1831.T5)	Thonga
	see M1831.T76
(M1831.X7)	Xosa
	see M1831.S5

M59	Other
	Previously, not subdivided by individual other stringed instrument
M110	Other
	Previously, not subdivided by individual other wind instrument
M142	Other
	Previously, not subdivided by individual plucked instrument
M174	Pianola and kindred instruments
	see M20+
M175	Other
	Previously, not subdivided by individual other instrument
M270	Other
	Previously, not subdivided by individual other wind instrument
M271	Other
	Previously, not subdivided by individual other wind instrument
M282	Other
	Previously, not subdivided by individual other plucked instrument
M283	Other
	Previously, not subdivided by individual other plucked instrument
M284	Piano and other instrument
	Previously, not subdivided by individual instrument
	For unspecified instrument, see M285.5
M285	Piano and other instrument
	Previously, not subdivided by individual other instrument
	For unspecified instrument, see M285.6
M1019	Other
	Previously, not subdivided by individual other solo stringed instrument
M1034	Other
	Previously, not subdivided by individual other solo wind instrument
M1034.5	Other
	Previously, not subdivided by other solo instrument
M1035	Other
	Previously, not subdivided by other solo instrument
M1038	Other plucked instruments. Scores
	Previously, not subdivided by individual solo instrument
	For individual solo instruments, see M1037.4.A+
M1038.5	Other plucked instruments. Cadenzas
	Previously, not subdivided by individual solo instrument
	For individual solo instruments, see M1037.4.A+
M1039	Other plucked instruments. Solo(s) with piano
	Previously, not subdivided by individual solo instrument
	For individual solo instruments, see M1037.4.A+
M1105	Solo instrument(s) with string orchestra. Scores
	Previously, not subdivided by individual solo instrument
	For individual solo instruments, see M1105+

TABLES

M1105.5	Solo instrument(s) with string orchestra. Cadenzas
	For individual solo instruments, see M1105+
M1106	Solo instrument(s) with string orchestra. Solo(s) with piano
	Previously, not subdivided by individual solo instrument
	For individual solo instruments, see M1105+
M1766.A-Z	Other Russian regions, peoples, languages, etc., A-Z
M1767.A-Z	Other Russian regions, peoples, languages, etc., A-Z
M1777	Spain and Portugal
M1831	Special. By region
ML484	Central America
ML567	Central America
ML568	South America
ML617	Central America
ML618	South America
ML667	Central America
ML668	South America
ML717	Central America
ML718	South America
ML817	Central America
ML818	South America
ML867	Central America
ML868	South America
ML1117	Central America
ML1118	South America
ML1216	Central America
ML1217	South America
ML1316	Central America
ML1317	South America
ML1416	Central America
ML1417	South America
ML1516	Central America
ML1517	South America
ML1616	Central America
ML1617	South America
ML1716	Central America
ML1717	South America
ML2516	Central America
ML2517	South America
ML2616	Central America
ML2617	South America
ML2816	Central America
ML2817	South America
ML2916	Central America
ML2917	South America
ML3016	Central America
ML3017	South America

ML3116	Central America
ML3117	South America
ML3216	Central America
ML3217	South America
ML3316	Central America
ML3317	South America
ML3416	Central America
ML3417	South America
ML3500	Pageants, folk festivals, community music
ML3572	Central America
ML3575.A2-.A26	General
ML3575.A3-Z	By region or country, A-Z
ML3770	Australia, Oceania, etc.
ML3775	Other, A-Z
MT720	Orchestral bells, bone playing, and other (not A-Z)

Alphorn
  History: ML990.A54
  Instruction and study: MT432
Alphorn music: M110.A47
Alto clarinet: M70+
Alto clarinet and piano music: M248+
Alto clarinet concertos: M1024+,
  M1124+
Alto flute and piano music: M240+
Alto flute concertos: M1020+, M1120+
Alto flute music: M60+
Alto horn
  Instruction and study: MT494
Alto horn and piano music: M270.A4,
  M271.A4
Alto trombone and piano music: M262+
Alto trombone concertos: M1032+,
  M1132+
Alto trombone music: M90+
Amaranth, Order of
  Vocal music: M1905.A55, M1906.A55
Amateur Hour Collection: M15 .A4
Ambrosian chants: M2154.6.A45
Amens: M6 .x14
American Association of Retired
  Persons
  Songs and music: M1920.A433,
    M1921.A433
American Cancer Society
  Songs and music: M1920.A44,
    M1921.A44
American Federation of Labor
  Songs and music: M1664.L3,
    M1665.L3
American Gold Star Mothers, Inc
  Vocal music: M1676.G6
American Independent Party
  Songs and music: M1664.A55,
    M1665.A55
American Legion
  Ladies Auxiliary
    Vocal music: M1676.A5+
  Vocal music: M1676.A5+
American Party
  Songs and music: M1664.K5,
    M1665.K5

American Revolution, 1775-1783
  Vocal music: M1631
American Revolution Bicentennial
  Songs and music: M1652
American sheet music: M1.A1+
  Civil War: M20.C58+
Amish
  Hymns: M2131.A4
Anabaptists
  Hymns: M2131.A45
Anacreontic song: M1630.3.S68
Ancient Arabic Order of the Nobles of
  the Mystic Shrine for North America
  Vocal music: M1900.M4, M1901.M4
Ancient Egyptian Order of Scioto
  Vocal music: M1900.M42,
    M1901.M42
Anglican chants: M2016.6, M2170.6
Anglican Church of Canada
  Liturgy: M2171.C3
Anglican Communion: M2016+
  Liturgy and ritual: M2167+
Animals
  Songs and music: M1977.A6,
    M1978.A6
  Vocal music: M1977.A6
Animals and music: ML3919+
Anklung
  History: ML1048
Antheil, George, Collection: M15 .A58
Anthems: M2020+
  Juvenile: M2190+
Anthony, of Egypt, Saint, 250-355 or 6
  Songs and music: M2149.5.A6
Antiphonaries: M2149+
Antiphons
  Sets, by language: M6 .x144
Antiquarian booksellers
  Catalogs: ML152
Antiques
  Songs and music: M1977.A65,
    M1978.A65
Antislavery movements
  Songs and music: M1664.A35,
    M1665.A35
Apollo harp music: M175.A5
Apostles' Creed: M6 .x32

343

Bağlama
  Instruction and study: MT654.B3
Bagpipe
  Bibliography: ML128.B17
  History: ML980
  Instruction and study: MT530
Bagpipe and piano music: M270.B3,
  M271.B3
Bagpipe music: M145
Bahai Faith
  Hymns: M2145.B34
Bajo sexto
  Instruction and study: MT599.B35
Balalaika
  Concertos: M1037.4.B3
  History: ML1015.B24
  Instruction and study: MT643+
Balalaika and piano music: M282.B3,
  M283.B3
Balalaika music: M142.B2
Balkan Peninsula
  History and criticism: ML3600+
Ballad opera: ML1950
Ballad operas
  Librettos: ML50.7
Ballet: ML3858
Ballets: M1520+
  Analysis, appreciation: MT95+
  Bibliography: ML128.B2
  History and criticism: ML3460
  Librettos: ML51+
  Stories, plots, etc: MT95+
Ballets Russes Archive: M15 .G75
Balloons
  Songs and music: M1977.B3,
  M1978.B3
Balo
  Instruction and study: MT725.B3
Baltic States
  History and criticism: ML3681.A+
Bambuso sonoro music: M175.B17
Bamun (African people)
  Music: M1831.B345
  Vocal music: M1831.B345
Ban hu
  Concertos: M1019.P3
  Instruction and study: MT335.P3

Ban hu music: M59.P3
Band music: M1200+
  Analysis, appreciation: MT135+
  Bibliography: ML128.B23
    Graded lists: ML132.B3
  Discography: ML156.4.B3
  History and criticism: ML1299+,
    ML3518
  Juvenile: M1420
  Performance: MT733+
    Juvenile: MT810
Band music, Arranged: M1254+
Bandolon
  Instruction and study: MT594
Bandoneon
  Concertos: M1139.4.B3
  History: ML1083
Bandoneon and piano music:
  M284.B33, M285.B33
Bandoneon music: M175.B2
  Juvenile: M1385.B34
Bandonion
  Concertos: M1039.4.B3
Bandora
  Bibliography: ML128.B235
Bands (Music)
  Dictionaries: ML102.B35
  History: ML1299+
Bandura
  History: ML1015.B25
  Instruction and study: MT654.B35
Bandurria
  History: ML1015.B26
  Instruction and study: MT592+
Bandurria music: M142.B3
Banjo
  Concertos: M1037.4.B36
  History: ML1015.B3
  Instruction and study: MT560+
    Juvenile: MT801.B3
Banjo and piano music: M274+
Banjo music: M120+, MT569
  Discography: ML156.4.B36
  Juvenile: M1385.B35
  Teaching pieces: MT563
Banjo ukulele
  Instruction and study: MT646

Blues (Music)
  Social aspects: ML3918.B57
Blues rock music
  Dictionaries906: ML102.B63
B'nai B'rith
  Vocal music: M1905.B5
B'nai B'rith International
  Songs and music: M1905.B5,
    M1906.B5
Boas, Franziska, Collection: M15 .B63
Bodhrán
  History: ML1038.B63
  Instruction and study: MT725.B55
Bombardon
  Instruction and study: MT480+
Bombardon music: MT484
  Teaching pieces: MT483
Bone flute
  History: ML990.B66
Bone pastor: M6 .x22
Bones (Musical instrument)
  Instruction and study: MT725.B6
Bongo (Drum)
  Instruction and study: MT663+
Bonkó
  History: ML1038.B66
Bonum est confiteri: M6 .x23
Bosnia and Hercegovina
  History and criticism: ML3611.B54+
Bouzouki
  Instruction and study: MT654.B69
Bowed stringed instruments
  Instruction and study: MT259+
Bowling
  Songs and music: M1977.S715,
    M1978.S715
Boxing
  Songs and music: M1977.S716,
    M1978.S716
Boy Scouts of America
  Songs and music: M1977.B6,
    M1978.B6
Bradbury, William B., Collection: M15
  .B7
Braille music notation: MT38
Brass decets: M957.4
Brass instrument music: M60+

Brass instruments
  Bibliography: ML128.B73
  Dictionaries: ML102.B7
  History: ML933
  Instruction and study: MT418
    Juvenile: MT801.B72
Brass nonets: M957.4
Brass octets: M857.4
Brass quartets: M457.4
Brass quintets: M557.4
Brass septets: M757.4
Brass sextets: M657.4
Brass trios: M357.4
Breath control
  Singing: MT878
Brethren in Christ Church
  Hymns: M2131.B6
British Americans
  Music: M1668.1
    History and criticism: ML3553
Broadsides: M1628.2+, M1630.3.S69,
  M1739.3
Bronze drum
  History: ML1038.B7
Brotherhood Week
  Songs and music: M1977.B7,
    M1978.B7
Bruderhof Communities
  Hymns: M2131.H87
Buddhist hymns: M2145.B8
Buddhist music: M2188.B8
Bugle
  Construction: ML961
  History: ML960+
  Instruction and study: MT452
  Maintenance and repair: ML961
Bugle and drum music: M1270
Bugle and piano music: M270.B8,
  M271.B8
Bulbultarang
  Instruction and study: MT634.B84
Bulgaria
  History and criticism: ML3602+
Bullfights
  Songs and music: M1977.B8,
    M1978.B8
  Vocal music: M1977.B8

Button-key accordion
  Instruction and study: MT681+
Button-key accordion music: M154
Byzantine chants: M2160.71+
Byzantine music
  History and criticism: ML188

C

Cadenzas: M1004.6+
Cajón (Musical instrument)
  History: ML1038.C25
Cajun music
  History and criticism: ML3560.C25
Cajun songs: M1668.8
Calliope music: M175.C3
Camaldolite rite: M2154.4.C34
Camp Fire Girls
  Songs and music: M1977.B6,
    M1978.B6
Campaign songs
  Bibliography: ML128.C13
  United States: M1659.7+
Campanula
  History: ML927.C36
  Instruction and study: MT335.C36
Campanula and piano music:
  M239.C36
Campanula music: M59.C36
Camping
  Songs and music: M1977.C3,
    M1978.C3
Canada
  History and criticism: ML205+,
    ML3484+, ML3563+
  Vocal music: M1678+
Canals
  Songs and music: M1977.C34,
    M1978.C34
Candlemas music: M2068.C2,
  M2078.C2, M2088.C2, M2098.C2
  Liturgy and ritual: M2150.4.C35+
  Songs: M2114.8.C2
Canon: MT59
Canons, fugues, etc. (Organ): M10
Cantata: ML3260

Cantatas
  Analysis, appreciation: MT110+
  Bibliography: ML128.C15
  History and criticism: ML2400
Cantatas, Sacred: M2020+
  Juvenile: M2190+
Cantatas, Secular: M1629.5
  Juvenile: M1996
Cantate Domino canticum novum,
  cantate Domino: M6 .x25
Cante hondo
  History and criticism: ML3712
Cantillation
  Instruction and study: MT860
Canun
  Concertos: M1037.4.C3
Capuchin rite: M2154.4.C36
Caribbean Area
  History and criticism: ML207.A+
Carillon music: M172
Carillons
  History: ML1039
  Instruction and study: MT710
Carmelite rite: M2154.4.C37
Carnatic music
  Bibliography: ML128.K37
  Dictionaries: ML102.K37
  Discography: ML156.4.C34
Carols
  Dictionaries: ML102.C3
  History and criticism: ML2880+
Carribean Area
  History and criticism: ML3486
Carrie Jacobs-Bond Collection: M15 .J3
Cars (Automobiles)
  Vocal music: M1977.M6, M1978.M6
Castanet music: M175.C35
Castanets
  Instruction and study: MT725.C4
Catá
  History: ML1038.C28
Catalogs, Booksellers: ML150+
Catalogs, Publishers: ML144+
Catches
  History and criticism: ML2670
Catholic Church
  Ambrosian rite: M2154.6.A45

Catholic Church
  Armenian rite: M2154.6.A76
  Hymns: M2119
  Liber usualis: M2151.A+
  Liturgy: M2010+, M2147+
  Mozarabic rite: M2154.6.M7
  Religious aspects of music:
    ML3921.4.C38
  Vocal music: M2069, M2089
Catholic Church music
  History and criticism: ML3002+
Cavaquinho music: M142.C38
Celesta and piano music: M284.C4,
  M285.C4
Celesta music: M175.C44
Celestial Church of Christ
  Hymns: M2131.C29
Celtic harp
  History: ML1015.C3
  Instruction and study: MT552
Celtic harp music: M142.C44
Celtic music
  History and criticism: ML3522
Cemeteries
  Songs and music: M1977.C4,
    M1978.C4
Cenda
  History: ML1038.C4
Centennial Exhibition (Philadelphia,
  1876)
  Songs and music: M1677.2.P4 1876
Central America
  History and criticism: ML3487.A+,
    ML3571+
Century of Progress International
  Exposition (Chicago, 1933)
  Songs and music: M1677.2.C3 1933
Chaconne
  Instruction and study: MT64.C48
Chaconnes
  Piano music (4 hands): M203
  Violin music: M220
  Violoncello and piano music: M232
Chaconnes (Band): M1203
Chaconnes (Orchestra): M1003
Chaconnes (Organ): M9
Chaconnes (Piano): M27

Chaconnes (String orchestra): M1103
Chalumeau
  History: ML990.C5
Chalumeau concertos: M1034.C5,
  M1134.C5
Chamber music: M177+, M180+,
  M300+, M400+, M500+, M600+,
  M700+, M800+, M900+, M990,
  MT728.2+
  Analysis, appreciation: MT140+
  Bibliography: ML128.C4
    Graded lists: ML132.C4
  Discography: ML156.4.C4
  For children: M1389+
  History and criticism: ML1100+
  Juvenile: M1413+
  Number of players: M177
  Performance: MT728+
    For children: MT810
  With voice: M1613.3
Chamber orchestra music: M1000+
Change ringing: MT711
  History: ML1039
Change ringing (Bells): MT710
Changgo
  Instruction and study: MT725.C45
Charango
  History: ML1015.C37
  Instruction and study: MT599.C45
Charles Hambitzer Music Manuscripts:
  M15 .H36
Charts, diagrams, etc: MT16
Chemistry
  Songs and music: M1977.C43,
    M1978.C43
Cheng
  Instruction and study: MT654.C47
Cheng music: M142.C49
Chicago International Exposition (1933)
  Songs and music: M1677.2.C3 1933
Child musicians: ML81, ML83
Children's Day music: M2191.C4
Children's songs
  Discography: ML156.4.C5
Chime music: M172
Chimes
  History: ML1039

Double bass
  Maintenance and repair: ML921
Double bass and keyboard instrument
  music
  Juvenile: M1400
Double bass and piano music: M237+
  Juvenile: M1400
Double bass concertos: M1018, M1118
Double bass music: M55+, MT333.4
  History and criticism: ML925
  Juvenile: M1385.D6
  Teaching pieces: MT333
Double keyboard music: M25.2, M38.2
Dramatic music: M1500+
  Analysis, appreciation: MT95+
  History and criticism: ML1699+,
    ML3857+
  Juvenile: M1995
Drinking songs: M1977.D7, M1978.D7
Druid and Druidism
  Hymns: M2145.D78
Drum
  History: ML1035+
  Instruction and study: MT662+
    Juvenile: MT801.D7
Drum and bugle corps music
  Performance: MT735
Drum and piano music: M284.D8,
  M285.D8
Drum machine
  Instruction and study: MT724.5
Drum majoring: MT733.5
Drum music: M146
  Juvenile: M1385.D7
Drum set
  History: ML1035+
  Instruction and study: MT662+
Drum set and piano music: M284.D83,
  M285.D83
Drum set music: M146
Duduk (Oboe)
  History: ML990.D76
Duets: M180+
Dulcimer
  Concertos: M1039.4.D85,
    M1139.4.D85
  Dictionaries: ML102.D85

Dulcimer
  History: ML1041
  Instruction and study: MT717+
Dulcimer and piano music: M284.D85,
  M285.D85
Dulcimer, Appalachian, music:
  M142.A7
Dulcimer music: M175.D84
Dulzaina
  History: ML990.D8
Dutch American folk music
  History and criticism: ML3555
Dutch Americans
  Music
    History and criticism: ML3555
Dutch Reformed Church
  Hymns: M2124.D7
  Liturgy and ritual: M2164

Đ

Đàn bâu
  History: ML1015.D35
Đàn tranh
  History: ML1015.D36

E

Eagles, Fraternal Order of
  Vocal music: M1905.E2, M1906.E2
Easter music: M1629.3.E3, M2066,
  M2076, M2086, M2096, M2148.3.E2,
  M2149.5.V54
  Bibliography: ML128.L2
  Juvenile: M2191.E2
  Liturgy and ritual: M2149.4.E25
  Organ: M14.4.E2, M14.5.E2
  Songs, etc: M2114.6
Eastern Star, Order of
  Vocal music: M1905.E3, M1906.E3
Ecce panis: M6 .x38
Ecce sacerdos: M6 .x382
Ecology
  Songs and music: M1977.C53,
    M1978.C53
Economic conditions
  Vocal music: M1977.E3, M1978.E3

Eric Johnson Collection of Ernest Bloch
   Photographs: M15 .J64
Ernest Bloch Collection: M15 .B56
Ernst Bacon Collection: M15 .B23
Ernst Bloch Photographs, Eric Johnson
   Collection of: M15 .J64
Eskimos
   Music
     History and criticism: ML3560.E8
   United States
     Music: M1668.9.E8
Ethics
   Songs and music: M1977.M55,
     M1978.M55
Ethnic songs: M1668+
Ethnomusicologists
   Biography: ML423.A+
Ethnomusicology: ML3797.6+
   Bibliography: ML128.E8
Ethnomusicooogists
   Biography: ML403
Euphonium
   Bibliography: ML128.B24
   History: ML970+
   Instruction and study: MT496+
Euphonium and piano music:
   M270.B37, M271.B37
Euphonium concertos: M1034.B37,
   M1134.B37
Euphonium music: M110.B33
Europe
   History and criticism: ML3580+
Evangelical Mission Covenant Church of
   America
   Hymns: M2131.E8
Evening service music: M2016.4
Ewe (African people)
   Music: M1831.E9
   Vocal music: M1831.E9
Ex-convicts
   Songs and music: M1977.C55,
     M1978.C55
Examinations, questions, etc: MT9
Exhibitions
   Vocal music: M1677.2.A+
Expatriate musicians
   Bibliography: ML128.E9

Expo 67 (Montreal, 1967)
   Songs and music: M1677.2.M65 1967
Expo 74 (Spokane, 1974)
   Songs and music: M1677.2.S65 1974
Eyes
   Songs and music: M1977.E84,
     M1978.E84

F

Famous people
   Vocal music: M1627.5.A+
Famous persons
   Vocal music: M1659+
Fang (Cameroon)
   Vocal music: M1831.F3
Fang (West African people)
   Music: M1831.F33
   Vocal music: M1831.F33
Farmer-Labor Party
   Songs and music: M1664.F15,
     M1665.F15
Farmers
   Songs and music: M1977.F2,
     M1978.F2
Farmers' Alliance (U.S.)
   Songs and music: M1664.F2,
     M1665.F2
Fathers
   Songs and music: M1977.F26,
     M1978.F26
Father's Day
   Songs and music: M2068.F3,
     M2191.F38
Father's Day music
   Songs: M2114.8.F3
   Songs and music: M2078.F3,
     M2088.F3, M2098.F3
Faust, d. ca. 1540
   Songs and music
     Discography: ML156.4.F35
Federal Music Project (U.S.) Collection:
   M15 .F43
Federal Party (U.S.)
   Songs and music: M1664.F4,
     M1665.F4

Hardanger fiddle
  History: ML927.H27
  Instruction and study: MT335.H4
Hardanger fiddle concertos:
  M1119.H37
Hardanger fiddle music: M59.H37
Hardwood drum
  Instruction and study: MT725.H37
Harmonica
  Concertos: M1039.4.H3, M1139.4.H3
  Dictionaries: ML102.H37
  History: ML1088
  Instruction and study: MT682+
    Juvenile: MT801.H4
Harmonica and piano music: M284.H3,
  M285.H3
Harmonica music: M175.H3
Harmonium
  Bibliography: ML128.H2
Harmony: MT50
  History: ML444
  Psychological aspects: ML3836
Harmony (Music): ML3815
  Philosophy and aesthetics: ML3852
Harold Bauer Collection: M15 .B43
Harp: ML1005+
  Bibliography: ML128.H3
  Construction: ML1006
  Dictionaries: ML102.H38
  Instruction and study: MT540+
    Juvenile: MT801.H43
  Maintenance and repair: ML1006
Harp and piano music: M272+
Harp concertos: M1036+, M1136+
Harp-lute guitar
  Instruction and study: MT634.H36
Harp-lute guitar and piano music:
  M282.H4, M283.H4
Harp-lute music: M142.H2
Harp music: M115+, MT544
  Bibliography
    Graded lists: ML132.H3
  History and criticism: ML1008
  Juvenile: M1385.H3
  Teaching pieces: MT543
Harp zither
  Instruction and study: MT634.H37

Harpola
  Instruction and study: MT634.H38
Harpsichord
  Bibliography: ML128.H35
  Construction: ML652+
  Dictionaries: ML102.H385
  Instruction and study: MT250+
  Keyboard instruments: ML651
  Maintenance and repair: ML652+
  Performance
    History: ML649.8+
Harpsichord concertos: M1010+,
  M1110+
Harpsichord music: M20+
  Discography: ML156.4.H3
  History and criticism: ML649.8+
  Juvenile: M1378+
  Teaching pieces: MT243
Harpsichordists
  Biography: ML397, ML417.A+
Hasidim
  Music: M1851
  Vocal music: M1851
Hát bòi
  Dictionaries: ML102.H4
Hausa (African people)
  Music: M1831.H39
  Vocal music: M1831.H39
Have mercy upon me, O God: M6 .x62
Hawaiian and piano music: M285.H35
Hawaiian guitar
  Instruction and study: MT590+
Hawaiian guitar and piano music:
  M284.H35
Hawaiian guitar music: M142.H3
Hawaiians
  Music
    History and criticism: ML3560.H3
Haymes, Joe, Big Band Arrangements:
  M15 .H397
Health
  Songs and music: M1977.H4,
    M1978.H4
Heckelphone
  History: ML990.H4
Heckelphone concertos: M1034.H4
Heckelphone music: M110.H4

Humor in music
  Bibliography: ML128.H75
Humorous songs: M1977.H7,
  M1978.H7
Hungarian Americans
  Music: M1668.9.H8
Hungary
  History and criticism: ML3593+
Hunger
  Songs and music: M1977.H77,
  M1978.H77
Hunting songs: M1977.H8, M1978.H8
  History and criticism: ML3780
Hurdy-gurdy
  Concertos: M1039.4.H87
  History: ML1086
  Instruction and study: MT725.H87
Hurdy-gurdy music: M175.H9
Husbands
  Songs and music: M1977.H85,
  M1978.H85
Hutterian Brethren
  Hymns: M2131.H87
Hymnals: M2115+
Hymns: M2115+
  Bibliography: ML128.H8
  Dictionaries: ML102.H95
  Europe: M2135+
  History and criticism: ML3086,
  ML3270
  Sets, by language: M6 .x43
Hymns, Afrikaans: M2132.A35
Hymns, Albanian: M2132.A5,
  M2142.A42
Hymns, Arabic: M2132.A57
Hymns, Armenian: M2132.A6,
  M2142.A6
Hymns, Basque: M2142.B38
Hymns, Bengali: M2132.B46
Hymns, Bulgarian: M2142.B8
Hymns, Cherokee: M2132.C35
Hymns, Cheyenne: M2132.C46
Hymns, Chinese: M2132.C5
Hymns, Croatian: M2132.C6
Hymns, Czech: M2132.C9, M2142.C9
Hymns, Danish: M2132.D3, M2140.D3
Hymns, Dutch: M2132.D7, M2135

Hymns, English: M2136
Hymns, Eskimo languages: M2132.E85
Hymns, Finnish: M2132.F3, M2142.F4
Hymns, French: M2132.F5, M2137
Hymns, Frisian: M2142.F7
Hymns, Galician: M2142.G3
Hymns, German: M2132.G3, M2138
Hymns, Greek: M2132.G5, M2142.G7
Hymns, Hawaiian: M2132.H3
Hymns, Hungarian: M2132.H8,
  M2142.H9
Hymns, Icelandic: M2132.I2, M2142.I2
Hymns, Irish: M2132.I55, M2142.I5
Hymns, Italian: M2132.I6, M2142.I6
Hymns, Latin: M2142.L2
Hymns, Latvian: M2132.L3
Hymns, Lithuanian: M2132.L4,
  M2142.L5
Hymns, Norwegian: M2132.N5,
  M2140.N6
Hymns, Polish: M2132.P5, M2142.P5
Hymns, Portuguese: M2132.P6
Hymns, Romanian: M2142.R6
Hymns, Russian: M2132.R7, M2139
Hymns, Sami: M2142.S26
Hymns, Serbo-Croatian: M2142.S35
Hymns, Slovak: M2132.S3, M2142.S4
Hymns, Spanish: M2132.S5, M2142.S5
Hymns, Swedish: M2132.S8, M2140.S8
Hymns, Tagalog: M2132.T2
Hymns, Ukrainian: M2132.U7,
  M2142.U7
Hymns, Welsh: M2132.W3, M2142.W3
Hyŏn' gŭm music: M142.H9

I

I AM Religious Activity
  Hymns: M2131.I2
I believe in one God, the Father
  almighty: M6 .x3
Ichigenkin
  History: ML1015.I3
Ichigenkin music: M142.I3
Ideal harp
  Instruction and study: MT634.I3

Jing hu
  Concertos: M1019.C5
Jing hu music: M59.C5
Job's Daughters, International Order of
  Vocal music: M1905.J6, M1906.J6
Joe Haymes Big Band Arrangements:
  M15 .H397
John Davis Batchelder Collection: M15
  .B4
Johnson, Eric, Collection of Ernest
  Bloch Photographs: M15 .J64
Joint Army and Navy Committee on
  Welfare and Recreation, Sub-
  Committee on Music, Papers: M15
  .U5
Joseph, Saint
  Songs and music: M2149.5.V545
Jouhikko
  Instruction and study: MT335.J68
Jubilate Deo omnis terra, servite
  Domino: M6 .x45
Judaism
  Religious aspects of music:
    ML3921.6.J83
Julius Gold Collection: M15 .G55
Junior republics
  Songs and music: M1977.J7,
    M1978.J7
Justus ut palma: M6 .x47
Juvenile delinquency
  Songs and music: M1977.J87,
    M1978.J87

K

Kabiye (African people)
  Music: M1831.K3
  Vocal music: M1831.K3
Kacapi (Lute)
  History: ML1015.K23
Kacapi (Zither)
  History: ML1015.K24
Kaen
  History: ML1089.K24
  Instruction and study: MT683
Kanklės
  History: ML1015.K27

Kanklės music: M142.K36
Kannel
  Instruction and study: MT634.K3
Kantele
  Concertos: M1137.4.K36
  History: ML1015.K3
  Instruction and study: MT634.K35
Kantele music: M142.K37
Karaoke
  Political aspects: ML3918.K36
  Social aspects: ML3918.K36
Kaval
  History: ML990.K36
Kaval music: M110.K4
Kayagŭm
  Instruction and study: MT654.K4
Kayagŭm music: M142.K39
Kazoo
  Instruction and study: MT533.K36
Kemp, Father, 1820-1897: M1677
Kern, Jerome, Collection: M15 .K4
Keyboard harmony: MT191.H4, MT224
Keyboard instruments: ML549+
  Bibliography: ML128.K5
  Dictionaries: ML102.K5
  Instruction and study: MT179+
    Juvenile: MT745+
  Music: M6+
Keyboard players
  Biography: ML416+
Keyed bugle
  Construction: ML961
  History: ML960+
  Instruction and study: MT452
  Maintenance and repair: ML961
Keyed fiddle
  History: ML927.K49
Keyed trumpet
  Construction: ML961
  History: ML960+
  Instruction and study: MT440+
  Maintenance and repair: ML961
Keyed trumpet music
  Teaching pieces: MT443
Khim music: M175.K45
Kiwanis clubs
  Vocal music: M1920.K5, M1921.K5

Kiwanis International
  Songs and music: M1920.K5
Kiwanis International b Songs and
  music: M1921.K5
Klezmer music
  History and criticism: ML3528.8
Knights of Columbus
  Songs and music: M1905.K5,
  M1906.K5
Knights of Labor
  Songs and music: M1664.L3,
  M1665.L3
Knights of Malta
  Songs and music: M1905.K54,
  M1906.K54
Knights of Pythias
  Songs and music: M1905.K55
  Vocal music: M1906.K55
Knights of the Golden Eagle
  Songs and music: M1905.K6,
  M1906.K6
Know-nothing Party
  Songs and music: M1664.K5,
  M1665.K5
Kobza
  History: ML1015.K6
Kobza music: M142.K55
Kodály, Zoltán, 1882-1967
  Music teaching method: MT23
Kokle
  History: ML1015.K64
  Instruction and study: MT634.K65
Kolisch, Rudolf, Collection: M15 .K63
Kŏmun'go
  History: ML1015.K65
Kŏmun'go music: M142.K58
Kong hou
  Instruction and study: MT555
Kopuz music: M142.K59
Kora
  History: ML1015.K66
Kora music: M142.K595
Korea
  History and criticism: ML3752+
Korea (North)
  History and criticism: ML3753+

Korea (South)
  History and criticism: ML3752+
Korean War, 1950-1953
  Songs and music: M1649
Koto
  History: ML1015.K68
  Instruction and study: MT654.K7
Koto concertos: M1037.4.K68
Koto music: M142.K6
Kotsuzumi
  History: ML1038.K7
Koussevitzky Music Foundation: M14
  0.3a+
Kreisler, Fritz, Collection: M15 .K7
Ku Klux Klan
  Songs and music
    Bibliography: ML128.K8
Ku-Klux Klan
  Songs and music: M1665.K7
  Vocal music: M1664.K7
Kuan concertos: M1034.K8
Kuba (African people)
  Music: M1831.K82
  Vocal music: M1831.K82
Kyriales: M2148.4.A+
Kyrie eleison: M6 .x5

L

Labor
  Vocal music: M1977.L3, M1978.L3
    History and criticism: ML3780
Labor Day
  Songs and music: M1629.3.L3
Labor songs
  Discography: ML156.4.L2
Ländler
  Instruction and study: MT64.L23
Latin America
  History and criticism: ML199+,
    ML3487.A+, ML3558
Latvia
  History and criticism: ML3681.L4+
Latvian Americans
  Music: M1668.9.L4
Lauda Sion: M6 .x52

Motion picture music
  Discography: ML156.4.M6
  Excerpts: M1505+
  History and criticism: ML2074+
  Instruction and study: MT64.M65
Motion pictures and music: ML3849
Motor transportation
  Vocal music: M1977.M6, M1978.M6
Mount Rushmore National Memorial
  Songs and music: M1677.3.M67
Mountaineering
  Songs and music: M1977.M63,
    M1978.M63
Mouth organ and piano music:
  M284.H3, M285.H3
Mouth organs: ML1088+
  Instruction and study: MT682+
Mozarabic chants: M2154.6.M7
Mridanga
  History: ML1038.M74
  Instruction and study: MT725.M7
Musette
  Instruction and study: MT373
Musette (Oboe) music: M110.M87
Music
  500-1400
    Bibliography: ML128.M3
  Acoustics and physics: ML3805+
  Africa
    Bibliography: ML120.A35
  Africa, Sub-Saharan
    History and criticism: ML355.S7+
  Almanacs: ML12+
  Analysis, appreciation: MT90+
  Anecdotes: ML65
  Arab countries
    Bibliography: ML120.A7
  Argentina
    Bibliography: ML120.A74
  Armenia
    Bibliography: ML120.A75
  Asia
    Bibliography: ML120.A78
  Australia
    Bibliography: ML120.A86
  Austria
    Bibliography: ML120.A9

Music
  Awards: ML75.5+
    Bibliography: ML128.P68
  Belarus
    Bibliography: ML120.B28
  Belgium
    Bibliography: ML120.B3
  Bibliography: ML112.8+, ML128.S29
    Catalogs: ML136+
    Graded lists: ML132.A+
  Bolivia
    Bibliography: ML120.B6
  Brazil
    Bibliography: ML120.B7
  Bulgaria
    Bibliography: ML120.B84
  Canada
    Bibliography: ML120.C2
  Caribbean Area
    Bibliography: ML120.C25
  Charts, diagrams, etc: MT15
  Chile
    Bibliography: ML120.C45
  China
    Bibliography: ML120.C5
  Collected works: M3+
  Colombia
    Bibliography: ML120.C7
  Competitions: ML75.5+
    Bibliography: ML128.P68
  Computer network resources: ML74.7
  Congresses: ML35+
  Cuba
    Bibliography: ML120.C85
  Cypress
    Bibliography: ML120.C87
  Czech Republic
    Bibliography: ML120.C9
  Denmark
    Bibliography: ML120.D3
  Dictionaries: ML100+
    Bibliography: ML128.D5
  Directories: ML12+
  Discography: ML155.5+
    Bibliography: ML128.D56
  East Asia
    Bibliography: ML120.A8

Panama
  Vocal music: M1684.P192+
Panama-California Exposition (San Diego, 1915)
  Songs and music: M1677.2.S3 1915
Pange lingua: M6 .x735
Panis angelicus: M6 .x737
Panpipes
  Concertos: M1035.P35
  History: ML990.P3
  Instruction and study: MT533.P3
Panpipes and piano music: M270.P3, M271.P3
Panpipes concertos: M1034.P35
Panpipes music: M110.P36
Pantomime: ML3460
Pantomimes with music: M1520+
Par dessus de viole and piano music: M239.P37
Parai
  History: ML1038.P38
Parent teachers associations
  Vocal music: M1920.P2, M1921.P2
Part songs
  Bibliography: ML128.P13
  History and criticism: ML2600+
Part songs, Sacred: M2060+
  Juvenile: M2193+
Part songs, Secular: M1547+, M1627+
Part-songs, Secular: M1574+
Parts (instrumental)
  Classification: M177+
Pasillos
  Discography: ML156.4.P27
Passacaglias
  Piano music (4 hands): M203
  Violin and piano music: M220
  Violoncello and piano music: M232
Passacaglias (Band): M1203
Passacaglias (Orchestra): M1003
Passacaglias (Organ): M9
Passacaglias (Piano): M27
Passacaglias (String orchestra): M1103
Passionist rite: M2154.4.P4
Pastoral music (Secular)
  Bibliography: ML128.P15
Pater noster: M6 .x74

Patriotic music: M1677.3.A+
  Bibliography: ML128.N3
  Discography: ML156.4.N3
  History and criticism: ML3544+
  United States: M1629.5, M1666+
Patriotic societies (U.S.)
  Vocal music: M1676.A+
Patriotic songs: M1627+
Patrons of Husbandry
  Vocal music: M1905.P3, M1906.P3
Peace
  Songs and music: M1977.P4, M1978.P4
  Vocal music: M1978.P4
Peace Jubilees, Boston
  Vocal music: M1642.2+
Peals (Change ringing)
  Instruction and study: MT710, MT711
Penny whistle
  History: ML990.P45
  Instruction and study: MT358.P45
    Juvenile: MT801.P46
Penny whistle music: M110.P46
Pentecost Festival music: M2068.W4, M2088.W4, M2098.W4, M2149.5.V56
  Choruses, etc., with keyboard: M2078.W4
  Organ: M14.4.W4, M14.5.W4
  Songs: M2114.8.W4
Pentecostal Holiness Church
  Hymns: M2131.P4
P.E.O. Sisterhood
  Songs and music: M1905.P2, M1906.P2
Percussion and piano duets: M284.P4, M285.P4
Percussion concertos: M1038+, M1138+
Percussion ensembles
  Performance: MT736
Percussion instruments: ML1030+
  Bibliography: ML128.P23
  Dictionaries: ML102.P4
  Instruction and study: MT655+
  Music: M145+
Percussion music: M146
  Discography: ML156.4.P4

Polonaises
  Instruction and study: MT64.P6
Polytonality: ML3811
Popular instrumental music: M1350+,
  M1356+, M1356
Popular music: M1627+
  Analysis, appreciation: MT146
  Austria: M1703.18+
  Bermuda Islands: M1681.518+
  Bibliography: ML128.P63
  Dictionaries: ML102.P66
  Discography: ML156.4.P6
  Greenland: M1777.18+
  Haiti: M1681.H218+
  History and criticism: ML3469+
  Instruction and study: MT67
  Kurdistan: M1825.K8718+
  Latvia: M1759.18+
  Malta: M1789.M318+
  Moldova: M1767.M518+
  Political aspects: ML3918.P67
  Religious aspects: ML3921.8.P67
  Serbia and Montenegro: M1721.18+
  Social aspects: ML3918.P67
  Solomon Islands: M1844.S618+
  Taiwan: M1807.18+
  Turkmenistan: M1825.T918+
  United States: M1630.18+
    History and criticism: ML3476.8+
  United States imprints: M1.A1+
  Yugoslavia: M1721.18+
Popular songs: M1622, M1627+
Populist Party (U.S.)
  Songs and music: M1664.P6,
  M1665.P6
Porter, Cole, Collection: M15 .P67
Portugal
  History and criticism: ML3717+
Post horn
  History: ML990.P67
  Instruction and study: MT456
Potpourris (Orchestra): M1075
Potpourris (Piano): M39
Pots and pans
  Instruction and study: MT722
Practice keyboards: MT258

Pre-recorded tape
  Concertos: M1039.4.T3
Pre-recorded tape and piano music:
  M284.E4, M285.E4
Pre-recorded tape music: M1473
Premonstratensian rite: M2154.4.P74
Prentiss Taylor Archives: M14 0.7
Presbyterian Church
  Hymns: M2130
  Liturgy and ritual: M2181
Preschool music: M1990+, M1990
  Instruction and study: MT920+
Preschool vocal music: M1990+
Presidential candiates
  United States
    Songs and music
      Bibliography: ML128.P66
Presidents
  United States
    Songs and music: M1659.A+
    Bibliography: ML128.P66
Printing
  Songs and music: M1977.P74
  Vocal music: M1978.P74
Printing Songs and music: M1978.P74
Prisoners
  Songs and music: M1977.C55,
  M1978.C55
Processionals
  Sets, by language: M6 .x75
Processionals (Liturgical books):
  M2150+
Program music: ML3855
  Bibliography: ML128.P69
  History and criticism: ML3300+
Progressive Party (1912)
  Songs and music: M1664.P7,
  M1665.P7
Prohibition Party (U.S.)
  Songs and music: M1664.P8+,
  M1665.P8+
Propers (Music): M2148.3.A+
Protest songs: M1977.P75, M1978.P75
  History and criticism: ML3621.P76
Protestant church music
  Bibliography: ML128.P7
  History and criticism: ML3100

Right hand piano music: M26.2

Rivers
  Songs and music: M1977.R58, M1978.R58

Robert Di Domenica Collection: M15 .D55

Rock music
  Bibliography: ML128.R6
  Dictionaries: ML102.R6
  Discography: ML156.4.R6
  History and criticism: ML3533.8+
  Political aspects: ML3918.R63
  Religious aspects: ML3921.8.R63
  Social aspects: ML3918.R63

Rockabilly music
  Bibliography: ML128.R65
  History and criticism: ML3535

Rockets (Aeronautics)
  Songs and music: M1977.S63, M1978.S63

Rodeos
  Songs and music: M1977.S726, M1978.S726

Rodgers, Richard, Collection: M14 0.58a+

Rodzinski, Artur, Collection: M15 .R64

Romania
  History and criticism: ML3608+
  Vocal music: M1718+

Romanian Americans
  Music: M1668.9.R64

Rome
  History and criticism: ML169

Rondo
  Instruction and study: MT64.R6

Roopill concertos: M1034.R66

Rotary clubs
  Vocal music: M1920.R6, M1921.R6

Rotary International
  Songs and music: M1920.R6
  Vocal music: M1921.R6

Rounds (Songs)
  History and criticism: ML2670

Rudolf Kolisch Collection: M15 .K63

Rugby football
  Songs and music: M1977.S7265, M1978.S7265

Russia
  History and criticism: ML3497+, ML3680+

Russian horn
  History: ML990.R8

Russo-Japanese War, 1904-1905
  Songs and music: M1675.R85

Ruund (African people)
  Music: M1831.R98
  Vocal music: M1831.R98

Ryūteki music: M110.R98

S

Sackbut
  History: ML990.S3

Sacred dramatic music: M2000+
  Juvenile: M2190+

Sacred duets, trios, etc: M2018+

Sacred music
  Bibliography: ML128.C54, ML128.S17
  Discography: ML156.4.R4

Sacred musicals: M2000+
  Librettos: ML52.65+, ML52.75+
  Scenarios: ML52.65+

Sacred operas
  Librettos: ML52.65+, ML52.75+
  Scenarios: ML52.65+

Sacred songs: M2102+
  Juvenile: M2193+

Sacred vocal duets: M2019.2+
  Juvenile: M2193+

Sacred vocal music: M1999+
  Bibliography: ML128.C2, ML128.S2
  For children: M2190+
  History and criticism: ML2900+
  Juvenile: M2190+

Sacred vocal nonets: M2019.4+

Sacred vocal octets: M2019.4+

Sacred vocal quartets: M2019.4+
  Juvenile: M2193+

Sacred vocal quintets: M2019.4+

Sacred vocal septets: M2019.4+

Sacred vocal sextets: M2019.4+

Sacred vocal trios: M2019.4+
  Juvenile: M2193+

Tanso
  Instruction and study: MT358.T3
Tanso music: M110.T36
Tantum ergo: M6 .x87
Tape and piano music: M284.E4,
  M285.E4
Tape (Music)
  Concertos: M1039.4.T3
Tape music: M1473
Tar (Lute) and piano music: M282.T3,
  M283.T3
Tar (Lute) concertos: M1037.4.T3
Tar (Lute) music: M142.T3
Tárogató and piano music: M270.T3,
  M271.T3
Tárogató concertos: M1034.T3
Tavil
  Instruction and study: MT725.T38
Taxation
  Songs and music: M1977.T3,
  M1978.T3
Taylor, Prentiss, Archives: M14 0.7
Te Deum laudamus: M6 .x9
Te Deum laudamus (Music)
  History and criticism: ML3090
Technicon
  Instruction and study: MT258
Techno music
  Dictionaries: ML102.T43
  History and criticism: ML3540
  Political aspects: ML3918.T43
  Social aspects: ML3918.T43
Tejano music
  Dictionaries: ML102.T45
Television
  Songs and music: M1977.R2,
  M1978.R2
Television and music: ML68
Television music: M176.5, M1527.7+
  Bibliography: ML128.T4
  Discography: ML156.4.T4
  History and criticism: ML2080
Television programs
  Indexes: ML158.4+
Temperance
  Songs and music: M2198+

Ten Intiyat Tiruccapai
  Ritual: M2184.C5
Tenor horn
  Instruction and study: MT495
Tenor horn and piano music:
  M270.T45, M271.T45
Tenora (Musical instrument)
  History: ML990.T46
Teresa of Avila, Saint, 1515-1582
  Songs and music: M2148.3.T48
Terra tremuit: M6 .x91
Texts: ML47+
Thanksgiving Day
  Songs and music: M1629.3.T4
Thematic catalogs
  Bibliography: ML128.T48
Theorbo
  Instruction and study: MT654.T54
Theorbo music: M142.T5
Theremin
  Instruction and study: MT723+
Theremin music: M175.T5
Tida (African people)
  Music: M1831.T53
  Vocal music: M1831.T53
Timpani
  History: ML1036
  Instruction and study: MT660+
Timpani and piano music: M284.T5,
  M285.T5
Timpani music: M146
Tinglik
  Instruction and study: MT725.T5
Tinglik music: M175.T56
Tiple
  History: ML1015.T5
Titanic (Steamship)
  Songs and music: M1977.T55,
  M1978.T55
Titles of musical compositions
  Dictionaries: ML102.T58
Titsŭ music: M110.T6
Toleration
  Songs and music: M1977.T6,
  M1978.T6
Tollite hostias: M6 .x914

GPO U.S. GOVERNMENT PRINTING OFFICE: 2010–357–308/40003